Shakespeare's Shrine

Shakespeare's Shrine

The Bard's Birthplace and th⟨

Invention of Stratford-upon-Avon

Julia Thomas

PENN

UNIVERSITY OF PENNSYLVANIA PRESS

Philadelphia

A volume in the Haney Foundation Series, established in 1961 with the generous support of Dr. John Louis Haney

Published by
University of Pennsylvania Press
Philadelphia, Pennsylvania 19104-4112
www.upenn.edu/pennpress

Printed in the United States of America on acid-free paper
10 9 8 7 6 5 4 3 2 1

Library of Congress Cataloging-in-Publication Data
Thomas, Julia.
    Shakespeare's shrine : the Bard's birthplace and the invention of
Stratford-upon-Avon / Julia Thomas.
        p. cm. (Haney Foundation series)
    Includes bibliographical references and index.
    ISBN: 978-0-8122-4423-6 (hardcover : alk. paper)
    1. Shakespeare, William, 1564–1616—Birthplace.   2. Shakespeare,
William, 1564–1616—Homes and haunts—England—Stratford-upon-
Avon.   3. Stratford-upon-Avon (England)—Description and travel.
I. Title.   II. Series: Haney Foundation series
    PR2916.T36 2012
    822.3'3—dc23

                                                    2012002583

Frontispiece: Victorian photographers set up camp outside the Birthplace. *Illustrated London News* supplement, 30 April 1864. Reproduced by permission of Special Collections and Archives, Cardiff University.

*To my parents for my first visit to the Birthplace,
and to Stuart for our many visits since*

Contents

Shakespeare's Shrine

Introduction

The Birthplace in Victorian Culture

> I will no longer conceal the fact from an excited world: I am
> the man—the miscreant—the morbid maniac—the
> misguided wretch, if you will have it so, who burned down
> Shakespeare's house, on the night of the eighteenth of March,
> one thousand eight hundred and fifty-seven.
> —J. Hollingshead, "A Startling Confession" (1857)

Fortunately for the modern-day tourist, Shakespeare's house was not really burned to the ground in the middle of the nineteenth century; it still stands on Henley Street in the English market town of Stratford-upon-Avon, where it attracts hundreds of thousands of visitors every year. This fictional act of destruction takes place in the context of "A Startling Confession," a short story that appeared in the *Train* magazine in 1857. The self-styled "morbid maniac," who narrates this tale, is driven to arson when his masterpiece, a tragedy in twelve acts with seventy-two scenes, fails to get staged in theaters saturated with productions of Shakespeare's plays; "I could have wrung the neck of the Swan of Avon," he, perhaps understandably, seethes.[1] The narrator's last hope quite literally goes up in smoke when his tragedy, which has been deposited in the (exceedingly strong) hands of a theater manager, is incinerated, along with the theater, during a performance of—you've guessed it—one of Shakespeare's plays. He determines to wreak a terrible revenge: "I decided at once to destroy the shrine of the saint,—the butcher's shop,—the miserable hut at Stratford-on-Avon."[2] The very next day sees him traveling to Stratford, setting fire to Shakespeare's Birthplace with breathtaking ease, and returning to London in the mail train from Warwick, the story thus neatly referring to the mode of transport that gave the magazine its title.

"A Startling Confession" is an ironic assessment of the state of Victorian theaters in the middle of the century when contemporary dramatists were marginalized in favor of Shakespeare. The author, John Hollingshead, went on to champion new talent, including Gilbert and Sullivan, in his management of the Gaiety Theatre in London. In addition to the theaters, "A Startling Confession" also satirizes the press (Hollingshead's other occupation was as a journalist), its second half brilliantly capturing the tones and prejudices of the newspapers as they report the disaster, from *The Times*, which calls for the culprit to be publicly horsewhipped, to the *Morning Advertiser*, which lays the blame for the event on the emissaries of the pope, and the *Athenaeum*, which refuses to mourn the destruction of the house because, it reveals, Shakespeare was actually born at Stratford in Essex rather than Stratford in Warwickshire. As one might expect of such a catastrophic event, the newspapers are dominated by reports of the burning of the Birthplace, but what is perhaps most startling, or at least curious, to modern readers of this tale is the privileged location of Shakespeare's house within the story.

Why, one might ask, does the narrator immediately decide to direct his vengeance at the Birthplace? Why doesn't he instead burn a first folio, or, if he insists on traveling by train to Stratford, deface Shakespeare's bust or the tombstone in Holy Trinity Church? For this "maniac," the Birthplace is the obvious choice: the house has an iconic status that is registered when the narrator throws his grenade into an upper window and compares himself to an "ancient Image-Breaker."[3] His dastardly deed, the reportage of the event in the press, and the horror of the public all attest to the pervasive presence of this house and the disturbing possibility of its absence, the story depending on the fact that a typical reader recognized and comprehended the importance of the Birthplace. And the typical Victorian reader would not have failed to recognize the exalted status of this building: the Birthplace was featured in biographies and criticism of Shakespeare, in poetry, and in fiction; it was described in guidebooks and travel narratives; it made news headlines at several key moments throughout the course of the century; and it was frequently represented in the form of prints and photographs. It was in this period that a door knocker in the shape of the Birthplace was designed, that models of the building were installed in zoological gardens and in the Great Exhibition, and that actual dwellings were constructed to look like Shakespeare's house.[4]

This book attempts to recapture the representations and meanings of the Birthplace and to describe how they became entrenched in Victorian culture. The significance of the building can be traced back to the eighteenth century and, most notably, to the Shakespeare Jubilee that the actor David Garrick organized in Stratford in 1769, but the focus of this book is on a more defining period in its history which began with the auction of the house and its purchase for the nation in 1847 and ended in the early decades of the twentieth century. During these years the Birthplace was actively created. This creation was both physical and ideological, the "making" of the house taking place in the forging of an association between Birthplace and bard, in the debates that surrounded its auction, in a restoration project that effectively rebuilt it, in the strategies of authentication and legitimization that "proved" its worth, and in the development of the property as a major tourist attraction. These events, beginning with the 1847 sale, gave the Birthplace an unprecedented position not just in Britain but across the world and inaugurated a new way of thinking about writers' houses and Shakespeare that has subsequently become the norm. Almost all of the developments in Stratford from the early twentieth century are largely continuations and embellishments of this Victorian phenomenon.

The events of 1847 were responsible for the formation of the Shakespeare Birthplace Trust, the body which continues to manage and promote the Birthplace today. The Trust had its roots in the Shakespeare monumental committee, which had been established in 1835 in order to preserve and restore Shakespeare's tomb in Holy Trinity Church. In 1847, and under the new name of the Shakespeare Birthplace committee, it focused its attention on buying the Birthplace itself, its efforts later being coordinated with a London committee set up for the same purpose. Following the purchase of the house, it was assumed that its ownership would transfer to the government, but by the 1860s when this had failed to happen, it was agreed that the management of the Birthplace should be given to a more organized and formal body of trustees. The first meeting of the Shakespeare Birthplace Trust was held in July 1866. By 1891, the authority of the Trust, not to mention its increasing income from admission charges, was such that it was incorporated by Act of Parliament, a gesture that signified not just its statutory but also its public recognition as the body which managed and maintained the Birthplace.[5] The Act gave the Trust a new legal status and a wider remit, encouraging it to use funds to acquire other lands or properties associated with Shakespeare. A year later, it bought Anne Hathaway's cottage, the home of Shakespeare's sweetheart.

The period I explore in this book also saw the invention of the Stratford tourist trail, which was pieced together from the houses that came into the possession of the Trust, each one marking a pivotal moment in Shakespeare's biography. At the center of this biography was the Birthplace itself, the house which gave the Trust its name and raison d'être. But how did such a seemingly unassuming edifice acquire such cultural significance in these years? Why Shakespeare's birthplace? Or, to rephrase the question, "why *Shakespeare's* birthplace?" One answer was that in the nineteenth century there was a distinct shortage of houses where famous writers had been born. John Milton's on Bread Street was the earliest English author's birthplace to be visited by tourists, but this building had been engulfed in the Great Fire of London (an inspiration, perhaps, for "A Startling Confession").[6] Other writers' houses were not identified or their locations had been forgotten, while several renowned authors were associated instead with the houses where they had worked or lived during their adult lives.[7] The answer to the question "why Shakespeare's *birthplace?*" might appear equally mundane. In 1866 an enterprising newsagent advertised his shop on Aldersgate Street, London, as the "Residence of the Immortal Shakspeare" when he was proprietor of the theater in Golden Lane, but the truth was that Shakespeare's residences in London were not known or had long disappeared, while New Place, the house that Shakespeare had retired to in Stratford, had been substantially rebuilt and was eventually demolished in 1759 by its then owner, the Reverend Francis Gastrell, who was subsequently hounded out of the town.[8]

Even with its unique heritage, however, the Birthplace has not always been at the center of the tour of Stratford. Well into the eighteenth century those visitors who sought out locations associated with celebrities focused on gravesides and monuments rather than on sites of nativity.[9] In this respect, Holy Trinity Church, where Shakespeare was buried, had initially proved far more of a draw than the Birthplace, which up until 1847 also had the disadvantage of being a privately owned and occupied building rather than a public site. As late as 1855, one visitor to Stratford could remark: "A birth place is never of so much interest to me as a grave. In the former are wanting the *remains*, dust though they be, that seem to bring us so near the presence of the dead."[10] This particular visitor, however, was a little behind the times. The public furor surrounding the auction of the Birthplace meant that by the middle of the nineteenth century it had superseded the Church as the principal tourist attraction in Stratford.

There were other possible reasons, more ideological than pragmatic, why the Birthplace became imbued with so much significance in this period, not least of which was the growing cultural significance of Shakespeare himself.[11] In an article published in *All the Year Round* in 1893, the cottage in Chalfont St. Giles, where Milton lived and completed *Paradise Lost*, was contrasted with Shakespeare's Birthplace, the writer concluding that the reason that Shakespeare's house had so many visitors while Milton's cottage had so few was that Milton, unlike Shakespeare, was not relevant to the Victorians; his ethics were not in tune with those of the nineteenth century.[12] Shakespeare, on the other hand, was very much in tune with the nineteenth century, so much so that he was frequently appropriated as an honorary Victorian, occupying an unrivaled position in the period. In *Shakespeare and the Victorians*, Adrian Poole describes how the bard was everywhere: in literature, the visual arts, the theater, in the Victorians' very utterances. "If not a god," he suggests, "Shakespeare was the most powerful of ghosts."[13]

This ghost haunted the Birthplace. The myth of this building contributed to the "myth" of Shakespeare: its location in the heart of England conveniently confirmed Shakespeare's role as a national poet, while its status as a burgeoning tourist site, which attracted visitors from around the globe, provided proof of Shakespeare's universal (and imperial) appeal. But the Shakespeare who haunted the building on Henley Street was not just the divinely inspired being who rendered this building a shrine. The importance of the house, which necessitated its purchase, restoration, and preservation in this period, also depended on the idea of Shakespeare as a real man to whose life the building bore witness. It might seem strange to visitors today, who flock to Stratford to see Shakespeare's works performed by the Royal Shakespeare Company, that for the majority of the Victorian period, plays were not staged in Stratford. Until the opening of the Shakespeare Memorial Theatre in 1879 every theater in Stratford had closed within a matter of years. Even early visitors to the Memorial Theatre were generally more interested in seeing the picture gallery that the theater contained than they were in attending the plays, and it was not until 1925 that the theater began to make a profit.[14] The attraction of Stratford for most Victorian tourists did not lie so much in performances of the plays as in the biography of the man who wrote them, a man who was born in the house on Henley Street.

With its prominent position in the nineteenth-century imagination, it is surprising that the Birthplace has been relatively neglected in critical studies. The most detailed account of the house was undertaken by the former director of the Shakespeare Birthplace Trust, Levi Fox, primarily in his memoir published in 1997.[15] Fox's research has been invaluable in providing a documentary account of the Birthplace based on the archival material of the Trust, but its focus on facts neglects the cultural meanings of the Birthplace, how the building intersects with and influences the world outside its timber-framed walls.[16] The Birthplace has also made appearances in discussions of the "myth" of Shakespeare and its associated industry.[17] Yet such discussions tend to conflate the Birthplace and Stratford, reading the Birthplace in the context of the town's other sites rather than as a building with its own distinct history and meanings.[18] Moreover, they often concentrate either on Garrick's eighteenth-century Jubilee or on the contemporary manifestation of the house, marginalizing its significance in the Victorian period.[19]

The potential for offering new perspectives on the Victorian creation of the Birthplace has emerged in recent research on literary tourism which looks at Shakespeare's house within the wider context of writers' dwellings.[20] This book takes a slightly different direction: I do not explore the relations between the Birthplace and other sites of pilgrimage such as Wordsworth's Dove Cottage[21] or Robert Burns's cottage in Alloway.[22] I am more concerned with how the Birthplace came to organize the experience of Stratford (not to mention the actual town) and played a part in shaping the meanings of "Shakespeare." This book therefore substantiates Balz Engler's claim that Stratford and its tourist industry contributed to the canonization of the bard.[23] I am also interested in what the appropriation and translation of Shakespeare reveal about Victorian culture itself. [24] As Harald Hendrix succinctly puts it in his discussion of writers' houses, such buildings "not only recall the poets and novelists who dwelt in them, but also the ideologies of those who turned them into memorial sites."[25] As a specifically Victorian edifice, the Birthplace offers a unique insight into the ideologies that informed and constituted this cultural moment. The making of the Birthplace and Stratford, then, is also about the making of the Victorians.

Victorian Values

Even those representations of the Birthplace that appear the most transparent are never entirely free from marks of their historical context. The tercentenary celebrations of Shakespeare's birth in 1864 saw thousands of visitors descend on Stratford and the house on Henley Street which had recently been restored. The event was commemorated by numerous publications, among them *All About Shakespeare*, a largely biographical account of the bard that was illustrated with drawings by Henry Fitzcook, including several of the Birthplace.[26] Fitzcook was a successful and accomplished illustrator, who went on in 1865 to promote the graphotype, a method of autographic printing that was advertised as half the price of wood engraving.[27] In *All About Shakespeare*, Fitzcook's images use the medium of wood engraving, fully exploiting the technical effects that this mode of reproduction could achieve and ensuring its position as the most popular method of printing images, despite the promise of the graphotype.

Fitzcook's picture of the exterior of the Birthplace is meticulously executed, from the cobbles in the road in front of the house to the meat hanging up in the butcher's shop that formed the central aspect of the property (Figure 1). Secured prominently to the wall is a wooden sign announcing that Shakespeare was born there. This gentle scene is not swarming with visitors, but, alongside the locals who go about their daily chores, a few figures are designated as tourists: the Victorian gentlemen standing opposite the house, one of whom points at it, and probably the man who rides on horseback toward the building.

Despite its attention to detail, however, there is something wrong with this picture of the Birthplace: its time is out of joint. It is in these anachronisms that its investment in the meanings and values of its Victorian context become apparent. Although the picture lays claim to a contemporary realism, the drawing does not show the Birthplace as it appeared in 1864 when this image was published. (The title on the engraving and in the list of illustrations is simply "Shakespeare's House in Henley Street," whereas illustrations showing the Birthplace at other historical moments usually announce this fact.)

SHAKESPEARE'S HOUSE IN HENLEY STREET.

Figure 1. An idealized and nostalgic view of the Birthplace in the nineteenth century. Henry Fitzcook, from [George Linnaeus Banks], *All About Shakespeare: Profusely Illustrated with Wood Engravings by Thomas Gilks, Drawn by H. Fitzcook. In Commemoration of the Ter-Centenary* (London: Henry Lea, 1864).

Between 1857 and 1862 the house had been extensively restored: the buildings on either side had been demolished and the three premises that made up the Birthplace (the tenement shown on the left of the picture with the woman in the doorway, the butcher's shop in the middle, and the Swan and Maidenhead pub on the right) were united as a single dwelling. Nor does Fitzcook's picture show the Birthplace as it appeared just prior to the restoration because, at the time, the butcher's shop was not in use and the Swan and Maidenhead's timber frontage was covered with brick. The house as it is represented by Fitzcook conforms loosely to how it might have appeared at the turn of the century (the brick frontage of the Swan and Maidenhead was added sometime around 1808), but the gentlemen tourists are unmistakably from the middle of the nineteenth century, their fashionable garb, which stands out against the rustic setting, emphasizing their contemporaneity. What initially appears as a realistic scene, then, is actually an imaginary one.

The fictionality of this picture might be surprising given that Fitzcook was skilled in depicting factual scenes. With the graphotype, he advocated a precision that was not possible with a technique like engraving, which required an intermediary process between the drawing of the picture and its printing. This artistic exactitude was demonstrated in images of Sweden that Fitzcook contributed to the *Illustrated London News* between 1856 and 1860. While he traveled to Sweden to make his drawings in situ, however, it is possible that Fitzcook never set foot in Stratford. So common and well known were images of the house that it was not unusual for artists to copy other pictures, adding their own flourishes, and mistakes.[28] (This might also explain another error in Fitzcook's picture in the form of the inscription on the sign, which actually read "THE IMMORTAL SHAKSPEARE WAS BORN IN THIS HOUSE.")

Whatever the story of its design, this image generates multiple and contradictory meanings that are bound up in the historical moment of its production and reception. Showing the Birthplace in its pre-restored state as a modest and unassuming abode, a mere "butcher's shop," as the narrator of "A Startling Confession" pejoratively puts it, emphasizes Shakespeare's humble beginnings, making his stellar rise to the heights of literary greatness even more impressive. It also suggests the bard's affinity with the common people, the lowly appearance of the house contributing to a leveling effect on visitors that is also remarked upon by the guide to the Birthplace in Hollingshead's story, who declares that kings enter this shrine as meekly as the poorest.[29]

Whereas the Birthplace is represented in Fitzcook's picture as a humble abode, one which, temporarily at least, offers the suspension of hierarchical distinctions, the figures who are situated outside the house are clearly demarcated in terms of class. The class divide, moreover, is also a gendered one: the local women, characterized by their country styles (aprons, plain bonnets, wicker baskets), who stand in doorways, do their shopping, and walk with their children past the Birthplace, contrast sharply with the stylish men, who maintain an authoritative and respectful distance from the house. It is this distance that defines the male figures as outsiders, the picture constructing an almost palpable separation between the country (women) and the city (gentlemen). While the men from the city are invested with authority in Fitzcook's picture, however, it is the values of a pre-industrial community that are privileged, the notion of a reassuring and uncomplicated way of life represented by the Birthplace and the Stratford locals. This visual iconography had textual analogues. The Victorian poet Mackenzie Bell wrote of Shakespeare that "sense guided thee/To live in this thy Stratford long ago—To live content in calm simplicity."[30] The "calm simplicity" represented in Fitzcook's image would have been compromised if the timber frontage of the Swan and Maidenhead pub had been covered in brick, or if the Birthplace had been displayed in the much grander form it had adopted as a result of its restoration.

In its depiction of an idyllic and idealized village life, this image draws on the genre paintings that were so popular in the nineteenth century. Caroline Arscott's account of Victorian genre suggests features of Fitzcook's drawing: "Built into the pictorial convention of genre is a response to a quaint old-world environment, with its haphazard jumble of different building styles that have been assembled over the years. Exaggeratedly pitched roofs, broken gutters, patchy plasterwork on walls: all this is the substance of genre painting, which attends to the picturesque rather than insisting on the grandiose."[31] Her context is the ways in which images of the past invade the Victorian present. In the case of Fitzcook's drawing, there are multiple pasts: the Elizabethan past of Shakespeare that its subject matter evokes, and the preindustrial and pre-Victorian past that made prints of the pre-restored Birthplace popular long after the restoration had actually taken place. This construction of a past that is set in the present of the Victorian spectator simultaneously establishes the distance and the immediacy of Shakespeare. It also constitutes a history for the Birthplace and, in so doing, situates the building as part of a wider narrative about national identity. Michael Hunter has suggested that the nineteenth century saw an increasing appreciation of historical relics as national antiquities, and the allure of the house on Henley Street is part of this cultural shift.[32] The Birthplace, in effect, is defined as a site of heritage.

It is a heritage, however, that is paradoxical and uncertain. The building, Fitzcook's image seems to announce, is timeless: it has been and will be there forever; life goes on in Stratford, tourists come and go, but the existence of the house is a certainty. It was, in fact, the need to ensure this continuity and to preserve the Birthplace that was the motivation for the purchase of the house on behalf of the nation. But Fitzcook's Birthplace does not depict the structure that stood on Henley Street in 1864; the drawing evokes a yearning for a past that has already gone or that never existed. According to Christopher Shaw and Malcolm Chase, buildings, along with objects and images, can become talismans, links to the past that, by suggesting how things were, create a sense of nostalgia.[33] These links, moreover, are not just about the past. As Shaw and Chase note, "Our dialogue with them is one-sided: the deep sense of connection with the past one might feel can be simply a unilateral projection of our own present anxieties and fantasies."[34] In its points of connection with a Shakespearean and pre-Victorian past, Fitzcook's image also has an ambiguous relationship with its nineteenth-century present, the Birthplace acting as a center around which contemporary desires, fantasies, fears, and anxieties are articulated and repressed.

Like the autographs of tourists which lined the walls and ceilings of its rooms, the Birthplace itself was the inscription of nineteenth-century meanings that were written all over its surface, which seeped into its very beams. These meanings, as Fitzcook's image demonstrates and as the following chapters show, were bound up not only in what "Shakespeare" signified in the period, but also in issues of class and national identity, gender and domesticity, commerce and tourism, and the visual, material, and textual cultures in which the Birthplace was represented. In Chapter 1, I look at how the Birthplace played its own part in constructing "Shakespeare" and his life, filling in the gaps in the bard's biography. Alongside its status as a shrine, which invited the veneration of Shakespeare as immortal and otherworldly, the Birthplace acted as a catalyst for imagining Shakespeare as a real historical being, whose childhood took place within its walls. The focus of Chapter 2 is on one of the most important events in the Birthplace's history: the auction and subsequent purchase of the house in 1847. The chapter examines the representation and contradictory meanings of this sale and the questions it generated concerning the ownership of the property and, by implication, of Shakespeare. In Chapter 3, I discuss the restoration of the Birthplace in the 1850s and 1860s, situating it in the context of Victorian anxieties about such projects. Chapter 4 concerns the documents, objects, and pictures that helped to authenticate the house, and in Chapter 5 I explore what tourists did and how they were expected to behave on their visit to the Birthplace and Stratford. Finally, the conclusion outlines how the Birthplace was, and still is, intertwined with the ways in which Shakespeare and the plays are read and interpreted. All of these chapters suggest the distinctive status of the Birthplace in the nineteenth century, its material and ideological construction in these years, and the importance of the house not only for an understanding of how

Shakespeare was perceived but also of Victorian values. The narrator of "A Startling Confession" might have set the house alight, but his act of destruction only exposes the cultural meanings of the property and its multiple incarnations at a historical moment that marks not the death but the birth of the Birthplace.

Chapter 1

The Birth of "Shakespeare"

Identity Crisis

Before the Birthplace was restored in the middle of the nineteenth century, a sign hung on the exterior wall between the window of a bedroom and the butcher's hatch: "The Immortal Shakspeare," it announced, "was born in this house." This sign established the provenance and authenticity of the building, marking the beginnings of the Stratford tourist trade. Some detractors suggested that the erection of this board was a conspiracy on the part of the townspeople to bring visitors into Stratford; others identified it as the work of an enterprising occupant of the house.[1] Despite its questionable origins, however, there is a sense in which the sign's statement about the origins of Shakespeare might have some validity: Shakespeare, or rather, an idea of what "Shakespeare" meant, was "born" in this house and in the debates and conflicting representations that surrounded it.

The history of the Birthplace involves a transition from an essentially allegorical, metaphorical, and metropolitan eighteenth-century representation of Shakespeare's immortality to a biographical and provincial sense of his mortality that became most prominent in the middle of the nineteenth century. The Victorians drew on earlier, mutually reinforcing conventions of viewing Shakespeare as godlike and the Birthplace as a site of pilgrimage and worship: the divinity of Shakespeare sanctified the house, while the house, as shrine, emphasized Shakespeare's otherworldliness. As one mid-Victorian writer remarked of the Birthplace, "There is a sense in which human genius consecrates the soil on which it flourished, and the material objects with which, while tabernacled in the flesh, it happened to be associated."[2] But Shakespeare, as this writer also serves to remind us, was not just a genius: he was human too. He might have been "tabernacled in the flesh," but he *was* flesh, and the Birthplace was the origin of that flesh. In seeming opposition to the insistence on immortality, the Birthplace became the symbol of Shakespeare's very mortality, the fact that he had once lived, breathed, and been part of a family. This cultural shift depended upon an investment in biography as an explanatory mechanism and, more specifically, on the importance of childhood in the writings that make up Shakespeare. As the home of Shakespeare's formative years, the Birthplace acted as the catalyst for "memories" of his life and was the kernel of a movement to domesticate Shakespeare that grew as the century wore on.

These multiple identities of Shakespeare emerged from and formed a key component of the growing connection between bard and Birthplace, which coincided with a more general attempt to unite people and places in the rise of the homes and haunts genre. Travel writing described visits to locations related to famous figures and thereby encouraged an association between the site and the person, so much so that, as one contemporary writer commented, the two become "inseparably connected" in the imagination.[3] In her account of literary tourism, Nicola J. Watson charts the development of the homes and haunts tradition from the eighteenth century as a textual movement that paralleled the burgeoning popularity of actual trips to these locations.[4]

The identification of the setting of Shakespeare's birth, though, does not fully account for the complex links that came to exist between this particular architectural edifice and "Shakespeare." Michel Foucault refers directly to Shakespeare's Birthplace, arguing that the discovery that Shakespeare was not actually born in the house would not affect what the author's name meant and how it circulated, whereas if it were proved that Shakespeare had not written the sonnets there would be a significant change.[5] Foucault's statement seems incontrovertible: the notion of what "Shakespeare" means would, of course, be modified if texts were proven not to have been written by him. However, Foucault's dismissal of the significance of the house, while perhaps justified today, would not apply to its Victorian reality. In the nineteenth century, the meanings of the building were in these points of connection which linked "Shakespeare" and the Birthplace, and, in so doing, fostered the contradictory notions of the poet that were inscribed in that little wooden sign: Shakespeare as immortal, with all the connotations of genius and divinity that came with this status, and Shakespeare as a real being, whose birth took place within these hallowed walls.

Immortal Willy

One of the earliest references to the material traces of Shakespeare's life in Stratford is in William Dugdale's monumental *The Antiquities of Warwickshire* (1656). Dugdale refers in detail to the tomb of Shakespeare in Holy Trinity Church and includes the first pictorial representation of the monument, remarking that "this ancient Town . . . gave birth and sepulture to our late famous poet *Will. Shakespere*."[6] Dugdale does not, however, mention the Birthplace, and the building does not make an appearance until over a century later in 1759 when Stratford's local surveyor, Samuel Winter, sketched the earliest plan of Stratford and identified the "House where Shakspeare was born."[7] Winter's map, which pinpoints all of Stratford's prominent streets and buildings (including the White Lion pub, which was located just up the road from Shakespeare's house), suggests that by 1759 the Birthplace had been identified as such and that the property was worthy of note, even if this was within the context of a provincial town plan.

It was not, then, until the second half of the eighteenth century that the attempt to construct and commemorate Shakespeare within the environs of Stratford-upon-Avon by using and exploiting the resources of the town really began. The key event in this movement was the Shakespeare Jubilee of 1769, which cemented the connections between Stratford and Shakespeare and signaled the formal beginnings of the tourist trade in the town.[8] In the words of Nicola J. Watson, "the Jubilee codified, expanded, and boosted a small-scale provincial industry by successfully linking different Shakespeares – the Shakespeare of the London stage, the Shakespeare of the printed page, the rural Shakespeare of Stratford, the increasingly mythic 'Shakespeare' praised by critics and nationalists – within a multimedia spectacular staged in a single location."[9] This "multimedia spectacular," organized by David Garrick, who had been approached to raise money for the purpose of erecting a bust of Shakespeare in a niche in the front of the town hall, effectively defined Stratford as the center of what became known as bardolatry. It also, as Watson indicates, established a discourse that articulated and shaped the growing bond between Shakespeare and Stratford.

Part of this bond was focused on the Birthplace. While the building on Henley Street, as the 1759 plan attests, was regarded as the Birthplace before the arrival of the charismatic actor in Stratford, no such tradition existed about the exact part of the house in which Shakespeare was born. Garrick, with typical bravado, strode into the building and confidently pointed out the room.[10] He went on to hang an emblematic transparency from the window of this "birthroom" showing the sun struggling through the clouds to enlighten the world, underneath which was printed a quotation derived from *The Third Part of Henry VI*: "Thus dying clouds contend with growing light."[11] Behind this glorious transparency glowed the warm light of commerce as Garrick's friend, the publisher Thomas Beckett, took his place as official Jubilee bookseller, selling a large supply of books and pamphlets, including a quarto edition of Garrick's *Ode on Dedicating a Building and Erecting a Statue to Shakespeare* and the collection of fourteen Jubilee songs.[12] Garrick also had plans for a fancy-dress parade past the Birthplace, which eventually had to be canceled because of bad weather.

Although the property was allotted a role in the Jubilee, it was not as eminent a venue as Holy Trinity Church or the huge octagonal amphitheater erected on the banks of the River Avon especially for the event. Designed in imitation of the rotunda which formed the centerpiece of the Ranelagh pleasure gardens in London, the amphitheater could seat one thousand people, had an orchestra pit for one hundred, and was decorated with a chandelier of eight hundred lights that hung from the dome. As stylish a theater as this rotunda was, during the three days of the festivities none of Shakespeare's plays was performed there, for "Shakespeare" and what he signified were more important than the drama itself. Indeed, what "Shakespeare" meant was there for all to see in the huge transparencies, illuminated by lamps, that adorned the front of this amphitheater and showed three allegorical paintings after compositions by Joshua Reynolds: Tragedy on the one side, Comedy on the other, and, in the central panel, Time leading Shakespeare to immortality.[13]

This iconography and language of immortality dominated the Jubilee festivities of 1769 to the extent that one of the songs Garrick performed celebrated the immortality of a mulberry tree which was said to have been planted by the bard's own hands in the grounds of New Place: "And thou like him immortal be!" was the catchy refrain.[14] Garrick's exclamation was not far from the truth since the wood from this tree continued to supply an endless number of relics, despite the fact that it had been chopped down a decade earlier by the infamous Francis Gastrell (whose destructive tendencies were then directed to the house itself). With Shakespeare revered as an immortal being, Stratford was defined as his shrine, the Jubilee applying the religious terminology used to label Shakespeare to descriptions of the town itself. This association was explicit in many of Garrick's lyrics: at dinner on the second day of the festivities, the assembled guests joined in with the lines "Untouched and sacred be thy shrine,/Avonian Willy, bard Divine."[15] The Avon was treated as holy water, some trees on the bank being cut down by express permission of the duke of Dorset so that visitors could get a better view of the river.[16]

Garrick's definition of Stratford as a sacred shrine might have jarred with the weary and wet participants of the Jubilee. For all its grand planning, the event succumbed to the British weather and was a complete washout. Some said that the thirty cannons lined up on the banks of the Avon made such a racket that they caused a shattering effect on the clouds.[17] Accommodation could not be found, prices soared, and coaches got stuck in mud trying to leave the town. Garrick himself was obviously jaded by the event. When he was asked to organize another jubilee by the Stratford Corporation, he declined, but offered some sage advice on how they could best honor Shakespeare in future: "Let your streets be well paved and kept clean, do something to the delightful meadow, allure everybody to visit the Holy-land, let it be well lighted and clean underfoot, and let it not be said, for your honour and I hope for your interest, that the town which gave birth to the first genius since the creation is the most dirty, unseemly, ill-paved wretched looking place in all Britain."[18]

For Garrick and his guests, Stratford was far from the ideal tourist destination, and it would take a century or so before his advice about cleaning up the town was heeded. His cynical comments (one can almost imagine him penning this letter wrapped up in several layers of clothing with his feet soaking in a tub of hot water) might explain why, although the Jubilee brought people to Stratford from different parts of Britain and especially from London, it did not result in an exponential increase in visitor numbers over the course of the following years. Tourism to Stratford remained an elitist activity, undertaken by the educated and wealthy visitor, or by the accidental tourist, travelers being lured inside the Birthplace because of its proximity to the White Lion, one of the major coaching inns on the great North Road, the main route through the country from Ireland and northern England. In fact, the irony of Garrick's Jubilee is that it moved Stratford to London, when Garrick transferred the festivities to the theater in Drury Lane, where they could not be disrupted by inclement weather or uncivilized locals.[19] This re-creation of the Stratford events within the security and comfort of a London theater was a huge success and resulted in almost one hundred performances during the course of the season. The show did contain some elements of the uncomfortable reality of the Stratford Jubilee: it opened with a scene in an inn-yard where the inhabitant of a post-chaise complains that he cannot get a lodging house for the night and is forced to sleep in his carriage.[20] Largely, however, the performance allowed for a celebration and veneration of Stratford, which was intensified because of its safe distance from the town.

The idea of Stratford and Shakespeare's connection with it that emerges from the Jubilee is primarily a metropolitan one, with Shakespeare hailed as "that demi-god!/Who Avon's flow'ry margin trod."[21] Eighteenth-century Stratford might have been more muddy than "flow'ry," but its idealization in the Jubilee festivities, along with Shakespeare's growing status as a divine entity, meant that the town had become the "Holy-land." And if Stratford was the "Holy-land" then the Birthplace, with its sparse interior, roughly timbered walls, and rudely paved floors, was regarded as the site of the nativity. Numerous texts and paintings glorified the infant Shakespeare, so it was not such a jump to venerate the setting of his birth in a similar fashion.[22] This trope continued into the nineteenth century. One visitor in 1824 described the tourist who comes to the house "as a pilgrim would to the shrine of some loved saint; will deem it holy ground, and dwell with sweet though pensive rapture, on the natal habitation of the poet."[23]

By the time of Victoria's ascension, the meanings of the Birthplace and the meanings of Shakespeare were so entangled that they became interchangeable. Frederick W. Fairholt, who visited the Birthplace in 1839 and went on to write one of the first guidebooks to Stratford, called the property the "immortal house."[24] In a letter to the editor of the *Examiner* in 1847, the poet Walter Savage Landor's description of the building makes explicit its connection with another glorious birth: "This edifice contained that illustrious cradle near which all human learning shines faintly, and where lay that infant who was destined to glorify and exalt our greatest kings."[25] Such religiosity is visually embodied in Thomas Nast's evocative painting *The Immortal Light of Genius* (1896), which was commissioned by the actor Henry Irving.[26] Nast's image, which is set in the birthroom, shows the bust of Shakespeare radiating with a supernatural glow as the figures of Comedy and Tragedy present laurel wreaths. The genius of Shakespeare, this picture suggests, will never be extinguished; it lives on in the light that emanates from the bust and shines on the bare walls and floorboards of the Birthplace.

This vocabulary of worship and pilgrimage was, of course, a rhetorical device: Shakespeare was not really a divine entity, and the Birthplace was a secular rather than religious shrine, but so effective was the language of spiritual devotion that the boundaries between the secular and the sacred began to blur. The "Bibliolatry of Bardolatry," as Charles LaPorte has recently termed it, was a characteristic feature of the way that the Birthplace was represented in this period.[27] Such pseudo-religiosity did not go entirely unobserved. A contemporary visitor to the house, who was compelled, as were many, to express his feelings in verse, warned that the worship of Shakespeare might threaten the worship of an even more divine being:

> Yet steals a sigh, as reason weighs
> The fame to SHAKSPEARE given,
> That thousands, worshippers of him,
> Forget to worship Heaven![28]

At Home with the Shakespeares

The idea of Shakespeare's immortality and the concomitant valorization of the Birthplace as a shrine was a main component of the commemoration of Shakespeare in Stratford beginning in the second half of the eighteenth century. The focus on Shakespeare's birth, however, signals a shift in his identification with the house; it represents a turn to biography and, with it, an emphasis on Shakespeare's mortality. More specifically, the Birthplace became the home of Shakespeare's imagined childhood and, as such, was bound up in contemporary ideas about the growing significance of youth as a distinct period of life and the importance of the domestic realm.[29] The Victorians are often credited with the invention of "the home" in the sense that they imbued this physical space with social and moral values about the family unit, the upbringing of children, and the differing roles of men and women. These attitudes are evident in the stories of Shakespeare's childhood that circulated around this particular building.

The emphasis on Shakespeare's early life in the Birthplace came to prominence in the beginning of the nineteenth century and initially ran alongside the discourse of divinity. One of the first instances of this development can be found in Washington Irving's description of the house in *The Sketch Book of Geoffrey Crayon, Gent.* (1819–20), a curious hybrid of fact and fiction that recounts the protagonist's trip to Stratford. Crayon's visit to the Birthplace does not bode well: his impression of the house as a "small mean-looking edifice of wood and plaster" is not helped by the fact that he is guided around the property by "a garrulous old lady in a frosty red face," who wears a wig under "an exceedingly dirty cap."[30] But when he is confronted with a chair that was said to have belonged to Shakespeare, Crayon leaps into imaginative biography, seeing the young William sitting on it and "watching the slowly revolving spit with all the longing of an urchin; or of an evening, listening to the crones and gossips of Stratford, dealing forth church yard tales and legendary anecdotes of the troublesome times of England."[31]

Irving's, albeit brief, account of Shakespeare growing up in the Birthplace set the tone for texts that followed. The sometimes strained juxtaposition of the language of divinity and domesticity reaches an unintentionally comic climax in Leigh Cliffe's poem, *The Pilgrim of Avon* (1836), which draws on Coleridge's *The Rime of the Ancient Mariner* but is somewhat lacking in its literary merit. The poem tells of the narrator's dream of an old man, who has come from afar, "A Pilgrim to the Poet's Shrine,/Led on by Genius' guiding star."[32] Cliffe's verse identifies Stratford as the last port of call before death, the final pilgrimage before the journey to the grave, a connection that was later made in an article on the town published in *Fraser's Magazine*.[33] It is the Birthplace, however, that receives the pilgrim's special attention, his emotions in the house almost parodying the enthusiasm displayed by so many nineteenth-century visitors:

> And was it here! Oh! was it here,
> His cry first charm'd a mother's ear?
> Here, where his first young wizard thought
>   To charm the wond'ring world was given. . . .
> Oh! that some mighty spell could raise
> A vision of the bygone days,
> A mirror, like his Banquo's, fling
>   In its reflecting radiance true,
>   His childhood's scenes before my view[34]

Fortunately, Leigh Cliffe's pilgrim did not have to wait too long before his wish to see Shakespeare's "childhood's scenes" was granted. Casting their own "mighty spell," Victorian biographies raised Shakespeare from the dead and placed him as a young boy sitting at the family hearth in the house on Henley Street.

The rage for biographies, in whatever form, was diagnosed by a contemporary critic as a "modern madness," and those of Shakespeare encouraged a particular frenzy.[35] According to Samuel Schoenbaum's account of Shakespeare's biographers, the abundance and varying quality of these Victorian life stories mark a move away from the "high road" of Shakespearean biography in the eighteenth century into various footpaths that are choked with foliage and sometimes lead nowhere.[36] Part of the problem, according to Schoenbaum, was that these years witnessed an explosion and proliferation of biographies of Shakespeare, with the result that they appeared in a bewildering array of publications: Schoenbaum mentions articles, monographs, editions, compilations, works of fiction, and large- and small-scale biographies, but he might also have added travel writing and guidebooks to Stratford and the Birthplace.[37]

Undeterred by the scanty details of Shakespeare's life (all that could really be said of him with any certainty was, to employ Groucho Marx's expression, that he was born at a very early age), these biographers sought to fill in the gaps. So effective were these imaginative Victorian accounts that Walter Bagehot, in his own biographical analysis, could confidently assert that "of no person is there a clearer picture in the popular fancy. You seem to have known Shakespeare—to have seen Shakespeare—to have been friends with Shakespeare."[38] And Stratford-upon-Avon was the place where one could properly acquaint oneself with the bard. Stratford provided the only trace, however faint, of Shakespeare's life, of the setting he grew up and grew old in, of the countryside he knew. As one Victorian writer recognized, "From the obscurity in which his life is shrouded, the coeval remains of Stratford-on-Avon have far greater importance than they would have possessed had Shakespeare received from his contemporaries notice such as has so frequently been lavished on inferior men."[39] Stratford, in effect, *was* Shakespeare's life; the town, it was argued, "is not the name of a place but the alias of a man."[40] There was a sense, however, in which Stratford did not simply elucidate Shakespeare's biography but actually played a part in constituting the details of his life: the houses that he occupied were seen as evidence of his position in society; the small market town was said to have given him a connection with the people; the surrounding countryside, it was suggested, led to his communion with nature.[41]

If Stratford brought the visitor closer to Shakespeare, then the Birthplace offered an even closer intimacy, the sense that one was walking on floors that Shakespeare had trodden, seeing things that his eyes had fixed upon. The presence of the young Shakespeare lingered in the very atmosphere. Although the house is barely mentioned in earlier biographies, in the nineteenth century it is inextricably woven into accounts of Shakespeare's life. This is the case in one of the most successful and respected of the Victorian biographies, which was written by Charles Knight and appeared as a single volume (1843) to accompany his edition of Shakespeare's works (published in parts between 1838 and 1841). Knight's biography attempted to contextualize Shakespeare, to relate his life to the manners and customs of his day. Despite its apparent historicity, however, Knight's style was as imaginative as Irving's before him, to the extent that he was compelled to justify it in the advertisement for the biography: "The form we have adopted may appear fanciful, but the narrative essentially rests upon facts," he proclaimed.[42] "Fanciful" is certainly an appropriate description of Knight's account of Shakespeare growing up in the Birthplace:

> The happy days of boyhood are nearly over. William Shakspere no longer looks for the close of day when, in that humble chamber in Henley Street, his father shall hear something of his school progress, and read with him some English book of history or travel,—volumes which the active presses of London had sent cheaply amongst the people. . . . At this season we may paint the family of John Shakspere at their evening fireside. The mother is plying her distaff, or hearing Richard his lesson out of the A B C book. The father and the elder son are each intent upon a book of chronicles, manly reading. Gilbert is teaching his sister Joan *Gamut*, "the ground of all accord;" whilst the little Anne, a petted child, is wilfully twanging upon the lute which her sister has laid down. A neighbour comes in upon business with the father, who quits the room; and then all the group crowd round their elder brother, who has laid aside his chronicle, to entreat him for a story.[43]

Knight's remarkable textual picture of the Shakespeares at home is accompanied by an illustration by the artist William Harvey (Figure 2).

Harvey's drawing of the fireside with its spacious chimney nook is an exact rendition of how it appeared in the nineteenth century (like the other vignettes of the interior of the house in the biography, this picture was drawn on the spot in the Birthplace when Harvey toured Stratford with Knight and his family),[44] but the illustration also makes a significant addition to the room, inserting into this interior the Shakespeares themselves. Harvey does not show William's siblings (a pity as one almost wants to see the spoilt Anne), but focuses instead on Shakespeare's mother, who plies her distaff alarmingly close to the fire, and a young Shakespeare, book in hand, who leans against his father's knee, a father whose domed forehead, beard, and mustache resemble portraits of the older William.

The inglenook fireplace in the Henley Street house that is described by Knight and pictured by Harvey had made its first appearance nearly half a century earlier in the form of an illustration of the Birthplace in Samuel

Figure 2. William Harvey, "The Fireside," from Charles Knight, *William Shakspere; A Biography* (London: C. Knight and Co., 1843).

Ireland's *Picturesque Views on the Upper, or Warwickshire Avon* (1795),[45] but it took on a fantasy life of its own in the Victorian period. When John Mounteney Jephson visited the house in the 1860s, he imagined Shakespeare sitting on a settle in the chimney breast learning his lessons, reading Holinshed, or drying off after one of his raids upon a neighboring park or warren (a reference to the story that Shakespeare was forced to leave Stratford after he was caught poaching deer in the nearby estate of Sir Thomas Lucy at Charlecote Park).[46] In a souvenir publication timed to coincide with the tercentenary celebrations in 1864, Shakespeare's mother, Mary Arden, is described sitting in the cozy chimney corner with William's baby brother, Gilbert, on her knee and William at her side and telling stories "such as Hermione used to tell her wonder-loving restless boy, Mamilius."[47] Another writer sees the Shakespeare family, including five children, gathered in the chimney corner, their laughter and talk making the winter nights pass quickly, although, he adds, "like most things written about Shakespeare, this is pure speculation."[48] Frequently, however, such stories move away from their status as "pure speculation," and many commentators assert as a matter of fact that the young Shakespeare loved to sit in the chimney nook in the kitchen.[49] The Victorian custodians of the Birthplace actively exploited this fascination with the fireplace, encouraging visitors to take a seat in this same chimney nook, which was carefully dusted each morning.

The descriptions of the young William Shakespeare listening to or reading tales in front of the glowing embers of the fire indicate the roots of his literary creativity and constitute part of a historical connection between fireplaces and storytelling that Shakespeare himself alludes to in several of his plays. Richard II advises his wife, "In winter's tedious nights sit by the fire/ With good old folks and let them tell thee tales/Of woeful ages long ago betid" (5.1.40-42); while Lady Macbeth exclaims that her husband's "flaws and starts" when he sees Banquo's ghost "would well become/A woman's story at a winter's fire" (3.4.63-65). Victorian writers also regarded the fireside as a site of inspiration: the stories that Shakespeare reads there, they imply, will influence his later works. They were probably right. Catherine Belsey has analyzed the debt that Shakespeare's plays owe to fireside tales, a debt that was frequently picked up on by the Victorians.[50] Charles Knight's description of the stories that Shakespeare recounts to his eager brothers and sisters bears an unmistakable similarity to the plays: there are tales of wars, tales featuring goblins and witches, and a tale of a tragic love affair between members of feuding families which scarcely leaves a dry eye in the house.[51]

The fireplace also has another function in these nineteenth-century accounts, capturing a particular notion of domestic felicity and comfort (Harvey's illustration even includes the family pets) that had particular resonance for the Victorians, for whom the hearth was at the heart of the sanctified space of the home. In this period, Shakespeare was reimagined as a domestic hero. A sermon given on the occasion of the tercentenary by Charles Wordsworth, the bishop of St. Andrews and a nephew of William Wordsworth, described Shakespeare as the quintessential Victorian poet, "especially in that we are a *domestic nation*."[52] Shakespeare, Wordsworth asserts, is "to us Englishmen, the national, the domestic Poet, whom we love as we love our own homes."[53] The fact that Shakespeare apparently left his wife and children and spent most of his life in London is no hindrance to Wordsworth, who portrays him as a "parent of such affection, such sensibility, such tenderness."[54] Even when Shakespeare lived in London, "time after time, he dropped, as it were, again into this his nest."[55] Another contemporary critic argued that amid the attractions of the metropolis, Shakespeare always found time to think about, if not to visit, Stratford and his family, "and here clustered all those hopes and fears for the future, all those dear remembrances of the past . . . . Then, all hail! our Shakespeare, for his love of home."[56]

The attempt to locate Shakespeare in an idealized domestic setting was fundamental to the the meaning of the Birthplace during the period, although there was the occasional objector, who pointed out the stark reality of this myth. Nathaniel Hawthorne, who visited the Birthplace before the restoration, observed that the dimensions of the Henley Street property meant that the family were quite literally too close: "A great fire might of course make the kitchen cheerful; but it gives a depressing idea of the humble, mean, sombre character of the life that could have been led in such a dwelling as this—with no conveniences, all higgledy-piggledy, no retirement, the whole family, old and young, brought into too close contact to be comfortable together."[57] According to Hawthorne, these claustrophobic domestic conditions serve ultimately to emphasize Shakespeare's greatness: "What a hardy plant was Shakspere's genius, how fatal its development, since it could not be blighted in such an atmosphere!"[58]

Other writers, however, fostered an appealing image of family life, which ignored the daily realities of Tudor existence and focused instead on Victorian gender roles, with the maternal figure as the linchpin of this domestic ideal. Another American visitor to the Birthplace, Harriet Beecher Stowe, was inspired to create an extraordinary account of young Shakespeare as a bright-eyed, curly-haired boy, who creeps up the stairs of the Henley Street house to explore the mysterious garret full of mice and rats and cobwebs. A belligerent relative finds William watching a mouse hole with his cat and sends him downstairs straight away, complaining that his mother does not control him better![59] For Stowe, who also imagines Mary Arden with a "lovely face" and John Shakespeare as "a man who wore his coat with an easy slouch," these visions emanate from the very walls of the house; one can almost hear the sound of voices and rustling garments in the deserted rooms.[60]

The genre painter Thomas Brooks (1818–1891) turned these imaginings into a visual reality (Figure 3). Brooks's painting, which was probably composed in the 1860s, was sold in reproductions to tourists in Stratford at the end of the nineteenth century.[61] A blanket box in the background of the picture inscribed with the name "Shakspeare" and "1564," the year of his birth, indicates the context of the image. Beside the cradle, where the baby Shakespeare is bathed in a divine light, his mother gazes dreamily across the picture space, perhaps contemplating the future that lies in store for her son, a clue to his fate being provided in the couple of books that lie scattered on the table and windowsill. This picture is the visual equivalent of the textual accounts of the Birthplace written by biographers and travel writers that attempted to recreate Shakespeare's birth and young life. It could almost have been the inspiration for the opening passage of George Henry Calvert's "biographic aesthetic" study of Shakespeare published in Boston and New York in 1879: "In Stratford on Avon, a small town of Warwickshire, England, in a small room of a cottage on Henley Street, lay, in the summer of 1564, a babe asleep in his cradle. Beside the cradle sat a young woman, with broad, open brow and large hazel eyes, that were a light to clear symmetrical features. This woman was Mary Arden, wife of John Shakespeare, and, three months before, the babe had been christened WILLIAM SHAKESPEARE."[62]

As well as textual equivalents, Brooks's image also has specifically pictorial counterparts, its iconography familiar from the hundreds of pictures of mothers, their babies in cradles at their sides, which crowded the walls of the Royal Academy in the nineteenth century and were frequently reproduced as engravings to adorn the walls of Victorian homes. Although the presence of an impossibly cherubic baby Shakespeare is the key to the meanings of this picture, it is actually Shakespeare's mother, the aptly named Mary, who is the focus of the image. For the Victorians, with their interest in physiognomy and

Figure 3. [Thomas Brooks], Mary Arden and the infant Shakespeare in the Birthplace, c. 1860s. Photograph by Chaplin, Stratford-upon-Avon (c. 1900). Reproduced by permission of the Shakespeare Birthplace Trust.

their fluency in reading such narrative paintings, her calm demeanor, neat dress, and serene expression would immediately suggest her worthiness to fill the maternal role. Indeed, costume aside, Mary Arden is the ideal Victorian mother (her hair swept back from her temples and placed neatly under her cap is, in fact, a fashion of the 1860s). Although Anne Hathaway was sometimes represented in the period as an ambiguous figure accused of seducing and entrapping the younger Shakespeare,[63] Mary Arden was viewed as a paragon of virtue, the inspiration for the "beautiful female creations" in the plays,[64] and even responsible for her son's love of flowers.[65] Stowe regarded Mary Arden as the embodiment of and model for Desdemona's purity: "I cannot believe that, in such an age, such deep heart-knowledge of pure womanhood could have come otherwise than by the impression on the child's soul of a mother's purity," she writes.[66] This association of Mary Arden with specifically middle-class values about female purity and maternal duty is exemplified in Brooks's picture, where the interior of the Birthplace, as humble as it is, is characterized by its cleanliness and tidiness, with the vase of flowers on the windowsill and the books, those symbols of learning and improvement, lying within easy reach.[67]

The iconography of pictures like Brooks's—the persistence of the image of the young Shakespeare hiding in the attic of the Birthplace or reading by the fireside—makes these scenes seem strangely familiar, less like fictional accounts and more like memories of how things really were. Gaston Bachelard has argued that houses are spaces of daydreams and memories, and this seems especially true of writers' homes.[68] Harald Hendrix emphasizes the importance of such houses in the making of memory, whether it is the self-fashioned memory of how the author wants to be remembered or the memories that others bring to these sites.[69] The growing status of Shakespeare's Birthplace in the Victorian period means that it assumes an even more symbolic value, functioning as what Pierre Nora calls a *lieu de mémoire*, a site of cultural memory that is invested with the meanings of the heritage of the community.[70] *Lieux de mémoire*, Nora asserts, are "rituals of a ritual-less society; fleeting incursions of the sacred into a disenchanted world."[71] Nora's terms characterize the nineteenth-century understanding of Shakespeare's Birthplace: a secular shrine with its own set of rituals that occupies an exalted status in a culture in which organized religion and orthodoxy were increasingly undermined. However, whereas for Nora the *lieu de mémoire* is the realm of true memory (as opposed to history, which is a construction of the past), the memories of Shakespeare's house are only ever imaginary.

This fictionality is exposed in Mary Elizabeth Braddon's *Asphodel* (1881), a novel set in the vicinity of Stratford, where the hero sneers at the tendency to recreate Shakespeare's young life through the environment in which he lived (although he does later gain his comeuppance by falling to his death off the Matterhorn):

"We may picture [Shakespeare] as a youth going across the fields to Shottery: because it is the shortest way, and a man of his Titanic mind would naturally have taken it: yes, over the same meadows we tread this day: on the same ground, if not actually on the same grass." Or again: "Seeing that Apostle-spoons were still in common use in the reign of Elizabeth, it may be fairly concluded that the immortal poet used one for his bread and treacle: for who shall affirm that he did not eat bread and treacle, that the inspired lad of the Stratford grammar-school had not the same weaknesses and boyish affections as his schoolmates? Who would not love to possess Shakespeare's spoon, or to eat out of Shakespeare's porringer?" That is the kind of rot which clever men write about Shakespeare; and I think it is because I have been overdosed with such stuff that I have learned to detest the bard in his private character.[72]

The inclination to bring Shakespeare back to life and turn him into a real bread and treacle-eating human being might be "rot," but it had an overwhelming appeal, which was evidenced just two years after the publication of this novel when Clement Mansfield Ingleby made the shocking suggestion that Shakespeare's body should be exhumed.[73] Ingleby, far from a madman, was an accomplished Shakespearean scholar and a trustee of the museum housed in the Birthplace. He argued that seeing Shakespeare's skull in the flesh, as it were, would authenticate or invalidate the numerous portraits of the playwright and the bust in Holy Trinity Church. Implicit in Ingleby's proposal was also the idea, motivated by his own interest in phrenology (the notion that character traits are laid out in the shape and size of the skull) that Shakespeare's bones would provide evidence of his personality. The skull might give vital clues to the man he was, a different man, Ingleby hoped, from the clownish figure represented in the bust, who looked like he was eating a sour apple.

But what if, after his body was exhumed, Shakespeare did not live up to the ideal? What if, in Ingleby's terms, he was just a clown after all? Such a possibility was at the heart of the problem that the unfortunate hero of *Asphodel* had stumbled upon and that was later described by Sigmund Freud. At Goethe's birthplace in 1930, Freud (speaking via his daughter, Anna) argued that a focus on biography can actually degrade its subject because it reduces the distance between the person and us: "It is unavoidable that if we learn more about a great man's life we shall also hear of occasions on which he has in fact done no better than we, has in fact come near to us as a human being."[74] Hawthorne had reached the same conclusion when he visited Shakespeare's Birthplace over eighty years before: "I think I can form, now, a more sensible and vivid idea of him as a flesh-and-blood man;" he muses, "but I am not quite sure that this latter effect is altogether desirable."[75] Writing in *Our Old Home: A Series of English Sketches*, Hawthorne elaborates on this effect in terms that anticipate Freud: "It is for the high interests of the world not to insist upon finding out that its greatest men are, in a certain lower sense, very much the same kind of men as the rest of us, and often a little worse."[76] The author of a book about Shakespeare and Stratford grappled with the same problem when he remarked, "Had we seen him, most likely we should have found him a man like ourselves, greater because he was not less but more of a man, suffering terribly from all the ills to which flesh is heir; and we should have been disappointed."[77] For this writer, "It is better as it is. We know not for certain even his likeness, or his form. The earth-dress falls away, the worthless mortal coil is shuffled off, and only what is pure and noble, the essence of all that is great in the man, remains for evermore as a precious birthright to all the world."[78] The essence of the poet is only fully revealed when his life is rejected, when the "earth-dress falls away." Part of this "earth-dress" is the Birthplace itself, a trapping of Shakespeare's real, historical existence in Stratford-upon-Avon that privileges his childhood and the setting of the family hearth and, in so doing, generates collective memories that are only ever fictions.

But while fictions might lack veracity, they can be alluring, as Henry James suggests in his short story, "The Birthplace," which was published in the collection *The Better Sort* in 1903.[79] "The Birthplace" (the building is never actually identified as Shakespeare's house, but the clues are explicit in text) recounts how Morris Gedge, the custodian, goes from being morally unwilling to tell visitors the dubious tales surrounding the history of the house to indulging in and embellishing the legends. It is the image of a child sitting beside the fire, so pervasive in accounts of Shakespeare's Birthplace, which marks the climax of Gedge's inventive storytelling:

> It is in this old chimney corner, the quaint inglenook of our ancestors—just there in the far angle, where His little stool was placed, and where, I dare say, if we could look close enough, we should find the hearthstone scraped with His little feet—that we

see the inconceivable child gazing into the blaze of the old oaken logs and making out there pictures and stories, see Him conning, with curly bent head, His well-worn hornbook, or poring over some scrap of an ancient ballad, some page of some such rudely bound volume of chronicles as lay, we may be sure, in His father's window-seat.[80]

In the context of the cynicism of James's story, Gedge's picture of the young boy reading ballads in front of the fire is highly ironic, but the reliance on this iconography for the denouement of his narrative suggests how familiar it had become. James exposes this image as a myth, but, even as Gedge recounts his tale, it has the resonance of a memory of what once was or what could have been. This story might be just a story, but it is still seductive, both for the fictional tourists to the Birthplace, who listen to Gedge, and perhaps even for the readers of James's text.

Shakespeare on a Pedestal

The Birthplace, then, was the catalyst for the two main impulses behind the commemoration of Shakespeare in Stratford: the first was a largely eighteenth-century rendition of the bard as a quasi-divine, immortal being, whose house was a shrine and a site of pilgrimage; the second was a nineteenth-century emphasis on Shakespeare as a young boy living within this domestic space. At times, these paradigms stood uncomfortably side by side, particularly when it came to ideas about how Shakespeare should be represented and the material form that his memorialization should take. The question of how to depict Shakespeare was central to debates that sprung up periodically throughout the nineteenth century concerning the erection of a national monument. Private, as opposed to publicly funded (and therefore "national"), monuments had been built, such as John Thomas's sculpture *Shakespeare*, which was shown in the Crystal Palace in 1864 and depicted Shakespeare on a throne made of swans and accompanied by the figures of Comedy and Tragedy. Such sculptures, however, had not been entirely successful: when Thomas's had been displayed in the 1862 International Exhibition, the bad reviews were said to have hastened his death.[81] As far as national monuments to Shakespeare went, there was the memorial that had been placed in Poets' Corner in Westminster Abbey in 1740, but this was generally regarded as a failure, a "sculpturesque caricature" that "failed to satisfy the commemorative aspirations of the nation."[82] The nineteenth century, moreover, constituted a different historical moment, a different nation, and this called for a different kind of monument. In 1820 the actor Charles Mathews proposed a "national monument to the immortal memory of Shakespeare,"[83] an idea that resurfaced at the time of the auction of the Birthplace and again during the preparations for the tercentenary celebrations. Visitors like Victor Hugo were horrified that England had no monument dedicated to its national poet: "When one arrives in England, the first thing that he looks for is the statue of Shakespeare. He finds the statue of Wellington," Hugo complained.[84]

The building of a national monument to Shakespeare, however, entailed a fixed idea of what "Shakespeare" meant and how he should be portrayed: a focus on the man, for example, might generate a statue or likeness; while an emphasis on the immortal genius of Shakespeare required something symbolic rather than representational. There was, of course, the possibility of trying to encapsulate both "Shakespeares." For something truly monumental that would also depict Shakespeare as a man, the French sculptor Pierre-Joseph Chardigny proposed the erection in London of a colossal statue of Shakespeare, which would stand one hundred feet high and be built from cast iron.[85] Inside this statue would be three floors and various attractions. Visitors could ascend right up to Shakespeare's head (the top of which was made of glass to let in the light) and see all of London through the orifices which formed the pupils of his eyes. The *Art-Journal* objected to this proposal on the grounds that its scale took away from the sense of Shakespeare as a mortal, representing him as "a monster instead of a man."[86] Portrait statues, it asserted, should not be so large as to lose all sense of human scale; only symbolic statues could get away with being so big. The enormity of Shakespeare's genius could not be captured by constructing an enormous monument, and critics often cited Milton's poem "On Shakespear" as proof that such transcendence could not be shown: "What needs my Shakespear for his honour'd Bones, / The labour of an age in piled Stones, / Or that his hallow'd reliques should be hid / Under a Star-ypointing *Pyramid?*"[87] The answer, of course, was that Shakespeare needed no such monument.

In 1864 the people of Stratford disagreed with Milton's sentiment. The tercentenary celebration was to be marked by three schemes: a festival to be held in Stratford, the endowment of scholarships to universities for those who had received their education at the local grammar school that Shakespeare was said to have attended, and the erection of a monument in the town. When the idea of a monument was originally vetoed in the committee responsible for the celebrations, the Stratford locals revolted, organizing a petition that forced the mayor to convene a meeting to reconsider the situation. "Public feeling at this time ran very high on the subject," writes Robert E. Hunter, secretary of the committee.[88] At this meeting, James Cox, a local timber merchant, delivered an eloquent speech in which he argued "that no scheme for the commemoration of the three hundredth anniversary of our great national poet can be considered complete that does not embrace as a prominent feature a statue or monumental memorial, to be erected in this his native town."[89] This motion was supported by E. T. Craig, a phrenologist from Warwick, and was carried unanimously, with a national subscription being established for the collection of funds.

But not everyone saw the desirability of a monument to Shakespeare. John Ruskin was privately dubious about the venture. Writing to the journalist E. S. Dallas, he recounts that he had received a letter from Stratford informing him that Alfred Tennyson, Lord Carlisle, and Charles Buxton had joined a monumental memorial committee and asking if he too would join. "I didn't like to look as if I thought myself wiser than Tennyson; so I wrote saying, as far as my own judgement went, I could only repeat what I had said—that Shakespeare needed no memorial, that I thought we dubbed ourselves idiots if *we* wanted one of him;—and that nothing could be done anyhow, but that nevertheless, if I could be of any use, my name was at the disposal of *those three gentlemen*."[90] So concerned is Ruskin by the business of the monument that he adds in a postscript: "You *can't* have a monument. No human creature alive is fit to do a stone of it."[91] The novelist, Anthony Trollope, concurred. When he was asked a decade or so later to contribute to the Memorial Theatre in Stratford, he remarked, "If there be any one who does not want more memorials than have been already given, it is Shakespeare!"[92]

Alongside discussions of how Shakespeare should or should not be monumentalized, the tercentenary revealed a shift in Shakespeare's geographical bearings. In 1861 a committee in London had been formed with the same purpose of raising subscriptions for a Shakespeare monument, and when this became part of the capital's own plans for the tercentenary, there was considerable bickering as the rival Stratford and London committees attempted to secure the most famous names and raise the most money. The *Illustrated London News* came out, predictably, on the side of London, arguing for a representation of Shakespeare the man: "We think that the statue is the form which the tribute should take, and that the metropolis is entitled to the custody of the statue, not only because London was the place where the poet flourished, but because it is only by placing the memorial in the capital that we shall afford the world a chance of seeing it."[93] *The Times*, on the other hand, while contending that "we do not like the idea of a monument," decided to support Stratford in terms that highlight the extent to which Shakespeare had become associated with the town of his birth: "All Europe and all America, when they give to Shakespeare a local habitation, think of him not in connexion with London, but in connexion with Stratford, where he was born, where he was educated, where he married and had children, where his family seem always to have lived even when he himself was in London, where he visited them from year to year, where as he grew in wealth he bought house and lands, where he retired in the fulness of his strength to enjoy his days, where he died, and where he now lies buried."[94] These comments have some significance because they suggest not only the global appeal of Shakespeare but also his local specificity, signaling a decisive move away from a metropolitan sense of the bard to a provincial one. Stratford and Shakespeare had become intertwined, so much so that the little English town had risen from obscurity to be recognized the world over as the home of the bard.

This ideological move became a literal one when the London committee's plans for 1864 collapsed, leaving Stratford to host the events. The tercentenary celebrations in London took on a more restrained and symbolic form. The sapling of an oak tree, taken from Windsor Park by permission of the Queen, was planted at the foot of Primrose Hill and was "christened" with water from the Avon.[95] Shakespeare here was defined as the poet of nature and of nation, the Windsor oak associated both with the plays and with a specific idea of Englishness. As the *Illustrated London News* commented, the "undertaking was to plant an oak, the English tree, at the foot of Primrose-hill, in honour of the English poet."[96] This gesture, which was organized by the Working Men's Committee and also signaled Shakespeare's appeal across class divides, was the most fitting way of commemorating a bard who was more allegorical than real. His status was made explicit in the speech of the chair of the committee, who asserted that the tree was planted "with a view to perpetuate to those who are to come after us the high and universal esteem in which our immortal poet is held at this period of our history."[97]

While Shakespeare's immortality was honored in London, in Stratford there was no sign of the promised statue that would depict his mortal form, despite the fact that more funds were raised for this monument than for any of the other tercentenary schemes. (The suggestion that persons subscribing a shilling or more would have their names inscribed on rolls of parchment preserved in the Birthplace was obviously a good inducement.)[98] Perhaps there was a growing realization that Stratford did not need a national monument to Shakespeare because it already had one: the Birthplace itself. This house was superior to any monument because it seemed to provide a link to the past and could accommodate the multiple identities of Shakespeare, inspiring "memories" of him as a real historical being while at the same time pointing to his genius and divinity. So effectively did the building fulfill the role of monument, that, according to the critic Sidney Lee, all other attempts at national memorials to Shakespeare were doomed to failure when the ownership of the Birthplace was in private hands.[99]

In the century between Garrick's Shakespeare Jubilee and the tercentenary, there had been a crucial shift in the construction of Shakespeare from divine to domestic, and this took place in tandem with a shift in the proper location of his commemoration from London to Stratford and from monument to Birthplace. This change, as Lee's statement recognizes, was bound up in a defining moment in the Birthplace's history: its transfer in 1847 out of private hands and into national ownership, the subject of the next chapter. The appeal to the public to purchase the house employed and depended upon the dual registers of Shakespeare's divinity and domesticity, fully exploiting the ability of the building to offer direct access to Shakespeare's life. This idea is suggested in one of the seminal works in the homes and haunts tradition, William Howitt's *Homes and Haunts of the Most Eminent British Poets*, which was published in the same year as the auction. Having written in some length about Stratford-upon-Avon in his earlier *Visits to Remarkable Places* (1840–42), Howitt turns his attention to locations associated with Shakespeare in London, but even within this context, he admits that it is in Stratford rather than London that we can see "the actual traces of his existence," including the house and the room in which he was born.[100] These "traces" provide the impetus for the campaign to save the Birthplace, a building that was increasingly recognized as the most fitting monument to the bard and that came to encapsulate what "Shakespeare" meant to the Victorians. As the popular writer Douglas Jerrold commented, "There has long been a public desire to testify this urgent feeling towards Shakespeare, and the sale of the house of his boyhood affords an opportunity. It is a better mode than a mere statue."[101]

Chapter 2

Bidding for the Bard:
The Auction of the Birthplace

The Show Home

For a perfect family outing in the summer of 1847, it was difficult to beat the Surrey Zoological Gardens. Children could peer through cages holding wild and exotic animals; mothers could visit the flower and fruit shows; while fathers and older boys could be entertained by a pyrotechnic display of the siege of Gibraltar and the blowing up of battering ships. In 1847, however, there was an added attraction. Occupying a prime position in the fifteen-acre plot stood a house. With its higgledy-piggledy beams and exposed brickwork, the property had seen better days, but this did not stop thousands of tourists from waiting in line to enter it. These visitors needed no reminder of why they were there, but if they looked up as they crowded through the quaint little timber door, they would have seen, just above the open hatch that constituted one of the downstairs windows, a sign that announced: "THE IMMORTAL SHAKSPEARE WAS BORN IN THIS HOUSE."

The immortal Shakespeare was not really born in this house, but, as far as replicas went, this was certainly impressive. In many ways, it was better than the actual Birthplace. For one thing, it was closer to London, and it also came with a complete interior and furnishings, in contrast to the dilapidated condition of the Stratford house following the recent death of its owner. Apart from location and interior (and the fact that the Surrey house had been aesthetically detached from the houses on either side of the Birthplace), the two properties were identical. As the *Illustrated London News* commented, "Nothing can exceed the minuteness of the copy."[1] The replica Birthplace was a mirror image, right down to the blackened and worm-eaten timbers and the broken paving stones outside the front door. Some pains had been taken to ensure this veracity, the artist Alfred Crowquill (Alfred Henry Forrester) being commissioned to make drawings of the Birthplace on the spot in Stratford and superintend the construction of the house in Surrey.[2] The result, according to the advertisement, was that Shakespeare's Birthplace was the most successful attraction that the Zoological Gardens had ever shown.[3] The house, the poster confidently asserted, appealed equally to those who had seen the Stratford property and those who had never visited it: "To the countless Thousands who are prevented from making a Pilgrimage to the Hallowed Spot, this cannot fail proving eminently gratifying, whilst to those who have had the satisfaction, the vraisemblance must be highly interesting."

But there was another reason why the Surrey house was proving such a success in the summer of 1847. Never one to miss an opportunity, the proprietor of the Zoological Gardens had built his replica in response to the public excitement caused by the probable fate of the Stratford Birthplace. Shakespeare's house was up for sale! This announcement (complete with numerous exclamation marks that emphasized the shocking nature of the event) dominated the press until the property went to auction in September. This chapter explores the representation and contradictory meanings of the sale and the problems and anxieties that it generated: problems concerning to whom the property belonged, or should belong, and wider, but interconnected, anxieties about the dangers of the marketplace. The publicity surrounding the auction positioned the Birthplace at the epicenter of what Ivor Brown and George Fearon have called the "Shakespeare Industry,"[4] or what Barbara Hodgdon has more recently termed the "Shakespearean exchange economy."[5] The marketability of Shakespeare has its roots in Garrick's Jubilee and even the preceding decade with its production line of mulberry-tree relics, but the Shakespeare industry that we recognize today, the economy that has transformed Stratford into a tourist mecca (a description that was frequently used by the Victorians), was a direct result of the auction of 1847.

A growth in the Stratford tourist trade had been predicted by Douglas Jerrold, who suggested that, if the Birthplace were bought for the nation, Stratford would be enlarged by "the thronging to the town of an increased number of visitors,"[6] and, according to commentators, such a rapid increase in tourist numbers did indeed occur.[7] Because figures for admissions to the Birthplace were not always totaled in the earlier years and sometimes not at all, it is impossible to calculate just how many tourists entered the hallowed doorway of Shakespeare's first home, but there seems to have been a significant rise from the 700 or so visitors per year recorded between 1812 and 1814, to 2,321 from 1852 to 1853, and over 30,000 from 1900 to 1901.[8] In addition to tourism, there were other commercial opportunities that evolved from the auction. In the months leading up to the sale, for instance, the Victorian consumer could buy his or her very own Birthplace. J. V. Quick, a toymaker, lived up to his name in his speedy production of a New Puzzle of Shakespeare's House, a drawing which showed the house on all four sides, and which, cut out and folded according to the directions, made "a splendid Chimney Ornament."[9] There were also lithographs, etchings, and engravings of Shakespeare's house (and, curiously, of the Surrey replica) that provided the perfect decoration for the walls of Victorian homes. Envelopes and letter paper came adorned with embossed pictures of the Birthplace, and a medal showing the house and the room in which Shakespeare was born was available in silver and bronze.

Publishers also jumped on the band (or should that be "bard"?) wagon. Frederick Fairholt's *The Home of Shakspere*, complete with thirty-three engravings, had sold few copies outside Stratford when it was first published in 1845 but was reissued and became a bestseller, the *Art-Union* referring to it as "well-timed."[10] Another timely, or as the *Athenaeum* described it, "seasonable" book was George May's *A Guide to the Birth-Town of Shakspere and the Poet's Rural Haunts*, which was "intended to supply what the writer says he has, in occasional visits to Stratford, found to be needed—a guide-book succinctly directing the worshipper of Shakspere to the several localities there more peculiarly connected with the poet's name."[11] Less expensive publications included a *Shakspere Newspaper* documenting the history of the Birthplace and events leading up to the sale, and a special edition of the *Illustrated London News*, issued on the Saturday following the auction and containing recent pictures of Stratford and the Birthplace. Even the auction catalogue was marketed as a souvenir. With sixteen quarto pages that included extracts about the Birthplace from numerous works and a decorated title page depicting a view of the house alongside other vignettes, the catalogue, as an advertisement proclaimed, "should be possessed by all who take an interest in the property."[12]

But prospective purchasers needed to hurry: "So great is the curiosity excited by the sale of this relic of the immortal bard, that the catalogues are already selling at half-a-crown each."[13]

Ownership of these goods provided only a momentary gratification, however, or rather, it both masked and exposed the fact that, at the very moment that they were on sale, there was another far more valuable object that had entered the marketplace: the Birthplace itself. With the imminent auction of the house in Stratford-upon-Avon, came concerns about who might purchase it. In the possession of the wrong sort of people, defined as foreigners and private speculators, there was the risk that it could turn into a vulgar tourist attraction. *The Times* expressed the typical view that "if the house be transferred out of the hands of its present proprietary by a private bargain, it will be traded upon as a common show."[14] The *Athenaeum* saw this prospect as an incentive for the British public to purchase the building: "One great inducement to the national appropriation of this monument is the desire to rescue a property so sanctified by its associations from the vulgarity of showmanship and the commonplaces of commercial speculation."[15] These frequent allusions to "showmanship" and "speculation" were shorthand for a more specific threat that was bound up in issues of national identity: there was a risk, whether real or imagined, that Shakespeare's house would be bought and moved brick by brick as a tourist attraction, not to a Surrey zoo, but to the birthplace of the showman and the speculator: the United States of America.

These anxieties about the fate of the Birthplace now that it had entered the marketplace had historical parallels. In 1847 factory closures, speculation in the railways, the high price of imported goods leading to the collapse of the loan market,[16] and a series of bad harvests (which had such devastating effects in Ireland), conspired to create an economic crisis. Frederick Engels regarded the situation as the most severe England had ever seen: "All the branches of England's vast industry have been paralysed at the peak of its development; everywhere there is stagnation, everywhere one sees nothing but workers thrown out on the streets."[17] Engels's words, appearing just weeks after the sale of the Birthplace, suggest the fragility of the economic prosperity brought about by industrialization. The capitalist world, Engels reminds the reader, is vulnerable and dangerous. And Shakespeare's house needed protecting from such dangers. At the very moment that the property was on the market, symbolic attempts were made to remove it, to suggest that this "shrine" was set apart from the commercial world.

Home Is Where the Mart Is

Mr. Robins had never seen anything like it. Despite years of experience as a London auctioneer, he was noticeably moved by the cheering that greeted him as he ascended the rostrum. Looking into the packed room of the auction mart, he would have noticed several famous artists and men of letters. There were, in fact, men everywhere—only one woman had braved the rush upstairs when the downstairs sales room proved inadequate to accommodate the crowds. Some prospective buyers anxiously thumbed their catalogues; others were there as witnesses to the event itself, glancing excitedly around or hurriedly copying what they saw in sketchbooks. This, after all, was no ordinary auction. The item up for sale on Thursday 16 September 1847 was Shakespeare's Birthplace in Stratford-upon-Avon (Figure 4).

This extraordinary event had been set in motion nearly a year before when Mrs. Court, the owner of the Swan and Maidenhead, the public house forming part of the Birthplace, pulled her last pint. Mrs. Court had a lucrative sideline showing round the odd tourist, and she had a business card printed, respectfully inviting "the nobility and gentry visiting Stratford-upon-Avon to gratify their own laudable curiosity, and honour her by inspecting the house in which the immortal Poet of Nature was born."[18] Her death meant that the whole premises, which also consisted of a tenement and butcher's shop, was up for sale. Even before her demise, a number of potential buyers were waiting in the wings. As early as 1843, Charles Knight made the case that the house should be bought by the government or a public society.[19] In April 1846, prior to Mrs. Court's death, such plans seemed to be under way. At a meeting to commemorate the bard's birthday, the chairman of the Royal Shakspearean Club, which had recently undertaken the restoration of Shakespeare's tomb and chancel in Holy Trinity Church, announced that "there might be a time coming when they could purchase one of the greatly authenticated relics connected with Shakspeare—namely, the house in which he was born."[20] One only hopes that the ailing landlady of the Swan and Maidenhead was not present in the town hall to hear his remarks. Despite the chairman's optimistic forecast, however, when the time eventually arrived, a lack of funds and a direction in the will of the late Thomas Court which necessitated that the

SKETCH FROM THE SALE OF SHAKESPERE'S HOUSE, AT THE AUCTION MART, SEPT. 16. 1847.

Figure 4. *Illustrated London News*, 25 September 1847. Reproduced by permission of Special Collections and Archives, Cardiff University. At the top left of the image is the only woman at the auction, Mrs. Fletcher of Gloucester. The tall man with the mustache opposite Mrs. Fletcher is the American actor George Jones. The seated figure with his arms crossed at the top of the picture is the editor Charles Knight, while in the foreground on the far left with the catalogue under his arm is John Payne Collier. The picture is full of other famous figures of the day, including George Cruikshank (his bare head can be seen next to the drawing of the Birthplace held by the gentleman in the right foreground).

property go to public auction, meant that the Shakspearean Club was unable to buy it outright from the trustee.

Not even the government was willing to intervene. A letter sent by the Royal Shakspearean Club to Lord Morpeth, Chief Commissioner of Woods and Forests, suggesting that the government purchase the house, came back with the response that "Members of the Government are disposed to think that the acquisition of so interesting a property pertains still more to the people of England than to the Government."[21] It was up to the "people," then, to buy the house and, with this in mind, the Royal Shakspearean Club set up a committee to take subscriptions. Their efforts in Stratford were aided by a London-based committee with high profile members including Charles Dickens as well as Prince Albert, the president of the committee, who pledged £250 to the fund.[22] The committees circulated posters and placed advertisements in newspapers and magazines imploring the public to donate money. So extensive was this publicity that there was the suggestion that the amount of press space devoted to the sale of the Birthplace was actually affecting the market value of the property, critics arguing that there should be no call for subscriptions until after the auction and that the committee should make it known that it was not willing to go beyond a fixed price for the house.[23] One writer anxiously remarked that because "the price rises in proportion to the curiosity excited by discussion," it was advisable to keep all further debate on the subject out of the newspapers, but conceded that, as a matter of such importance, the sale "ought to be kept before the public."[24]

It is no wonder that the nervous energy in the auction mart was almost tangible when Edmund Robins started the bids on that September day in 1847. A sum of 1,500 guineas was offered immediately, followed by a bid of £2,000 from a Mr. Butler of Clapton, then £2,100. But before Robins could even get into his stride, something extraordinary happened: he was handed a letter. Robins read aloud its contents to the excited audience:

> We the undersigned, deputed by the united Committees of Stratford and London for raising subscriptions for the purchase of Shakespere's House, hereby offer a bidding of £3000. The Committees having purchased another property, which really constitutes an integral portion of Shakespere's house, have expended a considerable part of the amount already raised by public contribution; but, looking at the duty imposed upon them in undertaking to represent the feeling of the nation, they have come to the resolution of making this large and liberal offer for the property now on sale, without regard to the funds which they at present command, in the confidence that the justice of the public will eventually discharge the Committees from the individual responsibility which they thus incur.—(Signed) T. Amyot, Chairman of the Committee of London, Thomas Thomson, Chairman of the Stratford Committee; Peter Cunningham, Treasurer of the London Committee; W. Sheldon, Treasurer of the Stratford Committee.[25]

After this letter had been read, Robins asked if anyone present proposed to offer a larger sum. According to one newspaper, "A few moments of anxious suspense ensued, when no other bidder appearing, the Stratford and London Committees were declared the purchasers for £3,000, amidst immense cheering, which clearly exhibited the gratification which those present felt at the circumstance of this most interesting national monument having been secured for the nation by the committees."[26]

The house had been "secured for the nation," but it had come at a cost, and not just to the Stratford and London committees, which, unable to pay off the debt, were forced to take out a bank loan.[27] By putting a price on what was commonly represented as priceless, the auction marked a clash of Victorian values, and it was in this clash that a specifically Victorian idea of Shakespeare and his worth began to emerge. The Birthplace, and, by implication, Shakespeare himself, had a value, and this value increased according to its apparent otherness from the market.

Home Economics

The contradictory status of Shakespeare and the Birthplace reached a climax in the auction mart, but it had been building up for months previously when potential subscribers were encouraged to part with their cash in a campaign that played on the notion that the house should not be on the market in the first place. This defining moment in the birth of the Shakespeare industry, then, was always already at odds with itself. By capitalizing on the religious terminology associated with the Birthplace, the call for subscriptions gave this construction of the house a new urgency and immediacy, with the building commonly described in the press as "hallowed," a "shrine," a "relic," a "monument," a "place of pilgrimage," and "a temple." A prologue to a performance of extracts from Shakespeare's plays held after the auction, which was written by Charles Knight and recited by the famous actor-manager Samuel Phelps, demonstrates the extent to which the identification of the house as a place of worship had become the norm:

> Yes! when a race unborn shall gather round
> *His* hallowed roof, and consecrated ground,
> And secret tears, and smiles of sudden glee,
> Attest his sway—the mind's own jubilee;
> Remembrance, perhaps, may turn to this "brief hour,"
> Which yields *our* feeble homage to his power:
> For here th'assembled Nation stands to say,
> Our Shakspeare's home is snatch'd from quick decay[28]

The religious imagery used to describe the house went hand in hand with a focus not only on Shakespeare's childhood but also on his ghostly presence, the *Daily News* writing that "there is a haunting presence which lingers round all in the midst of which the hero has lived, moved, and had his being"[29] and the *Athenaeum* referring to the Birthplace as "a site which is haunted and glorified."[30]

The idea that the Birthplace was worth rescuing because of its intimate, even supernatural, connection with Shakespeare did not go entirely unchallenged. The earl of Ellesmere, the vice president of the London committee, gave a personal subscription of £100, but argued that "a single copy of Shakspeare in the backwoods of America was a more enduring monument to the genius of our immortal dramatist than any structure of marble could possibly be."[31] The explicit reference here was to the call to build a monument to Shakespeare, but there was also a veiled reference to the "monument" that the Birthplace was becoming. Dissenters, however, were in a minority. The conflation of bard and Birthplace was a rhetorical and ideological device that was frequently employed during the campaign for funds, where the purchase of this house was regarded as a display of affection for Shakespeare. Thus, at the meeting to establish the London committee, it was suggested that buying, and thereby "saving," the property would demonstrate an "expression of public reverence towards Shakspeare's memory."[32] Harriet Martineau used a similar persuasive argument in her campaign to secure subscriptions from the poor. In a letter that was reproduced in local newspapers and working-men's magazines, she wrote that the auction of the house marked the "last and precious opportunity of showing that we truly revere and love our own glorious Shakspere . . . . Our neglect now will not be mere carelessness; it will be ingratitude."[33] When the house was eventually purchased, Douglas Jerrold poured scorn on those who saw it as a type of relic-worship, arguing that because Shakespeare was human it was only natural to feel a human affection for him; the Birthplace intensified this affection by offering the possibility of contact with the dead author: "We are by these means sensuously informed of his actuality, and seem able to expand in affection towards him."[34]

The representation of the Birthplace as an embodiment of Shakespeare and a divine place of worship gained force particularly when the marketplace was considered its opposite. As *The Times* remarked, "There is something grating to the ear in the announcement that SHAKSPEARE's house is about to be submitted to the hammer, and will be knocked down without reserve to the highest bidder."[35] Other magazines and newspapers stressed the absurdity of a situation in which the Birthplace had "become a matter of pounds, shillings, and pence!"[36] The *Athenaeum* summed up these sentiments: "It must have sounded strangely in the ears of foreign enthusiasts to hear that this place of pilgrimage was *in the market!* Considering the worship which Shakspeare has in England, there is something remarkable in the very language which announces the fact—that a dwelling which has been glorified by his familiar presence should have found its way to the Auction Mart, as if it were any other hereditament—and its 'haunting memories' have become an argument for the cant of the auctioneer."[37] The point that is made emphatically here is that the Birthplace is not any old building: its status arises from an association with the mortal and immortal "presence" of Shakespeare and its evocation of "memories" of him. In this respect, the fact that the house was for sale in England, the country that had given birth to and nurtured this literary genius, is presented as especially deplorable. Indeed, the prospective purchase of the Birthplace provided an opportunity to distinguish between the commercial and intellectual character of the British: "Are we for ever and a day to be looked upon as a commercial race only,—a nation of shopkeepers?" asked *Sharpe's London Magazine*. "Oh! it may be well to call us a mercantile people, plodders and workers in base metal; but we have our intellectualities about us."[38]

The commercial potential of the Birthplace, it was argued, should be cast aside and scorned upon; the marketplace threatened the "hallowed roof" and "consecrated ground" with "spoliation"[39] and "desecration."[40] The nearer the sale got, the more emotive the language became. Referring to the Birthplace as a "heart-stirring relic," a phrase also used in the auction catalogue, the *Athenaeum* stated that "of all the heart-stirring relics which this old country boasts, there is not one so deeply interesting as this—there is not one which we would less willingly suffer to disappear—there is not one on the removal of which by the sacrilegious hand of modern avarice or utilitarianism would inflict a more lasting reproach upon the nation: and yet, the house is to be sold by auction; and may be carried away piece-meal and cut into tobacco-stoppers!"[41] If it did not get cut into tobacco stoppers, there were other "sordid purposes" that might lie in store.[42] The *Morning Herald* saw it transformed into snuffboxes by the French, pipes by the Dutch, and card cases by the Chinese.[43] "The Oldest Inhabitant" of Stratford wrote in *Punch* that he had heard rumors that the timber from the house was to be made into bootjacks and clothes pegs,[44] while the *Athenaeum* warned that the house could be demolished to construct railway tracks, or, even worse, the whole site could become a modern Shakspeareton, with Timon terraces, Rosalind Rows, and Cordelia Squares.[45] And Shakespeare himself was not free from the taint of economics. One letter sent to a campaign organizer parodied the typical doorstep response to the subscription campaign: "Subscribe indeed! daresay this Shakespear has ruined himself in railway speculations, and now comes to us for money to pay his debts."[46]

Of course, there was always the unsettling possibility that the construction of the Birthplace as a shrine set apart from the commercial world could itself become a marketing tool. This was exploited to full effect in the following poem, which appeared in the *Shakspere Newspaper* and was written by the infamous "Poet of Moses," the author of numerous advertisements in verse for the clothing retailers Elias Moses and Son:[47]

> Where is the senseless heart that has not felt
> An interest in the House where Shakspeare dwelt?
> Who hears announced the melancholy tale,
> Of such a mansion being up for sale?
> Could one be met with who could tamely hear
> The final knock-down of the auctioneer?
> No—all with fondest feelings would regard
> The sacred dwelling of the immortal bard.
> O! may the public still this feeling cherish,
> And never may the House of Shakspeare perish;
> Protect it for the facts which it discloses,
> As warmly as you do the house of MOSES!
> For Shakspere as a poet was displayed
> Almost as great as MOSES in the trade.
> The House of MOSES stands upheld by all;
> Nor will the public suffer it to fall.
> MOSES & SON a glorious part have "play'd."
> In all their "acts" upon the stage of trade.
> Their mighty mountain ne'er produced a mouse,
> And hence they boast an overflowing house.
> Long may the trading house of MOSES stand
> The universal wardrobe of the land:
> Where garments beautiful in make and style,
> Will ever merit an approving smile.
> But pardon me—for, through the warmth I've felt,

I've quite forgot the house where Shakspeare dwelt—
And let me say before this tribute closes,
Protect IT as you do the house of MOSES.[48]

The poem, followed by a list of made-to-measure prices for dress coats, vests, and tweed trousers, beautifully exemplifies the complex relation between Birthplace and marketplace that was such a defining characteristic of the auction. The verse is a call for subscriptions and an advertisement, a celebration of Shakespeare and shops, the religious imagery it uses to describe the house echoed in the very name of the store: Moses and Son. As this advertisement implies, it was sometimes difficult to maintain the distinction between Birthplace and marketplace. Not only was Shakespeare's house up for sale, but, as any contemporary visitor knew, this "sacred dwelling" also happened to be a butcher's shop and a pub.

The People's Property

Maintaining a distinction between Birthplace and marketplace was imperative to the appeal for funds to secure the property. The call for subscriptions was primarily an attempt to ensure that the house did not become a vulgar commercial enterprise. It was an objective, however, which very nearly failed. Perhaps people were spending their money in Moses and Son; perhaps, with the economic depression, they did not have the money to spend; it may even have been the case that they were not convinced by the association between bard and Birthplace on which the purchase of the house depended. Whatever the reasons, the subscriptions did not come in as fast as the committee organizers had hoped. The assumption has generally been that because the Birthplace was eventually purchased for the nation, the call for funds was a success. Louis Marder, for example, comments that "the public did discharge the Committee's obligation, and has responded many times since then."[49] Despite this generous view, the truth of the matter was that the committee bought the Birthplace without the requisite money, and the public did not absolve this debt. Even the plays put on in aid of the fund failed to attract audiences. A performance of *The First Part of Henry IV* concluding with an opera of *Rob Roy* (it must have been a long night) did not collect as much as £10.[50] (Admittedly, this might have had something to do with the abilities of the cast, the *Daily News* reporting that "the forgetfulness or incompetency of the greater part of the

actors was too obvious to escape the laughter and ridicule of the audience.")[51]
Another performance by the Metropolitan Dramatic Society was also a
failure.[52]

Despite all the language of religious fervor and desecration, the appeal was
greeted with apathy. The public might have agreed with the "Fast Man," who
wrote in *Punch* that he could not understand what all the fuss was about: "We
don't care about SHAKSPEARE, or his house either."[53] In such desperate circumstances, newspapers attempted to shame people into parting with their money.
This frequently involved bringing "foreigners" into the debate in order to
compare their regard for Shakespeare with the neglect of the English, who
seemed quite willing to sit back and watch the house being bought and shipped
abroad. The Germans, for example, were well known for their love of Shakespeare: they treat "the name of Shakspeare with a reverence and ceremony that
become the homage of the Foreigner," claimed the *Illustrated London News*.[54]
The English, on the other hand, being too close to Shakespeare, often fail to
recognize his power.[55] Some papers were less forgiving: "Shakspere, to the
whole world akin, and his memory cherished by every people from the Wolga
to the Ganges, from the Thames to the Mississippi, from the Glommen to the
Niger, from the Rhine to the Maranon, is threatened with a Vandal desecration in the land of his birth, and on the very spot of his nativity. The home in
which he lived is advertised for sale! to be pulled down and carted away, as if it
were the common rubbish of the world, and not precious in every atom."[56]
Such remarks, which were typical of the press reaction to the sale of the Birthplace, highlight the wider implications of the nineteenth-century notion of
Shakespeare both as a universal poet with global appeal and as a distinctly
national one. On the one hand, the interest of foreigners in the English bard
and the apparent flocking of so many to the Birthplace gave credence to his
greatness. On the other hand, Shakespeare was used to keep foreigners out.
Throughout the commentary on the auction, there is a need to defend Shakespeare against foreign annexation and to define him as a figure around which
patriotic sentiment might cohere.

This patriotism is in evidence, and at stake, in appeals to the locals to support the cause. Walter Savage Landor called specifically on the people of
Warwickshire to come to the aid of the Birthplace: "If the Crown and Parliament are so insensible to disgrace, if the English people at large are so ungrate-
ful to the teacher of whom they have been boasting all their lives, let me exhort
and implore his more immediate neighbours to protect his deserted mansion."[57]

Likewise, a local newspaper pointed to the example of Scotland, which had honored Robert Burns and Sir Walter Scott, its literary heroes. "Let it not be said of the County of Warwick," the article commented, "that when the swarthy Indian, the hardy Northman, and the enterprising American have come forward to recognise and commemorate the genius of Shakespeare, the men of his own County have been found lukewarm in the cause."[58]

Shakespeare's own county, however, proved positively cold in its fundraising. Theodosius Purland, a wealthy dentist, who was a member of the London committee, canvassed his acquaintances to collect funds. One respondent wrote back, "I have tried my best to stir the Warwick and Leamington people in this subject but have found a plentiful overflowing of apathy—they are rather more delighted with people who balance poles, coach wheels and that sort of thing."[59] The *Royal Leamington Spa Courier and Warwickshire Standard* confirmed this view, stating that the sale "does not appear to excite much interest in the County which has the honour of claiming his birth-place."[60] The *Athenaeum*, unwilling to blame the lack of funds on indifference, pointed instead to the incongruity of the Birthplace being on the market. The contrast between public apathy and avowed idolatry, it claimed, lay in the "very singularity of the announcement."[61] The public did not believe that such a situation could have arisen; the event seemed unreal.

These attempts to canvass particular groups of subscribers (whether locals or the "English") expose the fact that the social fabric of mid-Victorian Britain was far from unified. Despite the government's view that the Birthplace should belong to "the people," there was no clear consensus of what "the people" constituted. Indeed, the relative failure of the appeal for money came about in part because "the people" were always fractured and heterogeneous. The campaign highlighted, and in some cases exacerbated, these divisions. The gap between Warwickshire and the rest of the country, alluded to by Landor and the *Royal Leamington Spa Courier and Warwickshire Standard*, widened into a gap between the capital and the provinces, which dogged the work of the London and Stratford committees. From the outset, there were concerns about making "the entire people of England parties to the purchase of Shakspeare's house,"[62] but having a metropolitan and provincial committee, along with other committees that were springing up by the week, seemed to compromise this inclusiveness. Separate proceedings, it was feared, "might seem to imply a want of union,"[63] and with this in mind, some commentators argued that although Stratford was home to the poet's ashes and relics, there should be only one committee based in London.[64] The result of these divisions, according to one magazine, was that "from opinions, gossipings, and gatherings, attained throughout the wide range of the county—in Coventry, in Kenilworth, Warwick, and Birmingham— there appears to be a conflict of feeling and an apathy of action."[65]

This apathy was as much a comment on contemporary attitudes toward Shakespeare and his works as on the Birthplace itself. The *Illustrated London News* wrote that there were many more people who admired Shakespeare than ever read him, and even this admiration was limited: "When a writer says that the admiration of Shakspeare is a national feeling, he means it is the sentiment of the part of it he represents and addresses. But what an abyss beneath, where the light has not yet penetrated?"[66] In terms of the appeal for subscriptions, the light only seems to have penetrated the elite, a factor that came to the fore in the subscription list with its famous actors, writers and artists, such as Charles Kemble, Charles Knight, Tom Taylor, and William Etty, and in the auction itself, where the attendees included Shakespearean scholars like Knight, James Orchard Halliwell (later Halliwell-Phillipps) and John Payne Collier.[67] Harriet Martineau attempted, unsuccessfully, to democratize the appeal. In her letter to the working classes, Martineau set out her plan: "In every town and neighbourhood set on foot a penny subscription. Speak of the matter, all of you, wherever you go. You will all of you give your pennies. Such of you as can spare a little time, and do not mind a little trouble, make yourselves agents and collectors."[68] But pennies, it was argued, would not buy the Birthplace. The *Athenaeum* drew attention to Martineau's scheme and saw in it an attempt to make the property "national in the most extended sense," agreeing with the "*universality* of right and interest" in the house which it encouraged.[69] Time, however, was short and the fate of the Birthplace should "not be left to chances so minute."[70]

What was represented as an appeal to "the people," then, increasingly failed to address them. The working classes, as the subscription lists indicate, did not respond in any significant way to the plea for money, a factor that might seem surprising considering that Shakespeare was evidently a popular writer with working-class theater-goers and readers.[71] This failure was largely due to the economic crisis itself, which meant that the working classes lacked the means to contribute to the funds, but they also seemed to have lacked the will. This could have been because they still perceived a gap (which the auction rhetoric itself did so much to bridge) between the plays and the Birthplace. The architectural structure on Henley Street might have seemed far removed from an enthusiastic appreciation of *Henry V.* Working-class disillusionment with the scheme might also have been exacerbated by the specifically middle-class vocabulary and ideology with which the papers couched their campaigns. This tone continued after the auction when the purchase of the house was seen as having an ameliorative effect on the working classes. The *Evening Sun* asserted that "The most unimaginative must behold in this proceeding a brilliant token of the advancement of civilization in these realms, and a lesson calculated to inspire the uneducated mechanic with aspirations beyond those which have, in bygone centuries, been prevalent throughout the humbler classes of society."[72]

The auction of the Birthplace served to emphasize the widening gulf between the classes that was to have its political expression in the last of the Chartist rallies which took place the following year. At the time that this most exalted of houses was up for sale, property itself, and the ownership of it, was at the forefront of these political discourses, the Chartists demanding the abolition of the requirement that Members of Parliament be property owners. When *Punch* complained that the aristocracy had not contributed enough to the fund (the rich, it wryly suggested, were too modest to open their purse strings), it framed its argument in terms of a class-based ownership of the house.[73] If the dukes, marquesses, earls, and barons failed to give subscriptions, then the "ready-money vulgar" would end up buying the Birthplace, leaving the aristocrats "without a single stake—as it is called—in the property." If, however, neither the nobility nor the moneyed come forward, then the millions should contribute their shillings: "It will—at the cost of only twelve-pence—be a pleasant fancy to a poor man to know that when he dies, he bequeaths to his successors twelve-pennyworth of the house of SHAKSPEARE. A mere splinter of one of the rafters: the smallest morsel of one of its bricks. Thus considered, every man and woman may, we repeat it, become fractionally, a household proprietor; leaving his and her property to the generations that are to follow."[74]

Home from Home

But Shakespeare's Birthplace, as the *Punch* article also implies, was not "private property": it was a "national monument."[75] Indeed, the aim of the committee purchasing the house was to bypass individual ownership and make the "nation" its proprietor. This strategy, moreover, was established in opposition to other nations that staked a claim to Shakespeare. With the auction looming, *Bentley's Miscellany* included a quotation from the American actor James Henry Hackett, copied from the visitors' book in the Birthplace, which suggested the extent of American interest in Shakespeare:

> Shakspeare, thy name revered is no less
> By us, who often "reckon," sometimes "guess";
> Tho' England claims the glory of thy birth,
> None more admire thy scenes well "acted o'er"
> Than we of "States unborn" in ancient lore.[76]

Despite America's apparent love of Shakespeare, in the discussions over the Birthplace it served as a foil to Britain, typifying everything wrong with consumerism and allowing the English to be defined in their difference from Americans. The country, it was argued, bred a particular type of speculator with no ethical values or, indeed, taste. In this way, the Victorians' concerns about speculation and the very marketplace of which they were a part were displaced onto a foreign other, a displacement that manifested itself in the widespread fear that the Birthplace would itself be displaced, uprooted from Stratford and taken to the States.

America came to embody two major anxieties about the marketplace: the dangers of speculation and free trade. In the economic crisis of 1847, caused in part by investment in the railways that could not be sustained, "speculator" was fast becoming a derogatory term. The merits or liabilities of free trade had also been the focus of recent attention in debates over the repeal of the Corn Laws in 1846. The repeal, a belated response to the Irish potato famine, and the debates that ensued grappled with the implications of "free trade," a trade that would not be restricted or controlled by national borders. These implications were central to the way America was represented during the sale of Shakespeare's Birthplace. The result of an international competition in the marketplace that was not curtailed or regulated by the government meant that the Birthplace could potentially be bought by American speculators and shipped abroad. A popular poem of the time uses this threat as a way of drumming up national support:

> Tis true, tis pity chaps from Yankee land
> Are coming over with the cash in hand.
> Blow winds, crack cheeks, their paltry lucre spurn

To what base uses may we not return,
Speculation—British nation, Oh, save the house from exporta-
tion![77]

The Times might have avoided such rhyming tactics, but it too stirred up the worst fears of the nation, reporting that "one or two enthusiastic Jonathans have already arrived from America, determined to see what dollars can do in taking it [the Birthplace] away. The timbers, it is said, are all sound, and it would be no very difficult matter to set it on wheels and make an exhibition of it."[78]

From one or two speculators in *The Times*, the *Shakspere Newspaper* warned that there were actually four Americans who were "on the alert" and asking detailed questions about the soundness of the timber and whether it could be transported.[79] Removed from Stratford, the Birthplace was in danger of losing its sacred status. No longer the fixed, permanent site of pilgrimage, which promised to enrich the soul of the visitor, it would become a house on wheels, part of a traveling show, which would enrich only the bank accounts of the investors. The vulgarity of the speculator and the spectator who participated in such an enterprise was used to motivate the public. If the English were to avoid the humiliating and degrading sight of this relic being lifted off its foundations and carried about on wheels around America like a "raree show" or "a caravan of wild beasts, giants, or dwarfs," they needed to make their donations.[80]

The generic "speculators" and "Yankees" actually had proper names: George Jones and Phineas T. Barnum. Jones, an American tragedian of questionable talents, was living in Britain at the time of the auction.[81] His greatest achievement was the authorship and performance of the "Original Oration upon the Life, Character, and Genius of the Poet," a celebration of Shakespeare that was peppered with dubious classical references and the "originality" of which was fast receding, Jones delivering it on every available occasion. Although he was praised as a gentleman and a scholar by his "friend" Leigh Cliffe, who dedicated his poem about Stratford to him, Jones was already a marginal figure of fun in the British press.[82] His attempt to purchase the Birthplace for "the people," however, was greeted with a censure and derision that seems strikingly out of proportion to the plans that he set out in his campaign. This might be explained by the fact that the journalists who disapproved of him were themselves members of the London committee for the purchase of the house. Tom Taylor, for example, an active member of the London group, who was writing for *Punch*, called him a "Human Blue-Bottle" and warned that "he must not be allowed to paw the revered head of the Poet—to bring his pinch-beck near the touch-stone of SHAKSPEARE's truth. There is desecration in it that makes *Punch* perfectly savage."[83]

Jones was actually one of the first public figures to come to the rescue of the Birthplace. On 13 August 1847 he held a public meeting in the Hanover Square Rooms, London, in order to organize a "People's Central Committee," which would raise a national subscription. True to form, the meeting was dominated by the actor. Giving apologies from an aristocrat, who was apparently supposed to have chaired the meeting, Jones chaired it himself and spent more than an hour reciting his "Original Oration upon the Life, Character, and Genius of Shakspeare" to an increasingly bemused audience.[84] Despite this unpromising start, the resolutions of the so-called "People's Committee" were remarkably similar to those later outlined by the London committee, which did not hold its first meeting until 26 August. (Jones complained that because he had been first, they should work with him.)[85] Dismay was expressed at the possibility of the Birthplace being "mutilated, removed, or destroyed by the hands of avaricious speculation, when it is regarded by the Nation as an heir-loom of the People of England"; and a resolution was made to start a subscription to buy the house, with any remaining money (Jones was nothing if not optimistic) going to the erection of a statue of Shakespeare in London or Stratford, the founding of a Shakespeare scholarship at Cambridge or Oxford, and the establishment of a Shakespeare charitable institution for the poor and infirm of Stratford.[86] With these objectives in mind, branch committees of the People's Central Committee would be set up in every city and town.

In some ways, Jones's campaign was more transparent in its aims than the London committee, where the purchase of the Birthplace was tied up with plans to insert Sheridan Knowles, the poverty-stricken playwright, as its custodian.[87] Certainly, Charles Dickens seemed as concerned with this outcome as he was with the actual purchase of the Birthplace.[88] The People's Central Committee, however, was doomed to failure, and, ironically, part of this failure stemmed from Jones's appeal to "the people." The day after the meeting, the *Daily News* reported that the majority of Jones's audience was made up of the working classes,[89] and, two weeks later, commented that "There is very suspicious indication that this committee is 'a people's central committee,' somewhat in the same way in which the three tailors of Tooley-street were the people of England."[90]

In short, Jones was represented as a con man. The papers reported with relish the fact that a gentleman by the name of Jones "wearing a very formidable pair of moustachios" disrupted the auction by calling on Robins to prove that the house he was selling was the identical one in which the bard was born.[91] After the hammer was down, Jones apparently complained that he had been authorized to bid more than £3,000. *Punch* preferred to represent Jones as not having attended the auction at all, being deliberately waylaid by gentlemen of the joint London and Stratford committee, who promised to listen to his "Original Oration upon the Life, Character, and Genius of Shakspeare."[92] The accompanying picture shows Jones as Bottom, asleep in a bower of flowers, his elbow resting on the manuscript of the oration as Punch flies in with an ass's head (Figure 5).

As both an actor and American (Jones had, in fact, been born in England, but this was conveniently forgotten),[93] Jones was regarded as a showman. A one-act "musical extravaganza" by J. Stirling Coyne, *This House to Be Sold; (The Property of the Late William Shakspeare.) Inquire Within*, which was performed at the Adelphi Theatre at the time of the auction, included a protagonist called Chatterton Chopkins, who, although the son of a London butcher (a reference to the butcher's shop in the Birthplace), seems to parody Jones's showmanship and claims to gentility (*Punch* commented that the American

Figure 5. The American actor George Jones is about to be given an ass's head by Puck (Mr. Punch). *Punch, or the London Charivari*, 2 October 1847. Reproduced by permission of Special Collections and Archives, Cardiff University.

tragedian wanted the Birthplace as a country residence).[94] Having failed at all previous attempts at notoriety, Chopkins buys the Birthplace simply because he wants to be famous: "I aimed at celebrity by going up in a balloon, but if I had never come down I believe the world would not have missed me;—then I made public speeches that nobody would listen to—and I wrote a novel that nobody but myself and my printer read:—after that I tried to be notorious in dress and wore stunning waistcoats and terrific hats, but if I had walked out in Adam's original surtout people wouldn't have minded me;—then I turned to private play acting and got laughed at; *that* however was something, but it did not satisfy me—I wanted to be notorious."[95] The references to public speeches that no one listens to, play acting that everyone ridicules, and even the ostentatious dress, could well be an allusion to Jones and the way he was represented in the press at the time of the auction. Richard W. Schoch has argued that Coyne's play embodies "middle-class fears about unrestricted access to Shakespearean culture."[96] It also suggests the dangers of the house falling into private hands, Chopkins only being redeemed when he decides to donate the building to "the nation."

Twenty years after the sale of the Birthplace, Jones was still up to his old tricks. In 1865 an American newspaper reported that a man who called himself "George, the Count, Johannes" had brought his tenth libel suit in New York, this time against the editor of the *New York Tribune*.[97] (Jones had left Boston the previous year after being found guilty of barratry: exciting and encouraging lawsuits and quarrels.) By a strange quirk of fate, one of the witnesses in this libel case was the other American who had his own role to play in the auction of the Birthplace: the showman Phineas T. Barnum. To the delight of the New York jury, Barnum compared Jones to the "What Is It?," the half man, half monkey, that was one of his curiosities.[98]

In 1847 there was a horrifying possibility that the owner of the "What Is It?" could also be the owner of Shakespeare's Birthplace. Allusions to the Birthplace being uprooted and traveling around the United States as part of a "raree show," along with wild beasts, giants, and dwarfs, refer specifically to Barnum's apparent plans to purchase the house. This rumor seems to have had little basis in fact, but it was effectively employed as part of the campaign propaganda. As the *Annual Register* remarked, such stories were "industriously put into circulation."[99] One of the chief circulators, and most probable source of the rumor, was *Punch*, which early on in the campaign published a fictional letter from Barnum to the mayor of Stratford:

Mr. Mayor, we—free Americans, children of the star-spangled banner—we, who are the only people on airth who understand English in the clear grit that that 'varsal critter SHAKSPEARE writ it—we ought to possess the location in which he fust saw the light, afore any other nation under the blue canopy. SHAKSPEARE'S house is a drug in England; but wouldn't it be a beauty, put upon wheels, and drawn through all the States?

And so, Mr. Mayor, jist say the number of dollars that your Stratford critters want for the immortal location, and I'll consign 'em slick; or if you'd like—in these tarnation hard times—the vally of the house in breadstuffs, or hams, or molasses, or any other airthly fixings, I'll swap strait ahead—I will. And as for gittin the house over here, I've a notion that I'd ship every crumb of it.[100]

Sharpe's London Magazine, inspired by these rumors, envisaged the dreadful scene of the Birthplace being turned into a traveling show, where an Englishman would be requested to "walk up" as he would to "some itinerant Mrs. Jarley's wax-work" for the low price of twopence.[101] Then he would hear the showman, already fed up with his labors, reply in a "country-fair fashion" to an urchin, who asked him for some information, "Whichever you please, my little dear." Such would be the consequences, the writer remarks, of the house being bought and shipped to America as the latest curiosity from England and the successor to Tom Thumb.[102]

In the British press, Barnum embodied everything successful, but also reprehensible, about showmanship and speculation. He had toured Britain to much acclaim with Charles S. Stratton, otherwise known as General Tom Thumb, in 1844–45, first traveling to Liverpool and then the Egyptian Hall in Piccadilly (incidentally, Tom Thumb had also appeared in the Surrey Zoological Gardens, whose proprietor, William Tyler, was a friend of Barnum's). In 1847 memories of Barnum and Tom Thumb were clearly still in the public imagination. Barnum's particular association with the Birthplace came from a trip he made there in 1844 accompanied by the writer Albert Smith, who reported the outing as "A Go-a-Head Day with Barnum," which appeared in two installments in *Bentley's Miscellany* in 1847 to coincide with the furor over the auction. Barnum himself recounts the story of the trip in his autobiography.[103] The event is a wonderful comic episode made all the more amusing because of Barnum's irreverence for the bard. In the Birthplace he offers to hang a portrait of Tom Thumb alongside a likeness of Shakespeare and leaves behind a quantity of visiting cards, advertising the fact that the general could be seen every day at Dee's Hotel, Birmingham.[104] One of these cards later gets stuck to the monument in Holy Trinity Church. As Barnum complains to Smith, "You talk a good deal about your Shakspere being the pride of England, but I can see nobody knew or cared a cent about him while he was alive, or else you'd have known more of him now. If he'd been a living author, and I'd had my exhibition, I'd have backed the general to have shut him up in a week."[105]

For all his boasting, perhaps Barnum was right. General Tom Thumb might have put Shakespeare out of business. After all, Benjamin Robert Haydon, the history painter, was known to have committed suicide after watching thousands turn up to see Tom Thumb while the number of visitors to his own exhibition across the road barely made it to triple figures.[106] And if no one cared a cent about Shakespeare when he was alive, the situation did not seem much better now that he was dead. Despite the threat of Barnum, the campaign to raise money for the purchase of the Birthplace ended disastrously. After years in debt, the committee members must have looked back with some dismay at those words written in the letter they gave to Robins, the misplaced "confidence that the justice of the public will eventually discharge the Committees from the individual responsibility which they thus incur." However, the mechanisms by which the house had been purchased—the founding of committees, the call for subscriptions, and the successful outcome of the auction—all ensured a distinct type of ownership: symbolically, the house belonged not to an individual, whether Barnum, Jones, or Chopkins, but to the "people." As the *Athenaeum* commented in the wake of the sale, "The relic is henceforth rescued from the chances of individual possession and has become the property of the nation."[107] Indeed, in some ways, public apathy actually worked to validate the venture, signaling the distance between this scheme and the popular traveling shows of Barnum or the tourist attractions at Surrey Zoological Gardens, which depended on transitory enthusiasm rather than on the more enduring approval of future generations.

In 1847 the fate of the Birthplace was secure. The house had been bought for the "people," if not actually paid for by them. And this was far better than the fate that lay in store for the Surrey replica. After the auction the following notice appeared in a magazine:

> We have been deeply concerned to hear that, by the will of the proprietor, the Shakspeare's birth-place, at the Surrey Zoological Gardens, will be pulled down at the close of the season, unless the

most extraordinary exertions are made to secure it to the nation. As this interesting tenement has an equal claim to be considered the actual birth-place of Shakspeare with the old house at Stratford-on-Avon, it is hoped that Government will take some steps to save it from the grasp of Mr. Barnum, who is already after it.

That the money can well be spared, the following calculation will show, made in round numbers. The population of England is 16,000,000: the sum raised amongst them, for the purchase of Shakspeare's House, with all the exertions of the worthy enthusiasts who believed in its authenticity, was, say £1000. This, by a simple sum, proves that it took about 16 persons and a-half to raise each separate farthing of the money. It will be seen that there is still some to be spared to secure the Surrey Shakspeare House to us for ever.[108]

In its parody of the articles that were published in the press in the months before the sale, this notice highlights the dismal sum raised by the call for subscriptions. There is a sense, though, in which this comic notice is disingenuous. The subscriptions might not have reached the desired levels, but in other ways the campaign was more successful than the London and Stratford committees could have hoped. It was in the widespread publicity surrounding the auction that the link between bard and Birthplace was forged. The humor of this notice depends on a comparison between the two birthplaces that actually exposes the disparity between them. As a replica, it is the Surrey house that is the true commodity, throwing into relief its very difference from the sort of property that the Stratford Birthplace had become. These birthplaces might look identical, but the meanings and validity of the real house lay in what could not be seen: in the "haunting memories" of the genius who once lived there.

The next chapter deals with the attempt to turn these "memories" into reality by restoring the Birthplace to how it looked, or was imagined to look, at the time of Shakespeare's childhood. The restoration transformed the appearance of the building into one that was more appropriate to its status as a monument and was also more attractive to the growing number of visitors to Stratford. Ironically, the result of the auction and the subsequent restoration project was that the "saving" of the Birthplace became increasingly bound up in its role as a tourist attraction, even if its tourists were refashioned as "pilgrims." Mr. Barnum might not have acquired it, but in 1847 it was the house on Henley Street that became the greatest show home of them all.

Chapter 3

―――――

Bringing Down the House:
Restoring the Birthplace

The Other John Shakespear

Today, we are all too familiar with the creative language used by real estate agents. In 1847 the auctioneering firm of Robins, which was responsible for the marketing of Shakespeare's Birthplace, possessed a similar verbal dexterity. One can imagine a potential buyer following the auction catalogue's advice and paying a visit before the sale to this "singular domicile."[1] Walking the length of Henley Street, and being muddied on the way by the puddles and animal excrement that collected in the rough paving, this visitor would eventually have arrived at the house, where he would have stopped to look at the catalogue, then at the Birthplace, then at the catalogue again. Instead of a "truly heart-stirring relic of a most glorious period" (the catalogue's words), he would have seen a neglected remnant of what was once a Tudor building but now bore no trace of its former splendor. The Birthplace could not even strictly be described as "singular" or a "domicile," being set in a terraced street and made up of not one, but three, premises: a cottage, which was built onto the northwest end of the house and at the time of Shakespeare's death was occupied by his sister, Joan Hart; a butcher's shop in the middle, complete with an open hatched window; and, on the right, the Swan and Maidenhead, the pub sign fixed prominently to the wall. It is perhaps for the best that this hypothetical visitor returns home, dispirited, but considerably more alive to the power of hyperbole and euphemism, leaving it to the Stratford and London committees to purchase these dilapidated buildings for the nation.

Figure 6. Photograph of the Birthplace c. 1850. Reproduced by permission of the Shakespeare Birthplace Trust.

Other visitors stopped to have their photographs taken. These early images provide a record of how the Birthplace appeared prior to its restoration, with gentlemen, and occasionally a lady, looking startlingly incongruous as they pose outside the shabby timber-framed house. One photograph shows three male tourists, one of whom looks up at the sign that announces the provenance of the house, and another who gazes off in the direction of the Swan and Maidenhead, his romantic sensibilities no doubt shaken by its brick frontage and the decorative plant pot on the windowsill (Figure 6). It is no wonder that the Swan was, in the auction catalogue's terms, "a thriving Public-house": after a visit to the Birthplace, many tourists were in need of a drink.

Following the auction, members of the joint London and Stratford committee might also have been forgiven for turning to alcohol. Despite an apparent promise from the Department of Woods and Forests to accept responsibility for preserving the house if it was bought, this support failed to materialize.[2] Without any funds (only in 1855 was the loan for the purchase of the house eventually paid off), the committee could do very little to protect it. In the first few years under its new ownership, the Birthplace barely changed. Some outbuildings were demolished, the road in front of the house was paved, and a sheet of opaque glass was fitted in a window at the front.[3] And there was no longer any respite for the thirsty tourist: the Swan and Maidenhead was let to a tenant with strict instructions that it should no longer be used to sell alcohol, ostensibly due to the risk of fire, but more probably because of the impropriety of serving beer in Shakespeare's house.[4] This, after all, was the heyday of the temperance movement.

Then, in 1856, the committee's luck seemed to change. A benefactor appeared in the form of none other than John Shakespear. This John Shakespear was not from Stratford-upon-Avon but Ashby-de-la-Zouch. He claimed to be a descendant of his more famous namesake, but was very particular to spell his name as "Shakespear," whereas he wrote the poet's name as "Shakespeare."[5] A scholar of the Indian language, who made his fortune as the author of books on Hindustani (this was also the heyday of the British empire in India), John Shakespear offered to do something for the Birthplace and gave the committee £2,500 for this purpose. The situation looked even brighter when John Shakespear died the following year, leaving a quarter of a million pounds in his will (he was notoriously careful with his money), £2,500 of which he donated for the creation of a museum in the house, along with £30 to be paid twice yearly from the rents of his estate for the wages of a custodian.

The Birthplace committee never had much luck with money. A group of trustees was established to administer John Shakespear's generous donation and restorative work on the house proceeded, but the principal legatees under the will, his nephews, refused to pay out. The case eventually went to the Court of Chancery, the major dispute arising because of the phrasing of the bequest: "I give to my said trustees and executors, out of my personal estate, and before any other legacies, the sum of £2,500, to be laid out by them as they shall think fit, with the concurrence of the trustees of Shakespere's house already sanctioned by me, in forming a museum at Shakespere's house in Stratford, and for such other purposes as my said trustees in their direction shall think fit and desirable for the purpose of giving effect to my wishes."[6]

Because John Shakespear had not declared that the museum for which the money was intended was for public benefit, the court could not recognize it as a charitable gift. This allowed the nephews to question the will under the Statutes of Mortmain: the Birthplace committee constituted an "immortal" institution and the Statutes of Mortmain declared that no estate should be granted to such a corporation without royal assent. Moreover, there was no direction in the will as to the trusts upon which the money directed should be laid out or held. When the case went to appeal in February 1860 the Lord Chancellor concluded that the gift was void because of uncertainty. As the *Royal Leamington Spa Courier and Warwickshire Standard* reported, the court might have overcome the difficulty of the nature of the museum which was to be formed, "but the words 'such other purpose as his trustees in their discretion should think fit' were fatal," as were "to give effect to my wishes," because there were no other documents that said what these wishes were; the court could not know the intention of the testator.[7]

The Birthplace committee was again in debt and in June 1860 turned to the British public for funds. When the appeal for money predictably failed, a bank loan of £400 was secured to pay for the work that had already been undertaken, some income being generated from the sale to visitors of small pieces of oak recently removed from the Birthplace.[8] In April 1862, Charles Holte Bracebridge, a member of the committee, came to the rescue and lent £300 without interest to complete the work. When the house was finally opened to the public, a collection box was placed in the birthroom for contributions to the restoration.

The unfortunate case of John Shakespear might almost stand as a symbol of the restoration project itself. This was a man whose ambiguous status as a "descendant" of Shakespeare was exacerbated by the equally ambiguous status of a bequest that was vague and indeterminate, where truth and veracity could not be ascertained. This chapter suggests that it was the search for legitimacy and validity that lay at the heart of the restoration venture and its attempt to recover the Tudor history of the house. Yet the foundations of this project, its reliance on an imaginative visual impression of the Birthplace and a distinction between past and present that could not be sustained, were as precarious as the foundations of John Shakespear's donation.

Shaking the Foundations

The question of what was to be done with the house on Henley Street had always been problematic. As early as 1835 when the Shakspearean Club met in Stratford to formulate an appeal to restore the monument in Holy Trinity Church, they indicated that if enough money were raised (unsurprisingly, it was not), they would "gladly extend their care to the *preservation* of the house in which Shakspeare's father resided, on Henley Street, the presumed birth place of Shakspeare" (my emphasis).[9] In the months leading up to and following the purchase of the house, this discussion became more urgent, Douglas Jerrold expressing his hope that "the local authorities will endeavour to maintain the predominance of a style of architecture of an Elizabethan character."[10] But what exactly this "preservation" or "maintenance" might entail remained unclear. In September and October 1856, after the committee had received John Shakespear's donation, John Payne Collier wrote two letters to Thomas Thomson, the chairman of the committee, imploring him to proceed with caution: "we must be especially careful in what is usually called 'restoration,'" he writes in his first letter.[11] He followed up with more specific concerns in the second: "What I am most anxious about is, that no scrap of the original fabric should be removed, and that who-ever may undertake the restoration should have sufficient reverence for the smallest relic that can be preserved. All ought to be kept, as far as possible, in the state in which it now is."[12]

Collier's comments about preserving the original fabric of the house are rather ironic when one considers that a year after writing these letters he was to publish a six-volume critical edition of Shakespeare that incorporated emendations from the "Perkins Folio," an apparent second folio from 1632, which had been "discovered" by Collier and annotated in a mid-seventeenth-century hand that later turned out to be the mid-nineteenth-century hand of Collier himself. Nevertheless, Collier's remarks are suggestive of a growing concern about restoration projects and of the differences between restoration (turning the building into what it once was) and preservation (retaining it in its current state). These differences were framed as oppositions in the writings of John Ruskin. Ruskin had been dismayed at restoration work carried out on monuments and buildings in Italy and frequently criticized such projects, coining the aphorism that restoration is "the worst manner of Destruction."[13] Indeed, according to Ruskin, restoration was actually impossible: an old building could never be restored because what was eradicated in the process was precisely its oldness, its spirit and life:

> Do not let us talk then of restoration. The thing is a Lie from beginning to end. You may make a model of a building as you may of a corpse, and your model may have the shell of the old walls within it as your cast might have the skeleton, with what advantage I

neither see nor care: but the old building is destroyed, and that more totally and mercilessly than if it had sunk into a heap of dust. . . . But, it is said, there may come a necessity for restoration! Granted. Look the necessity full in the face, and understand it on its own terms. It is a necessity for destruction.[14]

For Ruskin, the solution was not to restore but to preserve buildings, replacing decaying brickwork or propping up parts of the structure that were essential to its stability. Any new work, Ruskin contended, should be strictly differentiated from the old, with stonework added to the building engraved with the date of its insertion so that future historians would be able to identify it.[15]

It was not only influential critics like Ruskin who were taking a concerned interest in restoration projects. In 1864, the year of the Shakespeare tercentenary celebrations, when the public gaze was on the Birthplace, the Reverend W. Heather, curate of Holmer and honorary secretary to the Hereford Diocesan Church Building Society, delivered a paper to the Herefordshire Philosophical, Literary and Antiquarian Society. The subject of his paper was the restoration of shrines, a subject that has some bearing on the secular shrine that the Birthplace had become. Heather, like Ruskin, took a stand against the improvement of buildings, arguing that as much as possible of the old fabric should remain. Restoration works, he argues, are little more than "acts of vandalism":[16]

> Timber roofs are dealt with in the same spirit. Either the old wood-work is removed altogether, or it is so wrought, and stained and varnished, that it presents to the eye the appearance of a new roof. Now, it must be conceded that this method of treating a church is not "restoring" it. It is not bringing it back to its original state. It is not preserving our archaeological landmarks, but on the contrary, giving an old friend a new face, and spoiling his countenance in the process. Instead of allowing us to hold converse with the venerable and time-furrowed features, we have been accustomed to, and our forefathers likewise, it is introducing us to a nicely got-up man of fashion of the nineteenth century.[17]

In the light of such activities, Ruskin suggested that a committee be set up with the aim of keeping an eye on old monuments and preventing unnecessary restoration,[18] a scheme that was eventually adopted in 1877 when William Morris established the Society for the Protection of Ancient Buildings, nicknamed the Anti-Scrape Society.[19] In a letter published in the *Athenaeum*, Morris made the connection between restoration and destruction that Ruskin had made almost thirty years earlier: restoration was an act of "barbarism" and this new society would "protest against all 'restoration' that means more than keeping out wind and weather."[20]

When the trustees received the £2,500 from John Shakespear in 1856, then, there were two alternative possibilities: either to preserve the house in its current condition or "restore" it with all the meanings that critics like Ruskin attached to this activity. The trustees called in as an advisor Edward Barry, the son of Charles Barry, who had designed the new Houses of Parliament on the banks of the Thames. In his preliminary inspection of the Birthplace, Barry outlined these two options:

> In dealing with the exigencies of the case, there are two courses open, one to uphold strictly all that now exists, removing nothing, and restoring nothing, but remaining content with upholding the building against the ravages of time, and transmitting it to posterity as far as may be, in its present shape; the other, to remove with a careful hand all those excrescences which are decidedly the result of modern innovation, to uphold with jealous care all that now exists of undoubted antiquity, not to destroy any portion about whose character the slightest doubt may exist but to restore any parts needing it in such a manner, that the restorations can never be mistaken for the old work, though harmonizing with it, and lastly to adopt such measures as modern science enables us to bring to our aid, for the perfect preservation of the building, and perhaps to endeavour to make Shakespeare's House a nucleus of such an institution as might prove eventually not unfit to bear so illustrious a name.[21]

Barry's proposal was either to leave the building alone, making only those repairs and additions necessary to preserve it in its current state, or to perform a sort of "anti-scrape" scrape, removing the modern additions of the building in order to reveal the ancient features beneath. Perhaps even Ruskin would have been content with Barry's recommendation that any repairs should be flagged as new, although exactly how recent work could be presented as such while "harmonizing" with the old is left unsaid.

The option chosen by the trustees is perhaps not surprising considering Barry's pointed remarks about the potential of the Birthplace, his indication that it could serve as the "nucleus" of an institution. Barry himself was quite clear about his own preference, warning that "If the first plan above named were adopted it would be necessary to uphold those portions of the building which in their modern ugliness so distress and confuse the present spectator and possess no sort of claim to historical interest, and for this and other obvious reasons, I do not feel called upon to recommend the adoption of such a course."[22] The trustees had probably already made up their minds. Letters and articles appearing in the press suggest that even before they received Barry's report, they had determined to restore the building. In the lengthy correspondence between John Shakespear's solicitor and William Oakes Hunt, the clerk of the Birthplace committee, Shakespear, no doubt under the committee's advice, offered the initial £2,500 specifically for the isolation and "restoration" of the house.[23] On 14 March 1857, John Payne Collier, writing for the *Athenaeum*, reported that in the previous week the trustees of the fund had held a meeting in which they decided to call in a well-known architect to determine how much of the modern additions to the house could be removed.[24] But, as in Barry's report, the methods of preservation and restoration are seen as complementary (rather than in terms of the oppositions posed in Ruskin's writing): restoration is actually presented as a type of preservation.[25] Reporting on the demolition of houses behind the Birthplace, the *Royal Leamington Spa Courier and Warwickshire Standard* commented that the committee had "never for one moment lost sight of the main object of their onerous mission—the conservation, in all its integrity, of the birth-place of the mighty Bard."[26]

Picture Perfect

The "conservation" of the Birthplace involved removing its modern aspects and revealing the ancient fabric. However, while the skeleton of the building gave some clues as to how it might have appeared when the first John Shakespeare purchased it, so little was surviving that its original appearance was difficult to ascertain. The Birthplace was to be restored, but restored to what? Perhaps the trustees of the John Shakespear fund should have followed the advice of a comic article published at the time of the auction in the *Man in the*

Moon. It showed the now familiar image of the terraced premises that made up the Birthplace alongside a picture of how the building might have looked when John Shakespeare bought it (a Tudor dwelling with prominent chimney stack and mullioned windows), how it might appear if Shakespeare was still living (an elegant Georgian villa, complete with glass house), and how it would look if it were restored by the Camden Society (an ornate Gothic building to rival the new Houses of Parliament).[27] The trustees sought advice from Edward Barry, who himself worked on the Houses of Parliament following his father's death in 1860,[28] but it was unlikely that they would favor a Camden or a Georgian version of the Birthplace. The *Man in the Moon*'s imaginative representation of what the house looked like when Shakespeare's father first took possession of it, however, did have some relevance for the restoration project because, as unlikely as it might seem, it was, in fact, a *picture*, the accuracy of which was as dubious as those comic drawings featured in the *Man in the Moon*, which served as the model for the entire restoration project.

With the architectural clues insufficient to indicate how the building appeared at the time of Shakespeare's birth, the restorers looked instead to a visual image. When John Shakespear made his donation, he concurred with the committee that the house be restored to "the state it appeared according to the old drawings."[29] This dependence on images was particularly apt in the restoration of a building that had already become a visual icon, the article in the *Man in the Moon* satirizing the proliferation of pictures that were appearing daily in the press at the time of the auction and that made the house instantly recognizable. The restoration project itself coincided with the growth of photography, a medium that was used to record the various states of the renovation. A local paper reported that when the restoration began and scaffolding obscured the front of the building, "the dismay of the multitude of peregrinating photographers, who have for the last six months been daily, nay, almost hourly, staring the poor old house out of countenance with the single eye of their mysterious machines, can be better conceived than described."[30]

These photographers might have sympathized with the decision of the Birthplace committee to turn to a picture for evidence of how the building looked in the past. The problem, however, was that this "past" was not the past of William Shakespeare, but of David Garrick. When Hunt wrote to Lord Carlisle asking his sanction as co-trustee for the restoration of the Birthplace, he revealed that the intention was to "restore the House to the state it is supposed to have been at the birth of the Poet according to the oldest Print extant and as it appeared at the time of Garrick's Jubilee in 1769."[31] But how the house appeared at Shakespeare's birth and how it appeared during the Shakespeare festival organized by Garrick two centuries later was not necessarily the same, nor was how it appeared at the time of the Jubilee and how it appeared in the "oldest Print extant" published in the same year. The camera never lies, or so the photographers outside the Birthplace might have claimed, but pictures frequently do.

The oldest drawing of the Birthplace and the one that was used as the template for the restoration project accompanied a letter written by "T.B." to the *Gentleman's Magazine* in July 1769 (Figure 7). T.B.'s letter, an example of the emerging fascination with homes and haunts, discusses the pleasures of visiting the burial sites and birthplaces of great men and refers directly to the attendant picture of Shakespeare's house: "My worthy friend Mr Greene, of this place, hath favoured me with an exact drawing of it (here inclosed), which may not possibly be an unacceptable present to such of your readers as intend to honour Stratford with their company at the approaching jubilee."[32] The "Mr Greene" responsible for this drawing was the antiquarian, Richard Greene, who himself contributed some thirty letters to the *Gentleman's Magazine* between 1751 and 1792.[33] Greene was famous for his Museum of Curiosities, an

Figure 7. R[ichard] Greene, illustration of Shakespeare's Birthplace, *Gentleman's Magazine*, July 1769. Reproduced by permission of Special Collections and Archives, Cardiff University.

eclectic collection of shells, stones, Roman coins, and other interesting objects, the admirers of which included Samuel Johnson. Significantly, his museum also consisted of items related to Shakespeare given to him by a neighbor, Peter Garrick, David's brother. An even closer connection to Stratford came in the form of Greene's brother, Joseph, who was headmaster of Stratford-upon-Avon grammar school and with whom he was in frequent correspondence. Joseph Greene took a keen interest in local affairs and was active in the appeal to raise funds for repairs to Shakespeare's monument in Holy Trinity Church. It is probable that Richard Greene drew this impression of the Birthplace on one of his visits to his brother.

Greene's image depicts a detached, timber-framed, gabled building with dormer windows and porch. Indeed, the success of the restorers in matching the Birthplace to this particular picture is demonstrated in the fact that the house we see on Henley Street today so perfectly mirrors this impression. Despite T.B.'s claims, and the apparent veracity of the image, however, this picture is anything but "exact." In 1769 the Birthplace was not a single house but was made up of several premises, as it was at the time of the auction. Nor was it detached from its neighboring dwellings or positioned in the middle of a field. The plan of Stratford executed by Samuel Winter in 1759 shows the house in the context of a terraced street. Rather than being an accurate representation of how the Birthplace really looked, Greene's drawing relies on an artistic convention, common to topographical images from the seventeenth century onward, that stressed the importance of buildings by setting them apart and isolating them from their surroundings. As the historian Lucy Peltz writes of antiquarian prints of London buildings, this convention ensured "clarity of visual information which could never be matched *in situ*."[34] The Greene brothers, who were interested in drawing and printing techniques and collected images of architectural structures as well as drawing them, would have been familiar with these conventions, which are also reflected in the decision to show the front profile of the building, to exclude any extraneous detail (people, for example), and to represent the house, despite its age, in such a remarkably good state of repair.[35] Shakespeare's Birthplace, like other important buildings pictured at the time, was meant to appear as it might have to its Tudor contemporaries, not as it was at the time it was drawn.[36]

What is revealing is that the trustees chose this particular image as the model for the restoration project. Apparently, this was because it was the oldest known engraving, but it also happened to represent the Birthplace in the most imposing way. Despite the questionable accuracy of Greene's image, it was the faithful transformation of the actual house into how it appeared in this picture that became the priority of the restorers. When advertisements were posted for architects, potential applicants were encouraged to view a copy of Greene's image at the local stationers.[37] Indeed, there was considerable anxiety during the restoration when the picture and the architectural features of the building failed to coincide. The trustees queried the fact that Barry's drawing of the house included in his report was at variance with the engraving, the minutes of the meeting recording "that Mr Barry be asked whether as his drawing differs in some respect from the old drawing there is any and what objection to introduce the dormer windows and porch as represented in that drawing."[38]

The fidelity of the actual house to the pictured one was also threatened when the red brick frontage of the Swan and Maidenhead was removed, revealing the ancient beams and exposing the mortises beneath. A plan of these beams was prepared, showing the distances of the mortise holes, and tests were carried out to ensure that the new timbers put in place corresponded exactly with those of the original structure. According to a local newspaper, these plans were considered "the more important inasmuch as they differ in some respects from the old drawing."[39] Such concerns about the conformity of the building to the 1769 engraving seem to have continued well into the twentieth century. Following architects' reports in 1922, the porch gable was remade at a slightly higher pitch and the roof was replaced with old handmade tiles consistent with Greene's picture. As Levi Fox comments, at the time of the original Victorian restoration, "It was not realized that the drawing showed a tiled roof and not a weather-boarded one, such as was then put on, and there were one or two other points of detail that had not been interpreted correctly. . . . These alterations, the Trustees were convinced, ensured that the appearance of the front entrance to the Birthplace was in strict keeping with the earliest known representation of the building."[40]

With the detached and commanding building represented by Greene as the model for the project, one of the first aspects of the restoration to be undertaken with John Shakespear's money was the purchase and destruction of the buildings on either side of the property and old stabling and a cottage behind. The trustees held a meeting on 21 January 1857 to receive tenders for this demolition. William Holtom of Stratford was employed and by March the buildings had been demolished, a process recorded by the eager photographers (Figure 8).

Figure 8. Photograph taken during the restoration, showing the demolition of the houses on either side of the Birthplace. Reproduced by permission of the Shakespeare Birthplace Trust.

This particular course of action had been mentioned as early as the year of the auction when *The Times* cited a statement from the committee that they needed funds to "remove certain premises adjoining, which injure the appearance, and endanger the safety of the house."[41] Interestingly, it was this "injury," not to the structure, but to the appearance of the house that was marginalized in later accounts, which emphasized the risk from fire posed by the connected buildings; no flames were now allowed in the building, which was heated by hot water pipes. Of the committee members, only Collier admitted that the isolation of the house should be undertaken "not merely for the sake of the property, but as an attractive site to the visitors of Stratford."[42]

In one fell swoop, the Birthplace was transformed from a terraced house to a detached one. This would have implications, as Collier predicted, for how tourists viewed the building, and it also had implications for how they viewed Shakespeare. Removed from the rest of the street, the house emitted a sense of its rural past and of Shakespeare's connection with the natural world. Perhaps more significant was the fact that the Birthplace was now the comfortable dwelling of a fairly prosperous Elizabethan landowner rather than a modest and unassuming country cottage. Shakespeare had, in effect, moved from the ranks of the working class into those of the affluent middle class. The identification of the social (and thus moral) status of the Shakespeares had become something of a preoccupation from the time of the auction, the Birthplace being looked to for evidence of their position in society.[43] When Charles Knight visited Stratford to gather material for his biography, for instance, he set out to prove that Shakespeare had been brought up in comfort, although this must have been a challenging task.[44] Victor Hugo took one look at the Birthplace and concluded that the "poor lodging sheltered a decayed family."[45]

The restoration of the Birthplace largely repressed this debate. Following work on the house, commentators could write with assurance that "There can be little doubt that during his childhood, and up to his eleventh or twelfth year, little William Shakspeare lived in careless plenty, and saw nothing in his father's house but that style of liberal housekeeping, which has always distinguished the upper yeomanry and rural gentry of England."[46] The strict adherence to the 1769 engraving gave the right impression of the building: it was set apart, important and unique. Just like the bard himself. Even the garden was laid out to make the house look more substantial, with a terrace running its width that, according to a local newspaper, "will give an idea of increased extent."[47]

Such descriptions provided a marked contrast to accounts of the Birthplace prior to the restoration, which often exploited the fact that this "cottage" was impoverished and humble. When Nathaniel Hawthorne visited the Birthplace in June 1855 before work on the restoration had begun, he was struck by its smallness and meanness: "To be sure, they say the house used to be much larger than now, in Shakespeare's time," he writes, "but what we see of it is consistent in itself, and does not look as if it ever could have been a portion of a large and respectable house."[48] Whether or not the Birthplace was much larger in Shakespeare's time, it had certainly expanded with the restoration of the building. One American tourist, who, like Hawthorne, visited the Birthplace prior to any structural modifications, was surprised when she returned in 1875 and found that the house "seems to have grown mysteriously."[49] The growth, in fact, was not so very mysterious: before the restoration, only the butcher's shop was shown as "the Birthplace," but Greene's drawing depicted a single dwelling that incorporated the Swan and Maidenhead part of the building and the tenement on the other side. The new Birthplace, therefore, was quite significantly larger than the old one. Some writers, however, preferred to retain a romantic notion of Shakespeare's humble beginnings. A writer describing the birthroom as the restoration project was reaching its end decried "how little Nature cares for her greatest children. She flings them by in obscure corners of the world, leaving them to fight their way."[50] But because Shakespeare's house no longer assumed the lowly appearance it once had, there is a qualifying explanation: we have to look at the room, remarks the writer, "and remember that probably it was much scantier and smaller."[51]

Indeed, the restoration of the inside of the house, including the room in which Shakespeare was said to have been born, proved somewhat problematic. While Greene's image was used as evidence for the exterior appearance of the building, there was no representation of what the interior must have looked like during Shakespeare's childhood. One of the earliest pictures of the interior was in Ireland's *Picturesque Views on the Upper, or Warwickshire Avon* and showed the kitchen with its commodious inglenook fireplace, but although this image spawned a tradition of representing this particular feature of the house, it was limited in terms of its focus on a single room.[52] Moreover, Ireland did not pretend to show the kitchen as it was in the past but as it presented itself to him on his visit. The absence of any historical evidence of the Tudor interior of the Birthplace might not have been such an obstacle, however. Taking into account the contemporary fascination with Shakespeare's youth, along with the Victorians' ideological investment in the idea of the home, the restorers could well have recreated an Elizabethan domestic interior, transforming the inside of the house into a space where one could easily imagine the young William living with his family.

Such a course of action would not have been without precedent. The house of the German writer Friedrich Schiller, which was often compared to Shakespeare's Birthplace, had been purchased by the municipality of Weimar with the intention of restoring and furnishing it as it was in his lifetime. One magazine article at the time of the auction recommended this as a viable option for the Birthplace: "In the case of Shakspeare we have not the means of attaining to this technical reality; but whatever future destination the amount of funds collected shall enable the public to give to the monument, something like a conjectural restoration to the probable condition of the interior when Shakspeare was there a living presence is an obvious feature of any scheme."[53] In Schiller's house, much of the original interior remained, unlike the Birthplace where there was no furniture belonging to the Shakespeares. As the writer points out, though, the reconstruction of the interior could be more "conjectural" than "technically real," and Elizabethan furniture could easily have been attained for the purpose.

This plan to present Shakespeare's Birthplace as an actual home was not put in place until the 1940s, another period during which people sought to cement family values. When it came to the inside of the building, Barry recommended only carrying out work that was absolutely necessary, such as removing the modern wallpaper and making the requisite modifications to convert the Birthplace from three separate buildings into a single dwelling. To achieve this, a new oak staircase was constructed, a partition and fireplace were removed from the Swan and Maidenhead, and a partition with an oak-ledge door was created towards the birthroom part of the building.[54] Underneath the birthroom, a new doorway allowed entrance into the former cottage. In the rooms upstairs, brickwork, wattle, and other filling were taken out of the framed timber partition between the two rooms, the timber was repaired, and the partition was left open. On completion of repair to the timbers throughout the house and extensive plastering work, the interior of the Birthplace looked as if it had always been one house.

Following these structural changes, the Maidenhead was lost: the pub that was attached to the Birthplace for centuries was transformed into something far more suitable—a library and museum.[55] The construction of this museum validated the house itself, reinforcing its connection with Shakespeare. It contained documents and objects collected by the local historian, Robert Bell Wheler (1785–1857), and donated to the Birthplace by his sister. In the absence of a recreated domestic space, these items gave a life to the bard: they include the desk, reputedly used by Shakespeare in his days as a pupil at the grammar school, and a gold signet ring engraved with the initials W.S., which had been found in a field near Holy Trinity Church. With its pictures, books, and objects, the museum was the most furnished part of the house. As contemporary photographs attest, the rest of the interior and, in particular, the birthroom, was left virtually empty, aside from the odd chair, small table, and bust of Shakespeare (Figure 9).

It was an emptiness that worked, paradoxically, to fill the rooms, to make them more evocative, allowing visitors to furnish them in their imaginations, to envisage what the house must have been like when Shakespeare lived there. It is this bareness that adds to the foreboding atmosphere when Daphne, the heroine of Braddon's *Asphodel*, says her farewell to the Birthplace. This

Figure 9. "The Birth Room," from John Leyland, *The Shakespeare Country Illustrated* (London: Offices of "Country Life Illustrated" and George Newnes, 1900).

nocturnal visit (she is allowed to enter by the custodians, who know her) marks a defining moment in the text, for she is discovered there by the man with whom she is in love and who, unfortunately, happens to be engaged to her sister. Daphne's sense that this is her last visit (which, indeed, it turns out to be: she is soon to commit suicide by rowing her boat in front of a steamer on a lake in Switzerland) is heightened by the sparse interior of the house: "It was more ghostly than the church—more uncanny in its emptiness. She felt as if the disembodied souls of the dead were verily around and about her."[56] Perhaps, as Daphne's experience suggests, there were certain advantages in leaving the Birthplace empty. Stripping the rooms back to their bare bones (or beams) gave the interior of the building a mystical, haunted atmosphere, suggesting the spectral presence of the bard. This ghostly atmosphere was captured in paintings of the Birthplace, such as Henry Wallis's *The Room in Which Shakespeare Was Born* (exhibited in the Royal Academy in 1854) and *In Shakespeare's House*, both of which were praised for their accurate rendering of the interior space. Because they were so empty, the rooms also appeared larger than they actually were, calling to mind more stately Elizabethan houses and baronial halls.

With its renovated external and internal structures, Shakespeare's Birthplace encouraged a return to the past. But however attentive to historical detail the restorers were, however much they attempted to transform the building into what it once was, the restored house was a Victorian rather than a Tudor construct. Even the notion of history on which the restoration depended was essentially a nineteenth-century one, the overriding aim of the project to reveal the Tudor structure of the building taking place in the context of a fascination with "merrie olde England," which assumed some complex forms and manifestations throughout the period, particularly in relation to architecture and design.

This fascination was suggested in James Hakewill's *An Attempt to Determine the Exact Character of Elizabethan Architecture* (1835), which sought to reclaim Elizabethan street architecture and expose the "hideous" imitations which were "disgracing our streets and public places."[57] The vogue for imitation Elizabethan architecture was not only present on the streets. Following the destruction of the original Palace of Westminster by fire in 1834, it was agreed to design the new Houses of Parliament as Elizabethan or Gothic structures, which were regarded as national forms. Charles Barry worked with fellow designer A. W. N. Pugin, who provided the ornate decorations and furnishings. Joseph Nash, who trained in Pugin's office, also played a part in the privileging of all things Elizabethan and followed up his lithographed album, *Architecture of the Middle Ages: Drawn from Nature and on Stone* (1838) with a no less lavish album, *The Mansions of England in the Olden Time*, which was published between 1839 and 1849 and focused on the interiors and exteriors of Tudor and Jacobean great houses. It is no wonder that George Fildes, one of the first speakers at the newly founded Decorative Art Society, remarked upon the "great prevalence of the Elizabethan style, both in the exterior and interior decorations of the present day."[58]

By the end of the nineteenth century, "merrie England" had taken on a decidedly radical edge, the early socialist Robert Blatchford using it as the ironically charged title for his collection of essays on the state of the country.[59] Blatchford's book, which went on to sell over two million copies, had its own proposals about contemporary housing, arguing that a truly "merrie England" could only be achieved if the towns were rebuilt with wide streets, gardens, fountains, and tree-lined avenues.[60] What is strikingly apparent in the restoration of the Birthplace is the way in which it coincides with and parallels these cultural and aesthetic developments, feeding directly into the Arts and Crafts movement and the so-called "Tudorbethan" or "Jacobethan" style of architecture with its characteristic half-timbering, mullioned windows, and jettied first floors that became a familiar sight in many British towns, including Stratford-upon-Avon. The restoration, then, stands as an embodiment not only of how the Victorians saw an Elizabethan, or more specifically, a Shakespearean, past, but also how they saw themselves and their own modernity.

Out with the New and In with the Old

Restoring the Birthplace involved "scraping away" the modern aspects of the building in order to uncover the ancient fabric beneath, assuming, of course, that these antique elements were in keeping with Greene's picture. Barry's recommendation had been "to remove with a careful hand all those excrescences which are decidedly the result of modern innovation, to uphold with jealous care all that now exists of undoubted antiquity, not to destroy any portion about whose character the slightest doubt may exist but to restore any parts needing it in such a manner that the restorations can never be mistaken for the old work." Barry's dislike for these modern additions, as much a comment on changing aesthetic tastes as an objective architectural judgment, was far from unique. In an account of his first visit to the Birthplace in 1839, Frederick Fairholt was highly critical of the brick frontage and the other features that made the building look like a "modern residence for a labouring man" of the type familiar in the London suburbs.[61]

But it was not always easy, or desirable, to identify the renovated aspects of the house. Indeed, such a strategy was at odds with the other aim of the project: to restore the ancient fabric. When alterations had to be made, there was a concerted effort to secure old materials. A delay in the work was caused when the restorers attempted to source oak timber from a demolished house owned by the earl of Warwick.[62] The earl refused, on the grounds that he was undertaking his own restoration projects, but at other times, the workmen were more successful.[63] Where the floorboards needed replacing, they acquired seasoned oak boards which looked older and more weathered, and gothic latches and handles were put on all of the doors to give the requisite antique feel. This emphasis on and preservation of the old went hand in hand with the eradication of the modern. Edward Gibbs, the local architect and surveyor, who was commissioned to manage the project, followed Barry's report, removing those aspects of the building which did not belong to the original structure and maintaining (and, arguably, "improving") what were regarded as the old features. It was its "originality" that was the deciding factor as to whether a part of the building should be removed or retained, but the repeated discussions throughout the project as to what was and was not "original" suggest that the distinction was not as obvious as it might have initially appeared. One of Gibbs's typical reports states that "Having thoroughly examined the projecting window at the west end of the aforesaid house . . . I find that it is not connected with the original structure except by nails, and I am of opinion that the date of its addition thereto must have been long subsequent to the date of the original structure. . . . I am decidedly of opinion that the aforesaid projecting window ought to be removed."[64]

The absolute distinction between the modern and the ancient on which the whole restoration project depended was never as clear-cut as Barry, Gibbs, and the trustees seemed to imply. It was not easy to locate the boundaries between what was old and what was new. Problems arose not just with the windows but with the garden, which was located on the site of so many demolished outbuildings (including the brewery attached to the Swan and Maidenhead) that it was difficult to determine where the grounds had originally been. This impediment was overcome by a landscaping that was intended to recreate the appearance of a Tudor estate (Figure 10).

Figure 10. A photograph of the Birthplace taken from the gardens, from John Leyland, *The Shakespeare Country Illustrated* (London: Offices of "Country Life Illustrated" and George Newnes, 1900).

An emphasis on historical accuracy was at the forefront of this design. The base stone of the ancient market cross which had stood at the top of Bridge street and was said to have existed at the time of Shakespeare was placed in the middle of the gravel walk. Unsurprisingly, a mulberry tree also turned up, which was presented by the owner of a garden on the site of the orchard attached to New Place. "Its 'pedigree,'" the public was assured, "is undoubted; it is only three degrees in descent from *the* mulberry, its 'ancestors' having being reared in their native soil."[65] And other "authentic" plants were used in the landscaping. John J. Cole, whose house was built on the foundations of Essex House, which fronted the Strand in London, offered a cutting of an ancient vine from his garden to be planted in the grounds of the Birthplace.[66] "I do not pretend that they [the vines] are as old as Elizabeth's time," Cole wrote in a letter that was published in the local newspaper, "but I have a fond hope that their ancestors' leaves gave grateful trellis-shade, as one of them does now. . . . My family is so romantic as to believe that Shakspeare must have many a time walked up and down our bit of terrace; have sat at the end with my Lord Essex and Lord Southampton, admiring the moonlight on the river, or jesting with 'night' templars over the parapet wall; must have drunk some sack in the cellar, and taken water 'at the stairs.' It is even believed that hardly at Stratford is there anything so little altered and so near to Shakspeare's footsteps as our paved garden."[67] The vine was, of course, gratefully accepted, although its planting in the garden was not an assurance of historical accuracy. In June 1861 the trustees received a letter complaining that they had the landscaping wrong: "Modern notions of laying out a Garden are totally opposed to the principles on which an Elizabethan Garden was constructed," wrote the irritated correspondent.[68] Despite the planting of mulberry trees and ancient vines, the idea of what was "authentic" was in dispute, subject to different and multiple interpretations, and, as this disgruntled visitor suggests, the "modern" always has a nasty habit of encroaching on the old.

This encroachment was recognized by some of the earliest tourists to the restored Birthplace. John Mounteney Jephson visited Stratford in 1863 and published his impressions in a book accompanied by photographs by Ernest Edwards, which was timed to coincide with the tercentenary (Figure 11). Jephson wrote despairingly of the house:

> I was not prepared to see it look so smug and new. Many of the old
> timbers remain, and the house is, indeed, substantially the same

Figure 11. Ernest Edwards, "Shakespere's House, Stratford-on-Avon," from J. M. Jephson, *Shakespere: His Birthplace, Home, and Grave. A Pilgrimage to Stratford-on-Avon in the Autumn of 1863* (London: Lovell Reeve, 1864).

house as it was; but new timbers have been inserted where the old were decayed, everything has been scraped and polished up, and the place looks as if it had been "restored," a word to strike terror to the heart of an antiquary, not to speak of a man of taste. The propensity to stain, and polish, and varnish, and substitute new work for old unnecessarily, is much to be deprecated. Perhaps the committee, who hold the property in trust for the nation, could not avoid giving to Shakespere's birthplace its present holiday appearance; but how often is the artistic eye offended by seeing a fine old building vulgarised by restorers! . . . The worst of it is, that the perpetrators of such enormities are generally such worthy, well-meaning people, that one is afraid to suggest a doubt as to their discretion, for fear of damping their zeal. Perhaps a few years' exposure to the weather may tone down the "neat" look of the house in Henley Street.[69]

For Jephson, the attempt of the restorers to retain the old and eradicate the new actually has the opposite effect: so much "new" work has been added to the old structures that the house adopts a "holiday appearance." As one early twentieth-century critic put it, Shakespeare's Birthplace "is but a feeble compromise between new and old."[70]

To the majority, however, this "newness" went largely unseen. The common opinion was that the Birthplace had been restored to its former state, and the project was hailed as among the most successful ever undertaken.[71] When the Birthplace was unveiled to the public during the tercentenary, one writer lavished praise on the architects and trustees:

> The sheltering pent house below and the dormer windows above have been reconstructed in accordance with early representations of the house, and the Birthplace has been made to resume its ancient form completely.
>
> Mr. Halliwell says: "The admirable care that has been taken to preserve to a nicety the various details, and to settle the accuracy of those details by the various indications of the original structure, confers the highest credit on the great ability of Mr. Edward Gibbs, and on the sagacity of the Birthplace Committee." As a restoration, one can safely regard the structure, in its present form, as the most careful and successful work of the kind ever accomplished.
>
> The interior of the central cottage, that is, the Birthplace, is in its original state, the old flagstones in the floor, and the old stairs leading to the room in which the Poet was born. The window of this room is the genuine old one, and was used as the model for the windows requiring restoration.[72]

The emphasis here on the validity of the restoration project and its exposure of the "ancient form" of the building typifies the Victorian attitude to the project. (Revealingly, this author quotes Halliwell but omits the lines immediately preceding those cited here in which Halliwell expresses his disinclination for restoration projects and his preference for leaving the Birthplace in the state in which it had been purchased.)[73] Indeed, so successful was the transformation of a group of unpretentious timber-framed and brick-fronted cottages into a detached "Elizabethan" dwelling that the fact of the restoration was silently erased. As Jephson predicted, the British weather did its work and the

Birthplace soon came to be regarded as a genuinely old building, the traces of its Victorian renovation more or less invisible. No longer a "restored" building, the Birthplace was the "real" thing, "the early home of the gifted Author, as it appeared in his day, now nearly three centuries past."[74] In the words of *Chambers's Journal*, the house is "one of those old edifices which are still frequently to be seen throughout Warwickshire, composed of a framework of timber, formed in squares, with the intervening compartments filled up with mud and plaster, or, as it is locally termed, 'wattle and dab'; latticed windows, and high-pitched gable roofs."[75]

Libraries and Tea Shops

The restored Birthplace was a product of mid-nineteenth-century values: values about the power of images, about what was regarded as old and new, and about an (imagined) Elizabethan past. At the turn of the century, these values were still very much in evidence. In 1903 the same debates about restoration, preservation, and historicity extended further down the length of Henley Street. A group of four cottages, known as the Hornby cottages, had been bought for the Birthplace Trust by Andrew Carnegie, the Scottish-born American millionaire (Figure 12). The Trust argued that the demolition of these cottages was necessary to prevent the risk of fire to the Birthplace (a fire had, in fact, destroyed several shops near the Birthplace in 1896),[76] although there was an aesthetic issue at stake here too: with the cottages removed, the Birthplace would further resemble the early engraving; it would be set, if not in the acres suggested by Greene, at least in its own distinct plot of land. This potential was not lost on Edgar Flower, the Chair of the trustees, who noted that, with the proposed demolition, "a considerable addition will be made to the garden" of the Birthplace.[77]

Carnegie's generosity extended beyond the purchase of these cottages, which he bought at some expense, for one owner planned to capitalize on the burgeoning tourist trade by opening a tea shop. He had also given money for the construction of a public library, which was to be built on Henley Street. These two events became linked in the public imagination, critics arguing that "historic" cottages were to be demolished in order to create a palatial Carnegie library that would dwarf the Birthplace.[78] This claim was strongly refuted by members of the Trust and the Corporation of Stratford, who argued, initially at least, that the Hornby cottages had no historic interest and pointed out that the library was not to be built on this site anyway but on the plot of an adjacent

Figure 12. The four Hornby cottages can be seen next to the china shop. Photograph from Sidney Lee, *The Alleged Vandalism at Stratford-on-Avon* (London: Archibald Constable & Co., 1903).

china shop, which was also to be demolished. These events caused a furor that one local historian described as "probably greater than at any time since 1847, when the nation waited, with trepidation and alarm, the result of the historic building being submitted to public competition at a London mart."[79] A writ was even brought against the Birthplace trustees by members of the British Archaeological Association.[80]

As with the restoration of the Birthplace, the dispute around the cottages and library involved questions about what was old and what was new, and, by implication, what should be restored and demolished, questions, it seemed, that still could not adequately be resolved. Opponents of the scheme attempted to trace the history of the buildings back to Shakespeare: the china shop that was to make way for the library had been the home of Shakespeare's cousin, while the Hornby cottages had housed the friends and neighbors of John Shakespeare, people whom William Shakespeare would have known and chatted to as he walked down the street.[81] Supporters of the project argued that the structures had no archaeological interest and were little more than hovels.[82] As Theodore Martin, a member of the Trust, put it: "How can the spending of money in propping up these two ruinous cottages be justified any more than in restoring cottages any where else in Stratford in which there happen to be a few old oaken beams of an uncertain date?"[83]

One of the most vocal objectors to the scheme was Marie Corelli, the author of *Vendetta* (1886), *The Sorrows of Satan* (1895), and numerous other popular novels, who had settled in Stratford, where she was often to be seen floating down the Avon on a gondola, complete with gondolier, that she had imported from Venice. In *The Avon Star: A Literary Manual for the Stratford-on-Avon Season of 1903*, a publication that was her campaign manifesto, she addressed the mayor and Corporation of Stratford in imitation of Othello's defense:

> And when mine eyes behold the vandal hands
> That would despoil these old streets' sanctity,
> And with their wood and plaster sacrilege
> Affront the name of him whose heavenly Muse
> Lights all the land with glory that outpours
> In broadening luminance o'er the darker world,
> Then doth my spirit rise in arms and use
> Its dearest action in the open field.[84]

On the other side of the dispute was the more sedate figure of Sidney Lee, the second editor of the *Dictionary of National Biography* and a biographer of Shakespeare, who took over as chair of the Birthplace Trust in 1903. His retort to Corelli, *The Alleged Vandalism at Stratford-on-Avon*, sought to undermine her claims and included photographs of the buildings which were intended "to restore to normal vigour all visual power that the heat of controversy has impaired."[85]

Corelli's objections to the library were bound up in the fact that it had been donated by Carnegie, who, despite being born in Fife and educated in a Lancastrian school, came to be associated with American excess and vulgarity, a fin-de-siècle version of Barnum. Thus, the library was described by Corelli as a "great temple to Mammon"[86] that would overshadow the Birthplace as a sign "of what the over-officiousness of moneyed men can do to dwarf the abode of genius."[87] Another critic saw it decorated with "the finest things in Pittsburg fixings."[88] Lee himself seems to have been embarrassed by this anti-American sentiment and dedicated *The Alleged Vandalism at Stratford-on-Avon* to his "Friends in America." But Americans were also put forward in support of the anti-Carnegie campaign. "What Americans love in England," remarked Lady Colin Campbell, a vocal supporter of Corelli, "are the evidences of the historic past, the old-world atmosphere of our little rural towns, which they cannot get at home. If Stratford is to be modernised . . . pilgrims may still come once to visit the birthplace, but will neither linger nor return as they have done hitherto."[89] The main danger was that the new Carnegie library would be constructed in a modern style that was not in keeping with the Birthplace: "Stratford should have none of the pagan music of a noisy modernity" was a typical view.[90] "Leave the sacred side of Henley Street uncontaminated by modern bricks and mortar!" was another.[91]

Ever the romantic, Corelli argued that the appearance of Henley Street should be retained "not only for ourselves but for all the unborn generations, that they might wend their way as we did, down the historic thoroughfare and find it spared from any touch of modernity."[92] Carnegie aside, Corelli's enemy was the "jerry builder," whom she accused of defacing Stratford and making it look like a cheap bit of Clapham.[93] Although one writer pointed out, with some glee, that the firm which constructed the "jerry-built houses" at the corner of Henley Street to which the novelist so objected was also responsible for restoring her own house "with its porch, and glass appendage in the style of an Earl's Court tea kiosk, which she calls a Winter Garden."[94]

For other commentators, the progress of modernity could not, and should not, be stopped. In his *The Errors of the Avon Star: Another Literary Manual for the Stratford-on-Avon Season of 1903*, J. Harvey Bloom suggested that the townspeople of Stratford needed to move with the times and that any imitation of the past was wrong:

> Imitations of old work, even were they wrought out in facsimile, would be shams, and therefore inartistic. It goes without saying that the life of to-day is not the life of Shakespeare's time, any more than a cosmopolitan drawing room, to be seen in Stratford, with its Cairene chairs, French embroidery, modern copper, German piano, Turkish carpets and what not, resembles in the remotest degree a withdrawing room in an Elizabethan mansion, though the writer has often heard it so called. . . . Modern needs require more room and must have it, and a simple imitation would be a ridiculous anachronism.[95]

Bloom's view, however, was in a minority. Once again, it was the language of "desecration" and "spoliation" that was used to describe the threat of modernization, with Henley Street as the "chief aisle of that Devotion" and the

Birthplace the altar.[96] The danger posed to the property by the demolition of these "Elizabethan" buildings and the erection of a Carnegie library depended, therefore, on the assumption that the Birthplace was itself the original Tudor structure to which others on Henley Street could be compared and contrasted. As one critic wrote, "It is to be hoped that steps will be promptly taken to prevent the destruction of buildings which may be said to be as full of historic memories of Shakespeare as his own birthplace in the threatened Henley Street."[97]

But perhaps the "historic memories" of Shakespeare's Birthplace did not go back far enough. By 1903 the history of its restoration had largely been forgotten. Lee attempted to rectify this, commenting that that a "murky cloud of misunderstanding"[98] enveloped Henley Street and that the truth about the history of the Birthplace needed to be told: "Many may learn with regret that the dormer windows and the porch were removed from the house in 1800 after they had so long resisted time's ravages, and that a brick front was erected in place of the ancient timber façade of the adjoining building," he reminded his readers.[99] Indeed, Henley Street underwent such complete renovation between the time of Shakespeare's death and the end of the nineteenth century that it could "never regain its pristine form or feature."[100]

It was increasingly recognized, however, that the future of Stratford depended precisely on its "regaining" its Elizabethan forms and features, whether these had ever actually existed or not. The demolition of the cottages and china shop intersected with wider ideas about what tourists wanted and expected when they visited the town, like the Americans, who, according to Campbell, were charmed by its "old-world" atmosphere. At the time of the restoration of the Birthplace, there was no objection to the destruction of the sixteenth- and seventeenth-century houses on either side of the building,[101] but now there was concern that the Birthplace was the only antique building on Henley Street, and that very little of the "historic" survived in Stratford.[102] Indeed, it might come as a shock to visitors to Stratford today to discover that some of its most historic-looking buildings did not assume an antique appearance for much of the nineteenth century. At the time of the tercentenary and well into the 1870s and 1880s, there was no half-timbering on the almshouses in Chapel Street, the grammar school, Hall's Croft (the Jacobean home of Shakespeare's daughter, Susanna), Nash's House (next door to New Place), the Shakespeare Hotel, or the Garrick Inn.[103]

Stratford itself needed to be restored. Rather than a library, Corelli argued, residents would prefer to uncover their fifteenth-century carved house-fronts, which had been plastered over.[104] Corelli herself provided the funds for undertaking such work. When it was discovered that a souvenir shop in the town contained architectural features belonging to the early sixteenth century, the novelist paid a large sum for the timber front to be restored, so that, in her own words, "the generations to come might look upon what the eyes of the Great Poet also saw."[105] Such restoration and the exploitation of the town's past would, Corelli suggested, turn Stratford into a gold mine: "If the half-timbered houses down the principal street were uncovered from their modern paint and stucco, it would be one of the most perfect old English thoroughfares in existence, and there are plenty of devotees who would visit it and stay in it for the sake of its beauty alone. If, instead of pulling down their old houses, the people would renovate and carefully restore them, they would find it well worth their while, even financially speaking."[106] Indeed, for all her romantic descriptions of Stratford, Corelli was acutely aware of its economic and commercial potential: "Modern progress is decidedly not the 'cue' for Stratford," she wrote. "Its good measures of gold, its full purses, its swelling bank-books, will be best and most swiftly attained by setting its back to the wall of the Sixteenth Century and refusing to budge."[107]

Corelli's argument seems eventually to have struck a chord with the Corporation of Stratford and the Birthplace Trust. While the two cottages farthest away from the Birthplace were demolished, the other two were left standing, apparently because old timber-work had been found inside that merited preservation. From being held up as the bastion of modernity, Carnegie was now appropriated as a savior of the old because his purchase of the cottages had protected the Birthplace "from peril of proximity to a most incongruous innovation": the restaurant or tea shop that would have been created on the site by its former owner.[108] Carnegie, so the argument went, had actually halted the progress of modernization: "so far from destroying 'historic Henley Street,' the Trustees and the Corporation, through the generous aid of Mr. Carnegie, are doing precisely the opposite."[109]

Carnegie had effectively removed the china shop too, the library being built in this renovated building and in a mock Elizabethan style that critics described as a "Norman Shaw faked Tudor structure."[110] Corelli was not satisfied; in her opinion the library was not authentic enough and she warned that "historic Henley Street will soon become a row of 'modern-antique' buildings, by which Shakespeare's house will be but sadly and incongruously companioned."[111] For others, however, this Tudor style was seen to be "quite in keeping with the oldest tradition of Henley street."[112] Or rather, this "oldest tradition" was being actively constructed in the transformation of the street from brick-fronted into timber-framed dwellings and the building of new houses in an antique style to match the restored Birthplace.

Such mysterious transformations were only to be expected in Shakespeare's Stratford-upon-Avon. The town, according to Corelli, possessed a magical quality that emanated from its association with the bard: "And as we push our punt slowly home along the peaceful Avon, and the light of the sinking sun reddens the fine old tiles of the houses not yet "slated" by the jerry builder, and gleams here and there on a picturesque thatched cottage, or a lattice window with a tuft of roses swinging on it, we forget the existence of all inharmonious things; and the little town looks like a poet's nestling dream of beauty, hallowed by the spirit of one to whom all things were as 'airy ministers' of thought."[113] As Corelli knew too well, the "inharmonious," or modern, aspects of the town needed to be expunged in order to create the vision of an ancient market town with thatched and timber-framed cottages. In Corelli's case, this was taken to extremes. It is telling, for example, that her vision of Stratford is only illuminated by the sun, the novelist having taken a dislike to electric lighting, although as Bloom sardonically remarked, "If Miss Corelli really wishes for the world of romance, why not relegate Stratford at once to the obsolete sway of horn lanterns and tallow dips, since gas is almost as modern, and certainly more dangerous and not much less glaring, than even an arc lamp."[114]

It is hard to imagine what Corelli would have thought if, floating down the Avon one evening in her gondola, she had seen, through the reddening glint of the setting sun, a vision of Stratford a century on. If she could have walked up from the river and visited the Birthplace, she might have been impressed with the attempts to keep the new at bay, especially in the ingenious masking of modern technologies, including lighting. A wonderful photograph from the 1940s in the collection of the Birthplace Trust shows an electrical engineer fixing switches behind the timber framework in the interior of the house. In the Birthplace, light is hidden not so much under a bushel as under a beam. And what would Corelli have made of Henley Street, the center of the thriving tourist industry that she had looked forward to in 1903? There are more "historic" timber-framed buildings than she would have been familiar with, and there are certainly more cafés. One thinks, with some sympathy, of the owner of the Hornby cottage, the would-be caterer, who must have regretted giving into Carnegie's offer, however generous. As for the two remaining cottages, they were restored and joined into one. The growing Shakespeare Birthplace Trust was desperate for space and this building could be adapted into a board room and secretarial offices. The terrible fate of having a restaurant or another equally "incongruous innovation" so near the Birthplace had, therefore, been narrowly averted. Or maybe it had not. Stepping into this building in the twenty-first century, Corelli would find herself at the altar of a devotional shrine to Shakespeare that is laden with cash registers rather than candles. The Hornby cottages are now the Birthplace's gift shop.

Chapter 4

Real Estate?
Authenticating the Birthplace

Making It Real

The restoration of the Birthplace brought to the fore the question of its authenticity. Supporters of the project pointed to the admirable objective of removing the modern, retaining the old, and marking up any restored aspects of the structure. This would have the effect, or so it was argued, of telling the truth about the house, of not allowing the pilgrims to the shrine to be misled, "for we may as well worship the Blarney stone at once as pay our devotions to imitative bricks and mortar which the fanciful eye of an architect may happen to select as *resembling* the original object of our admiration."[1] The problem arose, however, when new additions masqueraded as the old, when tourists were unwittingly led to "worship" elements that were not original. This danger was acknowledged by Edward Barry himself some thirty years later when he delivered his lectures on architecture to the Royal Academy. Although Barry plays down his involvement with restoration projects in his address, it is perhaps Shakespeare's Birthplace that he has in mind when he asserts that the imitation of original features of buildings and the passing off of new work as old amounts to "an elaborate forgery."[2]

The issue of the authenticity of the Birthplace does not only relate to its physical manifestation, however. There is another, perhaps more urgent, question of authenticity that lies beyond the attempt to reconstruct it as a Tudor building. Was William Shakespeare actually born in this house on Henley Street? From the number of tourists who gather outside the building and take photographs today, the Birthplace certainly seems to be regarded as the real thing. Those who explore inside are invited to discover the story of William Shakespeare's early years, to see where he was born, grew up, and started married life.[3] The authenticity of this house is not in question; in the guidebooks, souvenirs, and postcards, the status of the Birthplace is a given. There is no doubt about it.

Or is there? In the nineteenth century, even as the Birthplace became a literary shrine, its authenticity remained in doubt. While actual Victorian commentators were not quite as farfetched in their theories as the fictional reporter in Hollingshead's "A Startling Confession" (who claimed that the whole of Henley Street was built by a Birmingham contractor over a century after Shakespeare's birth), they nevertheless returned to the same troubling question: was Shakespeare born in the Birthplace?[4] In 1847 this question complicated the campaign to purchase the building. Supporters of the scheme such as Charles Knight were eager to defend its authenticity, not least because they were reliant on public subscription. Others had different opinions. In a letter to the editor of the *Examiner*, a former inhabitant of Stratford revealed that the Birthplace was a "deception,"[5] while a writer for *Man in the Moon* was even more explicit: "The rubbishing mass of lath and plaster in which the Poet was no more born than was the MAN IN THE MOON himself, is now nearly the 'property of the British Nation'– barring five hundred pounds. (We wish the committee may get it.) The legatees are laughing in their sleeves at the result of their well-planned hoax."[6] During the auction, when George Jones caused a commotion by daring to ask the auctioneer if the house that he was about to sell was the identical one in which the poet was born, Robins responded by saying that there was no doubt that Shakespeare's father lived in it and that Shakespeare was born there and spent the best part of his life there—and that he wished that skeptics had stayed away.[7]

In the nineteenth century, the skeptics never quite stayed away. But how can this be reconciled with the more secure status of the building in the twenty-first century? This chapter suggests that it was in the very articulation of doubts about the Birthplace and the responses to these doubts that the property was authenticated. My concern, therefore, is less with the question of whether or not Shakespeare was born in the house on Henley Street than with the raising of this question, the differing notions of "the authentic" that it reveals, and the conscious and unconscious strategies by which this legitimacy is established or undermined. "Authenticity," of course, is a highly problematic and unstable term: while seemingly transcendent and transhistorical, the concept is defined by its cultural, textual, and material contexts.[8] The "authentication" of the Birthplace is an important aspect of all the stories told in this book: it lies at the heart of the purchase of the property and its subsequent restoration; it can be seen in the way that the house generates specific notions of "Shakespeare" and the role it plays in the Stratford tourist industry. One could also point to the incorporation of the Shakespeare Birthplace Trust by Act of Parliament in 1891 as an event that authorized the workings of the custodians of the Birthplace and the properties they managed. This chapter, however, is concerned specifically with the material objects that were connected to and helped to legitimize the Birthplace, from the archival documents relating to the house and the relics it contained to the engravings and photographs that were published in books and sold as souvenirs. It was these texts, objects, and pictures, and the ways in which they were circulated and viewed, that turned the Birthplace into the genuine article.

Home Truths

For the Shakespearean scholar James Orchard Halliwell(-Phillipps), the truth of the Birthplace could be found in deeds, contracts, conveyances, indentures, and other archival material that connected the Shakespeares with the house on Henley Street. Described by Schoenbaum as "antiquarianism incarnate," Halliwell was an unrivaled expert on the manuscripts contained in the Birthplace, having in 1863 arranged almost five thousand documents that related to Stratford from the thirteenth century to 1750.[9] His defense of the Birthplace followed that of the other great Stratford antiquarian, Robert Bell Wheler, whose *An Historical Account of the Birth-Place of Shakespeare* (1824) Halliwell reprinted in 1863.

Wheler had traced the provenance of the Birthplace from the time of the Shakespeares and its mention in Shakespeare's will of 1616—where it was left to his eldest daughter, Susanna, with a life interest for his sister, Joan—to its owners and tenants in the nineteenth century. The zeal with which he undertook this task is indicated in the fact that he went to the length of citing as evidence a forgotten manuscript that alluded to the damages suffered by occupants of the house during the Civil War.[10] Such strategies established a history for the Birthplace, legitimating a property that had passed through numerous hands, unlike, for example, Anne Hathaway's cottage, which was still occupied by descendants of the Hathaway family. In constructing this historical narrative of the Birthplace's ownership, Wheler prepared the way for its acceptance as a site of national heritage.

But Wheler's history of the Birthplace did not go unchallenged. Halliwell was familiar with disputes over the authenticity of the property, which went back at least to 1808 when a disagreement had broken out between Wheler and John Jordan, the Stratford poet and historian who claimed in the *Gentleman's Magazine* that Shakespeare had been born in Brook House (which was located in grounds now opposite the Swan Theatre). Wheler responded by pointing out that at the time of Shakespeare's birth, Brook House was no more than a barn and garden.[11] When Halliwell came to publish a collection of Wheler's manuscripts, he included a note in which Jordan claimed, in no uncertain terms, that the Birthplace was a fake: "Even the house that for upwards of half a century has been shown for and venerated as the place of his nativity is a most flagrant and gross imposition, invented purposely with a design to extort pecuniary gratuities from the credulous and unwary, who fired with an enthusiastic admiration and regard for the poet's memory, are induced by the loquacious ignorance of low-bred mercenary and illiterate people to visit and pay for entering this paltry hut."[12] Jordan's assertion is immediately quashed by an editorial intervention from Halliwell: "This disreputable note was written by Jordan after he had quarrelled with the owners of the Birth-Place. Previously to that, he had been of an entirely different position."[13] Jordan's subversive opinions are blamed on a local squabble. And Halliwell might have had a point. Certainly, in Jordan's manuscript, *Original Memoirs and Historical Accounts of the Families of Shakespeare and Hart* (c. 1790), which was edited by Halliwell in 1865, he had included a drawing of the house on Henley Street under the title "A View of the House Where Shakespeare Was Born."[14] Jordan's erstwhile belief in the authenticity of the Birthplace was also implied in the fact that he openly defended the veracity of a document claiming to be the spiritual will and testament of John Shakespeare, a document which had apparently been found in the rafters of the house in 1757.[15]

When Halliwell asked on behalf of his readers, "But why is it called Shakespeare's Birth-place? What evidence have you that the spot was not consecrated under this title at a late period to answer the selfish purposes of its owners?" he provided the answers, as had Wheler before him, in the form of documentary evidence, the type of evidence that enabled Wheler to counteract Jordan's claims about Brook House.[16] The documents at Halliwell's disposal showed that in 1552 John Shakespeare, William's father, had been fined twelve pence for allowing a dunghill to accumulate outside a property on Henley Street; in 1556 he had purchased a copyhold in the same street consisting of a tenement and garden; this was followed in 1575 by the purchase of freehold premises and land on Henley Street and in 1590 by another copyhold tenement. A deed executed in 1597 stated that John Shakespeare had sold a narrow strip of land to the side of the Birthplace to a neighbor.[17]

According to the documents, John Shakespeare probably owned up to four houses, any one of which could have been the Birthplace. Moreover, the house thought to have been the Birthplace (even its boundaries were uncertain) was not actually purchased until 1575, when William would have been eleven years old. The facts might seem problematic, to say the least, but this was no impediment to Halliwell. He considered the evidence: Shakespeare's father must have resided on Henley Street in 1552 when the dunghill appeared, and the locality of his residence in the Birthplace could be ascertained by the details of the deed of 1597. The most probable supposition, he concludes, is that John Shakespeare lived in the Birthplace during the whole of his residence in Stratford, first as a tenant and then as an owner.[18]

Simple. And convincing, as it needed to be. For, at the time that Halliwell was attempting to prove the authenticity of the Birthplace, this authenticity was coming under threat, a threat that emerged, ironically, in the attempt to emphasize the unique history of the building: the restoration project. While Halliwell acknowledged that this restoration was "probably the most successful work of the kind ever accomplished," he was no supporter of the scheme, having preferred the option of protecting the building against the weather and the risk of fire and leaving it in the state in which it was purchased.[19] The material in the Halliwell-Phillipps collection in the Folger Shakespeare Library, which includes detailed sketches of every room before, during, and after the restoration, suggests Halliwell's concerns about the changes made to the building.[20] However much care had been taken to preserve various architectural details and to recreate an idea of how the property must have looked in its Tudor past, so extensive was the restoration that it was hard to believe that anything remained of the original property (indeed, the drawings in Halliwell's collection reveal an extensive replacement of the timber beams). Sidney Lee commented that the only part of the structure that existed as it was at the time of the poet's birth was the cellar,[21] and it is no coincidence that Halliwell seems to have held a particular fascination for this hidden part of the building, which lay beyond the reach of the restorers.[22]

Halliwell's most concerted efforts to prove the authenticity of the Birth-place took place between 1863 and 1865, dates that coincided with the interest generated by the tercentenary celebrations of Shakespeare's birth and with the immediate aftermath of the restoration of the house, which had taken place between 1857 and 1862. His edition of Wheler's *An Historical Account of the Birth-Place of Shakespeare* appeared in 1863, along with his *Stratford-upon-Avon in the Times of the Shakespeares*, which reproduced extracts relating to John Shakespeare from the council books of the Stratford Corporation. In 1864 Halliwell published a collection of abstracts and copies of indentures relating to estates on Henley Street, and in 1865 *The Abstract of Title to the House in Henley Street*, which had been drawn up by the vendor's solicitors when the premises were put up for auction in 1847 and included the first mention of the property in Shakespeare's will of 1616. These publications all established a trail of evidence that authenticated the property alongside, and perhaps in opposition to, a restoration project that sought to turn the house into what it was at the time of Shakespeare's birth and childhood.

Halliwell's reliance on the textual evidence relating to the Birthplace was supported by numerous attempts from the late eighteenth century onward to discover references that situated the Shakespeares firmly within the walls of the Henley Street property. It was in this period that many of these references were found, antiquarians carrying out forensic searches on the most seemingly insignificant court rolls, parish registers and legal documents. When he discovered an old well stuffed with refuse, Halliwell had its contents sifted four times in the hope of finding something of relevance to Shakespeare.[23] Occasionally these searches proved fruitful: Halliwell had waded through rubbish, but it was the Reverend Joseph Hunter who was lucky enough to stumble on the dunghill that John Shakespeare had let pile up outside his house on Henley Street.[24] John Payne Collier also had some luck in recovering documents, including an inventory of corn and malt from 1598 that referred to William Shakespeare, a resident of the Chapel Street ward (Chapel Street being the location of New Place), receiving ten quarters of grain.[25]

Collier, however, was a little too lucky. One of the major events to disrupt the world of Shakespearean scholarship in the nineteenth century was the discovery that this most respected scholar had forged several documents relating to Shakespeare in the possession of the earl of Ellesmere at Bridgewater House. Shakespeare and the Birthplace could bring out the worst in people. Collier followed in the disreputable footsteps of another Shakespearean forger in the late eighteenth century: William Henry Ireland, who seems to have been motivated in his fraudulent activities by a research trip he made to Stratford with his father, Samuel, who was gathering materials for his *Picturesque Views on the Upper, or Warwickshire Avon* (1795). Ireland still held some fascination for the Victorians, the novelist James Payn telling his story (or the story of William Henry Erin, the not too inventively named and barely disguised character) in *The Talk of the Town* (1885). Stephen Orgel has described the eighteenth-century forgers as "a genuine symptom of the intellectual pathology of the age."[26] Without doubt, there seems to have been an overwhelming desire, even a downright need, to discover information regarding Shakespeare's life, a need that was later described by Sigmund Freud: "We feel this very distinctly," Freud writes, "if the legacy of history unkindly refuses the satisfaction of this need—for example in the case of Shakespeare."[27] Some of the Stratford locals were more than happy to exploit this desire for information. A Warwickshire farmer managed to convince the Irelands that, just a fortnight before they turned up, he had burned several baskets of letters with the name Shakespeare written on them; he later confessed to Wheler that this had been a joke.[28]

This cultural desire provided the backdrop for the authentication of the Birthplace in the nineteenth century. Even as he was painstakingly searching for his evidence, Halliwell was acutely aware that texts did not always tell the truth; he had, after all, been one of the first critics to reveal Collier's forgeries, publishing his findings in 1853. Fortunately for Halliwell and for thousands of visitors to the Birthplace, however, the documentary evidence did not stand alone. The texts relating to the history of the house were accompanied by an oral tradition that identified this property as the one in which Shakespeare was born. Victorian commentators proved the authenticity of the Birthplace by pointing to this combination of textual evidence and verbal tradition. Thus, in the words of John R. Wise, "though there is no absolute evidence that he was born there, yet we know that his father rented it in 1552, and this, *coupled with the tradition*, makes the fact nearly certain" (my emphasis).[29] The antiquarian Charles Roach Smith makes a similar point: "Documentary evidence and tradition combine to vindicate the house in Henley Street as his birthplace; for although John Shakespeare, his father, had other houses in and about Stratford, yet the honour has never been claimed for any other; and it is pretty certain he lived in Henley Street about the time of the Poet's birth. Here we may safely trust to tradition."[30]

Halliwell, however, did more than simply trust to tradition: he attempted to verify it. This was a matter of some importance because, as Halliwell recognized, between the sixteenth-century references to John Shakespeare's dunghill and the 1759 surveyor's plan, which designated the Birthplace as such, tradition is all that existed. Moreover, the example of Garrick striding into and "identifying" the birthroom suggested the dangerous possibility that tradition could be invented, a possibility counteracted in Halliwell's attempts to textualize these oral stories, to make them more like documentary evidence. The first step in this process was to define tradition as fixed and stable, or, in Halliwell's own word, "unvarying": "The fact that Shakespeare was born in the house in Henley Street, which is now assigned as the place of his birth," he writes, "rests solely, as to the event itself, on tradition—on the unvarying tradition of the inhabitants of Stratford."[31] In this, Halliwell follows the opinions of Wheler, who in 1814 referred to the "invariable tradition" that Shakespeare's father inhabited the house when the poet was born.[32] It is also revealing that Halliwell's notion of tradition seems to gain more authority by locating the source of these legends not with an outsider like Garrick but within the local community itself.

With tradition defined as stable, it could also be represented as truthful. This strategy is central to Halliwell's (then Halliwell-Phillipps) last defense of the Birthplace, which he wrote just before his death. In response to a claim made by the German critic, Karl Elze, that Shakespeare could have been born in a house on Greenhill Street, Halliwell draws attention to the traditions surrounding the Henley Street property: "Those traditions are, I believe, as well authenticated as any of the kind, referring to so remote a period, can be expected to be," he asserts, "there is certainly not the shadow of a known fact that is inconsistent with their truth."[33] Later in the pamphlet, he makes the point more forcefully, commenting that "In former days truthful traditions were truthfully carried down through mere hearsay for many generations."[34] The insistent repetition of "truth" overturns the unreliability conventionally associated with an oral tradition, "mere hearsay," and works simultaneously to legitimate the Birthplace and the stories that surround it.

The eagerness to believe in the house, even against the odds, which Halliwell demonstrates, had taken root earlier in the century in Irving's *Sketch Book*. When the narrator, Crayon, visits the Birthplace he is shown the relics that the house then contained, and, while acknowledging that they are perhaps not all they seem, he is more than happy to go along with the story: "I am always of easy faith in such matters, and am ever willing to be deceived, where the deceit is pleasant and costs nothing. I am therefore a ready believer in relics, legends, and local anecdotes of goblins and great men; and would advise all travellers who travel for their gratification to be the same. What is it to us whether these stories be true or false, so long as we can persuade ourselves into the belief of them, and enjoy all the charm of the reality?"[35] Although Victorian tourists often failed to distinguish between the author and the narrator of *The Sketch Book* (as I suggest in the next chapter, the Irving—rather than the Crayon—tourist trail became a popular way of exploring Stratford), one can clearly identify in this extract the naïve, forgiving, and nonjudgmental voice of Geoffrey Crayon, ever the "Gent." His acceptance of the Birthplace and its relics is hardly surprising. It is questioned, however, by the suggestion opened up in the text that the truth of the Birthplace is anything but. In the acknowledgment that Crayon has to be "persuaded" into believing in the Birthplace and that he is "willing to be deceived," there is the implication that a deception has taken place. This is intimated later in the narrative when the local sexton expresses his doubts as to whether Shakespeare was actually born in the Birthplace, although, as Crayon acknowledges, the sexton's opinion might be colored by the fact that he regards the house as competing with the grave for the attention of tourists. "Thus it is," comments Crayon, "that historians differ at the very outset, and mere pebbles make the stream of truth diverge into different channels even at the fountain head."[36]

Crayon's ready "faith" in the Birthplace does not necessarily make him a dupe. Rather, it anticipates an almost religious belief in its authenticity that became dominant in discussions of the Birthplace during and following the auction. This is suggested in Charles Knight's revised and augmented version of Shakespeare's biography (interestingly, these lines do not appear in the original biography, which was published before the auction in 1843), where Knight remarks that "the want of absolute certainty that Shakspere was there born, produces a state of mind that is something higher and pleasanter than the conviction that depends upon positive evidence. We are content to follow the popular faith undoubtingly. The traditionary belief is sanctioned by long usage and universal acceptation."[37] For Knight, as for other Victorian commentators, an acceptance of the tradition surrounding Shakespeare's Birthplace produces a "higher" state of mind than reliance on documentary evidence because it depends on one's belief in the house. The religious overtones here are unmistakable, but this faith in the Birthplace is also bound up, as Freud might have argued, in desire: there is a need to believe in the traditions. Even if the authenticity of the Birthplace was an illusion, this illusion should not be shattered. This willing suspension of disbelief was often blamed for the very propagation of the Birthplace traditions. As one detractor remarked, "It is the easiest thing in the world to deceive people who themselves wish to be deceived."[38]

Halliwell certainly wished to be deceived. In his biography of Shakespeare, published in 1848, the shattering of the illusion of the Birthplace is regarded almost as a crime:

> Let not our poetical sympathies be measured by the argument of reality. It suffices to know and to feel that the spot was trod by Shakespeare, that there he "prattled poesy in his nurse's arms," and, more than this, that the associations remain and have not been destroyed. The worldly wise will tell us sympathies such as these are visionary, that our interest has arisen solely from our own imaginations, or they will cast the purest relic of the poet on one side, because truly it does not now appear as in his days. To descend to this destroys whatever that is good and noble it is in the power of association to bestow, for eyes will daily glisten at memorials far more changed from what they were—far less like the great originals. Breathe not a whisper to dissipate the solemn thoughts of such a power—tell us not how changeable are the records of men. If there be one spot in old, in historic England, sanctified by past association, it is the cottage where the poet of the world passed his youth, where he wooed and won, and encountered the struggles of early life—the birthplace of William Shakespeare.[39]

This is a striking moment in a biography that the author is openly determined to keep free from flights of fancy. The Birthplace, it seems, gets the better of Halliwell and his Gradgrindian facts, transforming the antiquarian incarnate into a romantic visionary. The connection between Shakespeare and the Birthplace, he contends, should never be questioned; indeed, it *cannot* be questioned precisely because "poetical sympathies" cannot be measured or judged against the "argument of reality." Halliwell's warning, "Breathe not a whisper to dissipate the solemn thoughts of such a power," echoes that of Frederick

Fairholt, who appealed to critics in his guidebook to the Birthplace: "Let no rude pen destroy such heart-homage."[40] Ultimately, for Halliwell, this "poetical" belief in the truth of the Birthplace is more robust even than supporting documents because it is sacred.

Shakespeare's Amazing Flying Chair

Geoffrey Crayon's willingness to believe in the myth of the Birthplace takes place in the context of a description of the questionable relics that the house contains. Among other curiosities, Crayon is shown Shakespeare's tobacco box, the sword with which he played Hamlet, the lantern with which Friar Lawrence discovers Romeo and Juliet, and Shakespeare's chair, which stands in the chimney nook of a small gloomy room at the back of the house and has been sat on by so many pilgrims that it is re-bottomed every three years.[41] The chair, Irving writes, "partakes something of the volatile nature of the Santa Casa of Loretto, or the flying chair of the Arabian enchanter, for though sold some few years since to a northern princess, yet, strange to tell, it has found its way back again to the old chimney corner."[42]

Shakespeare's chair features in other, more "factual," travelogues. Samuel Ireland, who traveled to Stratford in the summer of 1793 (along with his soon-to-be-disgraced son)[43] gave Irving's "northern princess" a name: Princess (Izabela) Czartoryska of Poland. According to Ireland, Czartoryska visited the Birthplace in 1790 and was desperate to purchase the chair but was informed by Mrs. Hart, a descendant of Shakespeare's sister to whom the house then belonged, that it was not to be sold on any account.[44] Hart's resolution wavered four months later when a secretary came from Poland and offered her twenty guineas, and the chair was duly sent to Poland complete with a certificate of authenticity. The certificate, though, was not worth the paper it was written on. Shakespeare's chair was "as spurious as that which immediately supplied its place," according to Wheler. "In this lowly dwelling," he writes, "some antiquated lumber was formerly imposed upon the world as its original furniture at the period of Shakespeare, but to none of which the least authenticity belonged. In the moment of unsuspecting enthusiasm, persons of easy faith in such matters too implicitly relied upon its originality; for it is well known that the furniture of this house has undergone more alterations than the building itself, and that it has, of late years at least, changed with every tenant."[45]

By 1793 when the next tenant of the Birthplace, Mary Hornby, arrived on the scene, the chair had magically reappeared, although it now had to compete with the little chair of Hamnet, Shakespeare's son, who had died as a boy. Hornby claimed that a letter from Shakespeare to his wife, written from the playhouse in London and kept in a cupboard in the birthroom, had been stolen by visitors.[46] Hornby's relics were shown in the Birthplace until 1820 when she was evicted by Mrs. Court, the owner of the property and proprietor of the Swan and Maidenhead, who must have looked on with some interest as her neighbor exploited the lucrative potential of the tenement where Shakespeare was said to have been born. Hornby's revenge was to whitewash the signatures that covered the walls of the Birthplace, including those of many famous writers and statesmen, and to take her relics with her to a house on the opposite side of the street where she was frequently to be seen fighting with her former landlady, a situation that was described in verse by one disillusioned tourist:

> What, Birthplace here! and relics there?
> Abuse from each! Ye brawling blowses!
> Each picks my pocket, 'tis not fair,
> A stranger's curse on both your houses![47]

This verse is typical of the cynical reaction to the Birthplace that can be identified from the 1790s to the late 1840s when Mrs. Court died and the property went to auction. Indeed, in her own occupation of the Birthplace, Mrs. Court, although relic-less, turned out to be as reckless as her predecessor, both women engaging in a war of authenticity, bandying about numerous documents that "proved" or disproved the authenticity of the relics.[48] Mrs. Hornby managed to secure a statement signed by the father-in-law of the late Thomas Hart (who was himself known to have sold numerous chairs), stating that the relics were genuine and had been in the possession of the Harts since the death of Joan Hart.[49] Mrs. Court responded by displaying a statement from another member of the Hart family in Tewkesbury, William Shakespeare Hart, which declared that when the property was sold to the Courts in 1806 it contained no relics. The statement added, "I further certify my positive belief, that anything advertized or shown there, or in the neighbourhood, at present, as such, must be spurious and deceptive."[50] As a final attack on her rival, Hornby turned to the only surviving daughter of Thomas Hart to certify that when the Hornbys rented the house, twenty years before the Courts purchased it, they bought all the relics; William Shakespeare Hart would have known nothing about the purchase because he was a young boy living in Tewkesbury at the time.

Crayon might have been willing to suspend his disbelief in these relics, but this disbelief still lingered. And where did this leave the true relic, the house itself? It is noticeable that Mary Hornby did not respond to Mrs. Court's rubbishing of her relics by calling into doubt the authenticity of the Birthplace. There was a sense, however, in which the meanings of the relics and the house were indivisible in this period of the Birthplace's history, the property often seen in the light of these dodgy leftovers from Shakespeare's life. As the disgruntled visitor remarks "What, Birthplace here! And relics there?" There is no difference between the two: both are used to extort money from the increasingly wary tourist.

An exposure of these relics was undertaken in an article published in *Bentley's Miscellany* in 1847 in the wake of the auction. Of Shakespeare's famous chair, the article asserts that the Harts actually sold four, all made by a well-known local craftsman, leaving a gap between the selling of the third and fourth to enable the new chair to acquire a "traditional reputation."[51] (Tradition, it seems, might not be as "unvarying" or as ancient as Halliwell assumes.) The uncovering of the relic trade in this article is not limited to the odd (or not so odd) chair, however. Indeed, as the writer comments, "As long as this was confined to chairs, tables, jugs, and walking-sticks, and the pious fraud benefited poor people at the expense of rich credulity, there was no great harm done; but the extraordinary sensation created by the purchase of this shabby sausage-shop deserves a prominent place amongst popular delusions."[52] For this author, the Birthplace itself is "the crowning fortune of the Stratford reliquary business."[53]

But the auction of the Birthplace and its purchase for the nation offered a fresh start for the house, the chance to recuperate it from the vulgar commercial concern it had become. The *Man in the Moon* depicted Shakespeare packing up his goods and saying goodbye to the autographs on the wall, the visitors' book, and his source of income: "And oh, you silver shillings, whose bright face / Our blessed Queen's fair portrait counterfeits, / Farewell. Poor Shakespeare's sole support is gone!"[54] The auction allowed a distinction to be made between the veracity of the house and the falsehood of the relics. When the house was sold, the majority of its furnishings were also disposed of, including an elaborately carved Elizabethan chair and a spectacle case made from the wood of the mulberry tree.[55] As for Mary Hornby's collection, this was now kept at a safe distance from Henley Street. By the time of the tercentenary, her relics, along with their new curator, Hornby's granddaughter, had moved to High Street, where the objects were regarded more as curiosities than as genuine artifacts.[56] In 1867 they were sold at auction.

The purchase of the Birthplace helped to differentiate between the residence and the relics. The dubious objects were eradicated, with only those items that helped to verify the property remaining in place. As with all things repressed, however, the relics were bound to return. The museum that opened in the interior of the Birthplace following its restoration needed exhibits, and these included a set of Long-beard jugs used in Elizabethan times, a goblet made from the mulberry tree that had been left to the Birthplace by Fairholt, and a drinking cup said to have belonged to Shakespeare and from which Garrick sipped at the Jubilee. Halliwell-Phillipps was responsible for these objects and moved them accordingly between the several properties that the Birthplace Trust owned. Among the items that were imported to the Birthplace was a coin from the reign of James I, a fragment of an old knife of uncertain date found in the excavations at New Place, and a small box made from a walnut tree which formerly grew in front of the house.[57] Any decisions about these transfers were made by assessing the veracity of the material: "Due regard has been paid to genuineness," Halliwell-Phillipps asserts.[58]

But "genuineness" is not so easy to ascertain or define. The issue of the authenticity of the objects on display in the Birthplace was resurrected in September 1903 on the death of a former custodian, Joseph Skipsey, the so-called "Collier Poet." The job of the custodian was, essentially, to legitimate the house by relating to visitors the authoritative (and authorized) history of the building since the time of Shakespeare, thereby carrying on the circulation of the local traditions. The task proved too much for Skipsey. Having taken up the post with his wife in June 1889, and with the support of key literary figures, including Browning, Tennyson, and Dante Gabriel Rossetti, he had resigned by October 1891. The reasons for this resignation became apparent following his death when his friend, John Cuming Walters, wrote to *The Times* citing a letter that he had received from Skipsey soon after the poet's return to Newcastle. In the letter, Skipsey confessed that he had lost faith in the Birthplace relics that it was his duty to show to visitors.[59] Among these relics, Cuming Walters's own disdain is reserved for the desk said to be Shakespeare's as a schoolboy, which had been taken from Stratford grammar school and exhibited at the Henley Street property.[60] The desk had proved especially popular with tourists, a lady from New York apparently falling on her knees and kissing it.[61] A more composed visitor in the 1870s imagined a young Shakespeare slyly cutting it with his knife.[62]

Despite the best efforts of the likes of Halliwell, the relics on show in the Birthplace could not simply be defined as true or false; the boundaries between these apparently stable categories kept slipping, so much so that the "authentic" relics that Cuming Walters *did* believe in—the signet ring apparently belonging to Shakespeare and a brooch bearing the poet's name that had been discovered in 1828[63]—are immediately called into question by another letter writer to *The Times*.[64] For Skipsey, the fakery of the objects went hand in hand with the dubiousness of those traditions that he was compelled to recite: "As to the idle gossip, the so-called traditions and legends of the place," he writes, "they are for the most part an abomination and must stink in the nostrils of every true lover of our divine poet."[65]

The reason for Skipsey's resignation was used by Henry James in "The Birthplace," a story in which Skipsey becomes Morris Gedge, the custodian who finds himself unable to tell the tales expected of him. Rather than resign, however, Gedge finally finds his voice, a voice that indulges in fantasy and romance to such effect that visitor numbers increase and he is rewarded with a pay raise. James's story calls into question the authenticity of the house and the possibility of an actual physical space where one can commune with the dead author, although recent readings of the text have suggested that even here the undermining of the veracity of the Birthplace is far from clear-cut.[66]

While uncertainties about the legitimacy of the Birthplace were expressed in the fictional context of James's story, the legitimacy of the Henley Street house was, to some extent, established in the very process of discriminating between the property and the material objects it contained. The relics might be an imposture, but this did not necessarily mean that the Birthplace was. Skipsey criticized the presence of the relics, but he was quoted by Cuming Walters as expressing his firm conviction in the validity of the house: "That our Shakespeare was born in Henley-street I continue fully to believe, and that the house yet shown as the Shakespeare House stands on the site of the house in which he was born I also believe (and it was sacred to me on that account)."[67] Some doubts might remain in Skipsey's passing reference to the Birthplace existing "on the site" of the current house, which could suggest that he believed, as did some historians, that the majority of the Henley Street properties, including the Birthplace, had been destroyed by fire after Shakespeare's death, or it may be that he viewed the restoration of the house as the erasure of the original structure. But conjectural doubts aside, Skipsey does, in this letter at least, profess his belief in the Birthplace.[68] Indeed, in his biography, Skipsey's resignation is blamed not on any personal reservations about the house, but on American tourists. Their questioning of the legends of the Birthplace and of the true authorship of the plays made Skipsey exhausted and bewildered: "The constant suspicion and doubts freely and often cleverly expressed had worked upon his mind. He felt that if he were to make this his life's labour he would end by doubting the very existence of Shakespeare, and so he resigned his place and came home to the North."[69] The fact that it was the inquisitive tourists, rather than the authenticity of the Birthplace, that forced Skipsey from his post is confirmed by Ernest Rhys, the founding editor of Everyman's Library, who reveals in his autobiography that Skipsey told him he had suffered in his job as custodian because, unlike Gedge, he could not play the part of the showman for the American tourist. Henry James's hero, writes Rhys, "is not in the least degree like Skipsey."[70] Likewise, for Skipsey's friend, Cuming Walters, the question of the authenticity of the Birthplace is not even raised; for him, it is Anne Hathaway's cottage that is the dubious property on the Stratford tourist trail.[71]

The debates about the truth of the Birthplace never entirely disappear, even when the nineteenth century draws to a close, but the terms of the debate shift from the house itself to the material objects that are displayed within it. Responding to Cuming Walters's concerns, Sidney Lee, who had become chairman of the executive committee of the Shakespeare Birthplace Trust earlier that year, declared that it was desirable "to distinguish by means of plainly worded labels what is certain from what is less certain."[72] Just as Halliwell needed the legitimization of documents to authenticate the house on Henley Street, so the resolution of the relics problem in 1903 seemed to reside in the apparent certainty and truth of written texts.

Seeing Is Believing

But the authentication of the Birthplace was a visual as well as a textual process. This was evident in the hundreds of images of the Birthplace that were in circulation in the nineteenth century and that transformed the building into a specifically visual icon. These pictures played a significant part in the process of recognition, establishing a notion of what the Birthplace looked like, even in its geographical distance from the viewer. When Sanford R. Gifford, the American landscape painter, visited Stratford in 1855, he regarded it as unnecessary to describe the building in his letters home to his father: "The prints have made you familiar with its appearance," he writes.[73] Visual familiarity and recognition were also bound up in authentication: images of the Birthplace showed the building *as* the Birthplace; the house was presented, in visual terms, as the real thing.

Following Greene's 1769 drawing of the property, other images of the house began to appear, including the pictures of the Birthplace in Ireland's *Picturesque Views*, images in magazines, such as the *Monthly Magazine* (February 1818), and the *Mirror of Literature, Amusement, and Instruction* (January 1823), and in travel books such as William Rider's *Views in Stratford-upon-Avon and its Vicinity, Accompanied with Descriptive Remarks* (1828). Although they constitute an important part of the history of the Birthplace, these early pictures were sporadically published in diverse contexts. In terms of volume and reach, it was not until the auction of the Birthplace that a more sustained practice of visually representing the house really began to emerge. The auction catalogue itself contained engravings of the building, while the images used in the leaflets issued by the Stratford and London committees in their appeal for subscriptions became so well known that they were satirized in the press. Victorian pictures of the Birthplace traveled the world, their presence suggesting the possibility of an instant connection with the real material building. This power of the visual was recognized in an illustrated publication sold at the time of the tercentenary celebrations, which stated that "As it is not possible for all the votaries of Shakspeare to make a pilgrimage to this literary Mecca, Stratford-upon-Avon, we will try—aided by our artist's pencil—to carry our readers there in imagination."[74] By the end of the century, images of the building appeared in book, magazine and newspaper illustrations, in editions of Shakespeare's works, in the form of stereographs, on postcards, notepaper, and pocket handkerchiefs, not to mention the prints that were sold as souvenirs in the Birthplace itself.[75] The American comic creation Artemus Ward comments that "them as sell picturs of his Birthplace, &c., make it prof'tible cherisin it. Almost everybody buys a pictur to put into their Albiom."[76]

The mass circulation of images of the Birthplace was made possible by the techniques of mechanical reproduction that shaped Victorian visual culture, among them etching, wood and steel engraving, lithography and photography.

In "The Work of Art in the Age of Mechanical Reproduction," Walter Benjamin makes the case that mechanical reproduction destroys the authenticity and authority of the original, what he terms its "aura."[77] In its copying, he argues, the unique object is removed from its context and location, and its value is depreciated. In the case of the Birthplace, however, there is an important sense in which the authenticity of the building was actually constituted in its pictorial reproduction. The images might have "removed" the Birthplace, transporting it from a street in Stratford to a drawing room in America, but they also pointed to the existence of the original house. And the more images of the Birthplace that were in circulation, the more assured the truth of the house seemed.

The authentication of the Birthplace was achieved not only in terms of the collective presence of these images, however, but also in individual attempts at artistic truth. For his illustrations in Knight's biography, William Harvey traveled twice to Stratford in order to make his drawings.[78] Fairholt also aimed for authenticity in his guidebook to Stratford, drawing his scenes on the spot rather than from recollection, even if this was sometimes a difficult task. In a letter to Wheler, Fairholt asked the historian if he might suggest any local person willing to make some sketches; Fairholt had been in the town earlier, but because it was a Sunday, he had been unable to do the drawings. "All could be done in 2 hours by any body at Stratford," he writes.[79] He did not have a satisfactory answer, for in his next letter he has determined to take the train to Stratford as soon as possible.[80]

Fairholt's sense of urgency was precipitated because he believed that the architectural structures and locations he sketched were on the verge of destruction: "In these days of change, when the birthplace of the Poet is scarcely safe, and Stratford is threatened with the spoliation of what little remains to it, it must be a work of interest to record and picture the few relics connected with the Bard of Avon, the more particularly as alterations are continually taking place there; which, if they do not destroy, do at least change the aspect of much that is interesting to all lovers of the poet."[81] Fairholt's images serve a documentary as well as instructive purpose: they attempt to capture for posterity objects and buildings that were about to change forever, including external views of the Birthplace and every one of its rooms. The review of the book in the *Art-Union* commented that while the localities in Stratford associated with Shakespeare "have been drawn and engraved over and over again," the majority of Fairholt's images were "quite new, and the others selected with great care."[82] Fairholt's "carefulness" was also recognized by Halliwell, who included

SHAKESPERE AND STRATFORD-UPON-AVON.
THE DRAWINGS BY E. DUNCAN, ESQ.

Figure 13. E. Duncan, "Shakspere's House," engraved by W. J. Linton, *Illustrated London News*, 18 September 1847. Reproduced by permission of Special Collections and Archives, Cardiff University.

the illustrations in his *Life of William Shakespeare*: "Nothing has been copied which will not bear the test of the strictest examination," Halliwell asserts. "Mr. Fairholt has also carefully abstained from those fanciful imitations which have so little real value, and in which the characteristic features of the original objects are so seldom preserved."[83]

Fairholt's efforts to provide an authentic visual representation of the Birthplace were paralleled just a month or so after his letter to Wheler when the *Illustrated London News* published a special edition of the newspaper to coincide with the auction. The pictures it contained were newly commissioned and had been drawn on the spot in Stratford by one of the newspaper's leading artists, E. Duncan, and engraved by W. J. Linton (Figure 13).

With its apparently truthful pictures and descriptions of the Birthplace, the *Illustrated London News* is able to sidestep the issue of whether or not Shakespeare was really born in the house: "We are not of those who attach much import to the question, whether this, in reality, is the tenement wherein he first drew breath? As has been well remarked, if it were not the Birthplace of the child, it was, unquestionably, the nurturing place of the Poet, which is of infinitely more consequence, and surely sufficient to entitle it to respect and

Figure 14. W. J. Linton, "The House in Henley Street as Restored," from John R. Wise, *Shakspere: His Birthplace and Its Neighbourhood* (London: Smith, Elder and Co., 1861).

preservation from the nation at large."[84] In a way, though, these remarks are highly ironic, for the pictures in the *Illustrated London News*, drawn in situ by one of its top artists, served to legitimate the Birthplace, forming part of a visual tradition of representing the house that was established not only in the wide circulation of these images but also in the interaction between them. Fairholt's images, for example, were published in several editions throughout the century and in New York as well as Stratford-upon-Avon. The same images were reused, though the text was changed, in Samuel Neil's *The Home of Shakespeare* (1871). Likewise, W. J. Linton, who engraved Duncan's pictures for the *Illustrated London News*, went on to picture the Birthplace himself in the illustrations for John R. Wise's *Shakspere: His Birthplace and Its Neighbourhood* (1861) (Figure 14). Some interactions were not quite so transparent, with artists like Henry Fitzcook failing to acknowledge debts to other drawings, but the mass reproduction of images and the interplay between them led to a distinct iconography that made the Birthplace instantly recognizable.

The pictures were part of a visual discourse that alluded to other pictures in a way that created a model for how the building should be represented and suggested the inherent truth and reliability of a representation. Although images of the house appeared in a range of different forms (as prints and illustrations, watercolors and wood engravings, in travel guides and criticism), they were part of an interpictorial web that generated a clearly defined visual vocabulary. Before the restoration, when the building was part of a terraced street, pictures of the Birthplace usually showed the three structures that made up the house—the tenement, butcher's shop (often depicted with joints of meat hanging up in the hatched window and the board on the wall proclaiming that Shakespeare had been born there), and the Swan and Maidenhead pub with a wisp of smoke blowing out of the chimney—along with a cut-off portion of the properties on either side (see, for example, Figure 13). The perspective was usually from the front of the house with the viewer positioned at the opposite side of Henley Street, facing the northwest or northeast corner of the house at a slight angle, so that the buildings recede toward the side of the picture space. The indistinguishable time of day and the absence of all but a few stragglers in the majority of these pictures add to the timelessness of the scene, while the focus on tumble-down, dilapidated buildings romanticizes the house, creating a sense of nostalgia.

By visualizing the Birthplace in such a prolific and uniform way, these images added to the truth of what they were showing, despite the fact that the representations themselves were not necessarily truthful. The location of the imaginary viewer across [a widened] Henley Street in a position that was actually occupied by other buildings gives a sense of air and space that was not entirely accurate. In a way, though, it made no difference whether the scene represented was real or not: taken together, images of the Birthplace constructed this reality, helping to create an illusion of stability and continuity. So established were these pictorial conventions that even differences in how the house appeared could be accommodated: the building might or might not have dormer windows, the Swan and Maidenhead pub might or might not have the brick frontage that was added early in the nineteenth century, but the building was still recognizable as the Birthplace.

This all changed, however, with the restoration of the house. Like Shakespeare's chair, pictures of the new Birthplace needed some time to acquire a "traditional reputation." Even as late as the 1880s, one visitor to Stratford wrote:

The house is recognised the moment it comes in sight. Every one has seen pictures of the building, but recollections of these pictures would be of little assistance were assistance needed in prompting the memory now, for all of them, all at least that I had seen, were executed in days when Shakespeare's birthplace wore a very different appearance. The prints I was familiar with depicted a somewhat tumble-down, weather-worn edifice, one of a row of like tumble-down, weather-worn edifices, with the highway running up to its very walls, and having two boards thrust out from the front to meet at an angle and inform those going by in either direction that beneath that modest roof Shakespeare saw the light.[85]

Images of the pre-restored Birthplace were still highly marketable in the second half of the nineteenth century, but if the authenticity of the building was to be consolidated, the "new" Birthplace needed to be as recognizable as the "old" one. To this end, publications turned to another visual convention that had run, though less conspicuously, alongside the images of the humble terraced street. These pictures recreated what the house apparently looked like in Shakespeare's day, showing a detached and relatively grand Tudor dwelling. The first such picture was Greene's, which served as the template for the restoration project. Now, however, it was employed to verify the Birthplace by providing an apparent visual history and legitimacy for its restored appearance. A duplicate of Greene's picture from the *Gentleman's Magazine*, but with the addition of a rather forlorn-looking dog taking a leisurely stroll in front of the house, was a copperplate engraving by Colonel Philip de la Motte. The engraving was originally published in 1788 and often reproduced after the restoration, including as the frontispiece for Halliwell's edition of Wheler's *An Historical Account of the Birth-Place of Shakespeare*, where the editor confidently asserts that it "represents the Birth-place as it appeared in the last century."[86] The reappearance of such images following the restoration of the Birthplace served to authenticate the restored building, connecting it to an ancient heritage and to an older and established visual convention.

The Camera Never Lies

In 1864 the *Illustrated London News* published an image of the Birthplace that showed its visualization in action. Set up outside the house, with a few curious children looking on, are three tripods and cameras, two of which are being operated by photographers (Figure 15). This image marks a shift in representations of the Birthplace, both in terms of its depiction of a recently restored building, and in the new mode of reproduction to which it refers. Up until the middle of the nineteenth century, pictures of the Birthplace were published primarily as wood engravings (a technique that had the advantage of allowing the images to be printed together with descriptive text) or as lithographs (which claimed a high level of factual accuracy). According to one print-seller, the chromolithographic views of the Birthplace sold in the 1860s and based on watercolor drawings "give the most exact representations ever offered to the public."[87] These techniques, however, were eclipsed by photography, a genre that continues to define images of the Birthplace today, and that came, moreover, with its own notions of "authenticity."

Roland Barthes has described the photograph as "indifferent to all intermediaries: it does not invent; it is authentication itself," and it is precisely this authentication that is at play in Victorian photographic images of the Birthplace.[88] The photograph seems to provide instant access to the reality of the house, without the interventions (or "inventions") that characterize mechanical processes of reproduction. In its apparently unmediated representation of the object, the photograph's own status as a representation is obscured: the

Figure 15. Victorian photographers set up camp outside the Birthplace. *Illustrated London News* supplement, 30 April 1864. Reproduced by permission of Special Collections and Archives, Cardiff University.

lines, cross-hatching, the very marks of the production that are inevitable in techniques like wood engraving, are hidden in the photograph. As Barthes writes, "A photograph is always invisible: it is not it that we see."[89] What we do see, however, is the referent of the image, the object that has stood before the camera lens, in this case, Shakespeare's house on Henley Street.

If the photograph is "authentication itself," if it seems to capture the reality and truth of what it shows, there is a sense in which the very presence of the photographic subject provides proof of its existence. In other words, photography is not only authentic in its own right, but also adds to the authenticity of what it represents. In her recent analysis of nineteenth-century photographic illustration, Carol Armstrong contends that architectural photographs, photographs of buildings and places, are those which most strongly privilege the subject matter of the image.[90] This can be seen to great effect in the photographically illustrated travel and guidebooks to Stratford that were so popular in the latter half of the nineteenth century and in which the Birthplace featured so prominently. Even as early as the 1850s, photographs of places and monuments were among the most commercially viable types of photograph,[91] with Shakespeare and the Birthplace outnumbering all other photographs associated with dead literary celebrities in the period.[92]

It was the ability of the photograph to document and record reality that came to the fore in contemporary discussions of the genre, Elizabeth Eastlake remarking in 1857 that the role of photography was "to give evidence of facts, as minutely and as impartially as, to our shame, only an unreasoning machine can give."[93] This seemingly objective display of facts was exploited in books that used photography or photolithography to reproduce facsimiles of historic texts, like Shakespeare's will.[94] The Birthplace Trust collection contains hundreds of Victorian photographs that set out to record all aspects of the existence of the Birthplace, from tourists posing at the front of the house and in the garden to interior shots of the rooms and different stages of the restoration project. When a model of Shakespeare's house by E. T. Parris was erected in the central transept of the Crystal Palace in 1864, visitors were given a photograph of the real Birthplace for comparison.[95]

The authenticity associated with the photograph rubbed off on the Birthplace itself: it was presented as the true building, which was captured by the camera lens. Indeed, there was a sense, as Eastlake had argued, in which photography was, by its very nature, documentary, its creative aspirations hindered by the technological restraints of the process. Whereas imaginative drawings like Greene's and de la Motte's could depict a full frontal view of the Birthplace (with the suggestion of expanse in the foreground, for example), the limitations of the camera lens and the fact that the houses opposite the Birthplace prevented the photographer from positioning himself farther back from the building, meant that such a view was more difficult to achieve in the form of a photograph. Thus, Victorian photographs tend to adopt the typical perspective of engravings of the pre-restored Birthplace, facing the corner of the house at an angle (see, for example, Figure 11).

Like the exterior shots, photographic representations of the interior of the Birthplace also depicted the same subject matter from the same perspective as previous engravings. Ernest Edwards, who took the photographs for Jephson's "pilgrimage" of Stratford, showed the inglenook fireplace downstairs and the hearth in the birthroom, the only difference between his photographs and earlier drawings being the spectral traces of Victorian tourists fleetingly captured by the exposure (Figure 16). This tradition continued well into the final decades of the nineteenth century with photographically illustrated books such as Henry Snowden Ward and Catharine Weed Ward's *Shakespeare's Town and Times* (1896), which also included the large inglenook fireplace and a photograph of the birthroom taken from inside the apartment and looking towards the hearth.[96]

Photographic images of the Birthplace, it seemed, needed their own legitimization, a legitimization that could be achieved by drawing on established conventions of representing the house. It is apt that the image of photographers outside the Birthplace in the *Illustrated London News*, which bears witness to the arrival of these new technologies, takes the form not of a photograph, but of a wood engraving. Despite its apparent veracity, however, the truth of the photograph, like the truth of the Birthplace, is always in doubt. The Victorians might not have had digitization software available, but there were ways of manipulating images. Capitalizing on the depth of perspective achieved by the camera, photographs of the Birthplace taken from opposite the northeast corner, with the ivy-covered chimney breast and the gabled roof in the right foreground made the house look broader, grander, and more isolated as it recedes into the distance, to the extent that some tourists must have been surprised when they visited the actual site (Figure 17).

Photography could construct a particular impression of the house, whether it was larger, more humble, or more idealized. This is exemplified in one of the most extraordinary publications of the period: James Leon Williams's *The*

Figure 16. Ernest Edwards, "Living Room in Shakespere's House," from J. M. Jephson, *Shakespere: His Birthplace, Home, and Grave. A Pilgrimage to Stratford-on-Avon in the Autumn of 1863* (London: Lovell Reeve, 1864).

Home and Haunts of Shakespeare (1892), a collection of images in five sections, lavishly illustrated with watercolors and photographs. The book went through several editions and over 12,000 copies were sold, with a specially bound copy presented to Queen Victoria. Williams, a successful American dentist (his claim to fame was discovering dental plaque), was an unlikely commentator on Shakespeare's country, but he spent four summer holidays attempting to re-create the Stratford of Shakespeare's youth. His motivation seems to have been the same as Fairholt's: he was distressed by the eradication of an older way of life. As his biographer, George Wood Clapp, relates, "He began to feel a sense of personal loss as he realized what the changes were destroying, and he knew that others would feel that loss in increasing degree as time passed. He resolved to perpetuate those conditions on paper for the benefit of Shakespeare lovers the world over."[97]

Figure 17. Photograph of the Birthplace, from James Leon Williams, *The Home and Haunts of Shakespeare* (London: Sampson Low, Marston and Co., 1892).

The Home and Haunts of Shakespeare, however, is far from a simple documentary analysis. Williams took hundreds of photographs, many of which, according to Clapp, required "painstaking preparations . . . in order to produce the conditions as they must have been when Shakespeare wrote."[98] These photographs, then, were "produced," staged, created to give the impression of a historic way of life that was in danger of obliteration. It was a way of life, moreover, that drew explicitly on the rural and pastoral genre paintings that had been so popular earlier in the century. The images had titles like "Waiting for the Ferry," "When We Were Boys," and "Crabbed Age and Youth." One photograph of a poacher that appears in the section on Charlecote, where Shakespeare was himself rumored to have poached, shows the culprit caught in the act and making his escape, gun and rabbit in hand. Williams's photograph of the exterior of the Birthplace (he also includes the familiar interior shot of the birthroom), entitled "Here Shakespeare was Born," is a wonderful image of the house as the nearest point in a long and beautifully framed expanse of Henley Street (Figure 18). The street is almost deserted, apart from a horse and wagon, the driver of which in the vicinity of the Hornby Cottages chats to another man standing on the road. The eerie emptiness and stillness of the photograph parallels the evocative atmosphere that many Victorian critics described inside the house. Despite its obvious artifice, the image seems to show the reality of the Birthplace, fulfilling the aim of the book as a whole, which, according to Horace Howard Furness who wrote the introduction, is to show life "almost as unchanged since the days when Shakespeare was a part of it."[99] It is noticeable that Williams's photograph of the Birthplace, like the others in the book, avoids depicting tourists but shows instead the Stratford locals engaged in their daily pursuits. Jennifer Green-Lewis has argued that "a photograph could change the narrative status of its subject from fiction to fact."[100] Williams's photograph asserts its own factual status, even as it seduces in its imaginative re-creation of Henley Street.

Photographic images like Williams's provided a new visual genre to match the newly restored house, a genre that existed precariously on the borderline between fact and fiction but that came to dominate the representation of the Birthplace. The case of Williams, the holidaymaker turned photographer, was symptomatic of the late nineteenth century when photographing Shakespeare's Birthplace had become a common activity, not just for the professionals shown in the *Illustrated London News*, but also for visitors, who were encouraged to

Figure 18. James Leon Williams, "Here Shakespeare Was Born," *The Home and Haunts of Shakespeare* (London: Sampson Low, Marston and Co., 1892). Reproduced by permission of the John Rylands University Library, Manchester.

take photographs as souvenirs. Guidebooks to Stratford advertised lessons in photography run in local studios, one such advertisement in 1886 promising proficiency in three lessons and free instruction to those who purchased the apparatus.[101]

But there were anxieties surrounding photographs of the Birthplace, a realization that photography had the power to generate rather than simply re-present the meanings of the house. In May 1904 the regulations for the management of the Birthplace, which included the ruling that no dogs, cycles, or perambulators be admitted, set out the following clause: "No interior or exterior photographs shall be taken on any of the premises without an order from the Secretary and Librarian; fee, £1 1s., and any person desiring to photograph any one or more special objects must first obtain special permission, through the Secretary and Librarian, from the Executive Committee. The negatives of all such photographs shall be the copyright of the Trustees."[102]

The charging of a fee to photograph the Birthplace must have provided a steady flow of income for the Birthplace trustees, but there is more to this regulation than a commercial opportunity. In the requirement that no photographs be taken without the permission of the secretary and the librarian and the statement that the trustees owned the copyright to the negatives, there is an explicit attempt to control these images. One wonders how such a regulation would have been enforced then, or how it could possibly be enforced today, when hundreds of tourists pose for photographs of the house.

Whether it was actually effective or not, the attempt to regulate the taking of photographs of the Birthplace suggests how pervasive, and persuasive, such images had become, and this is precisely why they needed to be controlled. Alongside Halliwell's archival documents and oral traditions, pictures of the house worked to quell doubts and anxieties about the authenticity of the shrine. Far from existing on the periphery of the Birthplace, circulating around it and simply reproducing it, these texts, objects, and images played a part in shaping the meanings of the building. The more the house was represented as the real thing, the more it came to be viewed as just that. Indeed, there is a sense in which the Birthplace itself is primarily a representation in this period, known across the world in its pictorial and textual manifestations.

As for the relics, while Shakespeare's chair has long since disappeared, his signet ring, which Cuming Walters was convinced was genuine, is still on display in the Birthplace, where it rests on the finger of a plastic hand under the glare of a spotlight. Although the Birthplace is now generally regarded as authentic, the status of this relic remains indeterminate. Could it really have once adorned the hand of William Shakespeare? The suggestion tantalizes visitors today just as it did their Victorian predecessors, whose ritualized itinerary and experience of Stratford is the subject of the next chapter.

Chapter 5

Eight Things to Do in Stratford-upon-Avon: A Guide for the Victorian Tourist

What did Victorian visitors do when they got to Stratford? How did they behave when they entered the sacred shrine of the Birthplace? This chapter takes the form of a list or guide for nineteenth-century visitors, which outlines what they did—or what they were meant to do—on their tour of the town, along with the ways in which some tourists attempted to defy convention. The list encompasses not only the attractions that were available for visitors to see but also how they were encouraged to respond to these sites. Perusing this itinerary, the tourist to Stratford today may notice a curious collapse of history. The emphasis of the trip might be different in the twenty-first century, as is the mode of transport, but there is still a recognizable Victorian aura to Stratford-upon-Avon. This aura is present in the Birthplace, but it is also there in the mock Tudor dwellings that line the streets, in the gift shops with their plentiful supply of souvenirs, and in the very fact that Stratford, "Shakespeare's town," remains such an appealing tourist destination.

1. Read the Guidebook

In 1847, amidst the furor surrounding the sale of Shakespeare's Birthplace, Stratford had a very special visitor. As reported by "The Oldest Inhabitant of Stratford," Queen Victoria, accompanied by Prince Albert and her young brood of children, arrived in the town.[1] The royal family looked like any other pilgrims as they made their way along Henley Street to the "immortal homestead."[2] Outside the Birthplace, Victoria broke into a smile, and, as she crossed the threshold, a tear could be seen in her eye. Inside the house, it was the turn of the town bailiff to almost burst into tears as the Queen told her children what a great man Shakespeare was and made them promise never to forget him. Before leaving the Birthplace for the church and the grammar school, the royal family signed their names in the visitors' book.

A young Victorian family paying their respects at the family home of Shakespeare, their royal status almost (but never quite) forgotten in their homage to the bard: it is a delightful scene and is recounted in a suitably delightful way by the "Oldest Inhabitant of Stratford." Unfortunately, however, this charming event never actually took place. The "Inhabitant" is the comic writer Douglas Jerrold, the magazine he is reporting in is *Punch*, and, rather than visiting Stratford-upon-Avon, the royal family had, in fact, spent the day at a Drury Lane theater, where there was a show of camels, Indian ponies, and elephants.[3]

Queen Victoria was genuinely enthusiastic about Shakespeare's plays (she sponsored many performances at Windsor Castle and the Princess's Theatre in London),[4] but throughout her long reign, she never visited Shakespeare's Birthplace. She went there once as a twelve-year-old, but even this visit to Stratford had more practical than literary concerns, made only because she might attend a local school.[5] The account of the visit in *Punch* is intended as a criticism of the royal family's apparent lack of interest in the Birthplace (despite the fact that Prince Albert was president of the London committee to purchase the house) and the frivolity of their leisure pursuits.

In her love of shows rather than Shakespeare, of beasts rather than bards, Victoria breaks the rules. By not visiting the Birthplace, not writing in the visitors' book, and not divulging her passion for Shakespeare, there is a sense in which the absent Queen Victoria is one of Stratford's most subversive tourists. This satire is effective, however, because the description of the tour of Stratford and the Birthplace is so believable. Members of the imaginary, if not the actual, royal family adhere to the conventional behavior of pilgrims to the shrine: they walk with reverence around the house, sign the visitors' book, and follow the tourist trail to the school and the church. Even the outpouring of sentiment and emotion, although exaggerated for comic effect, has the ring of truth. Ironically, this visit that never took place epitomizes the ideal tour of the Birthplace, a tour that is textually determined, marked out and defined by the numerous accounts of visits to Stratford that appeared in the nineteenth century. These narratives were so prolific and pervasive that they constitute an intertextual web, of which the *Punch* article is itself a part. The repetition in these travel accounts of descriptions of the sites and the experiences, behavior and emotions of visitors render the tour of Stratford familiar, formulating a perception of the Birthplace that was so ingrained in the public imagination that the "Oldest Inhabitant of Stratford" is able convincingly to recount the details of a royal visit that never was.

Descriptions of Stratford as a tourist destination took numerous forms and crossed generic boundaries in the nineteenth century. Irving's *Sketch Book* might have been fictional, but it influenced later travel narratives and even came to be viewed in its own right as a "guidebook" to Stratford. When Barnum visited the town, he immediately requested that the waiter in the hotel bring him a guidebook and was more than gratified on being presented with a well-worn copy of Irving.[6] Stratford also appears together with other destinations in seminal works of travel writing like Howitt's *Visits to Remarkable Places* (1840–42) and *Homes and Haunts of the Most Eminent British Poets* (1847) and John Dick's *Here and There in England; including a pilgrimage to Stratford-upon-Avon* (1871). In addition to these multidestination works, there were texts that focused exclusively on Stratford, like Charles Vaughan Grinfield's *A Pilgrimage to Stratford-upon-Avon* (1850) and Charles Roach Smith's *Remarks on Shakespeare, his Birth-Place, etc.* (1868–69). Later in the century, American tourists were seen walking around Stratford with their copies of William Winter, whose *Shakespeare's England*, published in 1892, was comprised of his *Trip to England* (1879) and *English Rambles* (1884).[7] Visits to the town were also reported in literary journalism and autobiographical accounts (by the likes of Benjamin Robert Haydon, Nathaniel Hawthorne, and Harriet Beecher Stowe), while poets described tours in verse (Henry Alford, Edwin Arnold, John William Inchbold, Robert Leighton, William Bell Scott, Algernon Charles Swinburne, and Lydia Howard Sigourney, to name but a few). There was also the odd novel in which the town featured, such as Braddon's *Asphodel* and Payn's *The Talk of the Town*.

Extracts from these diverse texts were sometimes collected together. One article published in 1844 advised that the portmanteau of the tourist should include Irving's *Sketch Book*, Howitt's chapter from his *Visits to Remarkable Places*, Wheler's guidebook, and a few biographies of Shakespeare.[8] Such anthologizing was catered to in contemporary magazines. In March 1857 *Reynolds's Miscellany* included an essay on Shakespeare's Birthplace that consisted of descriptions by Hugh Miller, Stowe, and Howitt.[9] *London Society* set Hawthorne's and Haydon's accounts alongside Irving's.[10]

Despite the generic and stylistic differences of these travel narratives, what is striking is the remarkable similarity with which they define the tourist experience, whether it is in the identification of the sites to be visited or the conduct of the visitor. They establish, in effect, a set of implicit and explicit rules for how actual or textual trips to Stratford should be conducted. These rules were also central to the nineteenth-century guidebook, which differed from travel writing in the sense that its main objective was to describe the features of Stratford for the benefit of the tourist whereas travel writing emphasized the narrator's personal experience and impression of the town. This objective of the guidebook resulted in some noticeable effects, with the text often directly addressing the tourist and assuming, and determining, a fixed starting point and destination. In this context, the narrator becomes a travel companion: "Come, we will go in and see the room where was born the man in whose pages live all the poetry," one Stratford guidebook invites the reader.[11] Another narrator almost nudges the reader out of bed in the morning:

> Now let us wake up and go for a walk. Where have you slept? At the Shakspere, the Red Horse, the Falcon, the Golden Lion, the Red Lion, the White Lion, the White Swan, or where else? If you are wise you will try to get there in the evening, attend to the first duty of man upon arrival in a strange town—find a place wherein to lay your head, have a quiet stroll to see nothing in particular, and leave visiting until next day.
>
> It is morning then, and we are standing, say, in the porch of the Shakspere Hotel, under its flower-laden balcony, quietly considering our movements. We are in Chapel Street, which is very short; but it, with High Street on the right and Church Street on the left, forms one long street running through the centre of town and parallel to the river.
>
> "Which are the places we *must* see?"[12]

With the narrator defined as the knowledgeable and authoritative source of information on the town and addressing a reader/tourist, the guidebook constructs a community of "pilgrims," of visitors linked across time and circumstances in their tours of the same buildings, witnessing of the same scenes, and experiencing of the same emotions.

The first dedicated guidebook to Stratford appeared in 1814 in the form of Robert Bell Wheler's *A Guide to Stratford-upon-Avon*. Wheler's guide was abridged from his earlier *History and Antiquities of Stratford-upon-Avon* (1806), the very fact of the adaptation of this more substantial history into a compact travel guide suggesting the growing public appetite for such a book. An anonymous, more generalized, travel guide followed in 1840, but it was not until 1847, the year of the auction, that the Stratford guidebook with its focus on the Birthplace really emerged. This was signaled by the publication of two texts, both of which ran through several editions over the course of the century: Fairholt's *The Home of Shakspere* and George May's *A Guide to the Birth-Town of Shakspere and the Poet's Rural Haunts*. While Fairholt's book was motivated by his shock at alterations that had been made to the courtyard of the grammar school,[13] George May had less elevated intentions: a bookseller from Evesham, he saw the need for a guidebook and produced it at a price that, according to a review in the *Illustrated London News*, "no reasonable tourist can complain of."[14]

Following the success of Fairholt and May, other authors and publishers took advantage of the growing tourist market, especially with the arrival of the train station in Stratford in 1859. This event saw a burgeoning of railway guides to the town, like the snappily titled *A Short Descriptive Guide to the East and West Junction Railway, Being the Shortest and Most Direct Route from London to Stratford-on-Avon via London and North Western Railway* (1886). With the changes that were occurring in Stratford throughout the century, including the purchase of other properties by the Birthplace Trust and the modifications to the collection in the Birthplace museum, it was sometimes difficult to keep these guides up to date. In 1868 *The Times* lamented that "a good "guide" to Stratford is yet a *desideratum* . . . . As for the older guide-book, it is altogether out of date."[15]

The demand for these books saw national travel guides (Baedeker's, Black's, Murray's, Shaw's, Ward and Lock's) competing against those produced by local printers and publishers. Edward Adams, a printer on High Street in Stratford, brought out his popular *Hand Book for Visitors to Stratford-upon-Avon* in 1860, which went through several editions. One of the cheapest and most successful guides later in the century was *Two Hours in Stratford-on-Avon* (1889) published by John Morgan, another printer on High Street, and written by the Reverend George Arbuthnot, the vicar of Holy Trinity Church. An enterprising local publisher of the 1890s was John Smith, who sold his guide for a penny (or twopence complete with a map of the town). Smith decided to capi-talize on the growing American tourist market and, instead of including the usual picture of the Birthplace on the cover, showed "Ye Ancient House" in Stratford, which, the caption informed the reader, was the early home of the mother of John Harvard, the founder of Harvard University. "Ye Ancient House" also had the added advantage of being situated next door to this very John Smith, whose pristine shop front is also pictured in the engraving.[16]

These guidebooks form a key element in how Stratford and the Birthplace were constructed in the Victorian imagination. They also appear to have played their own part in shaping and determining the actual tourist experience, although this effect is more difficult to gauge, not least because the records of these "real" visits are themselves part of the same textual tradition. It would seem unlikely, however, that the visitor to Stratford could not be influenced by accounts of other visits. Indeed, so descriptive were many of the guidebooks, which were frequently adorned with illustrations of the sites to be visited, that they provided a virtual tourist experience that made an actual excursion un-necessary. More often than not, they seem to have whetted the appetite and even to have motivated the trip. George May's guidebook, for example, was meant to "either vividly recall the glad emotions of a visit past, or act impul-sively to bring about the journey or the trip so long intended."[17] Certainly, the growth of the tourist trade in Stratford went hand in hand with the growth of guidebooks to the town.

In Stratford, these books provided the only guides, human guides being actively discouraged from frequenting the tourist attractions. Reports of un-desirables pretending to be guides (Artemus Ward describes being duped by a boy who shows him to the wrong grave,[18] while Hawthorne writes of old men who hang about the churchyard trying to pick up sixpence from visitors)[19] led to attempts to curb this problem. The title page of a publication aimed at those visiting Stratford for the first time cautions them about giving money to per-sons loitering in the streets or churchyard who pretend to be local guides.[20] Such strictures seem to have been effective, a visitor from the 1880s stating that because the town has no guides the tourist in Stratford is free to go wher-ever he or she wishes: "One of the chief charms of Stratford is that it is not, in the ordinary sense of the word, a show place. The guide, that ghoul-like cre-ation of modern civilisation and modern travel, the dark Efreet who plagues the wanderer abroad, has, happily, no existence here in Shakespeare's town. The visitor may go as he pleases where he pleases; no one will trouble him with importunate offers to show this or to lead to that."[21]

But if the human guide had no place in Stratford, then the textual one certainly did. So ubiquitous were descriptions of visits to the town that tourists were never entirely free to go or do as they pleased. These accounts, whether in the form of travel writing or guidebooks, established rules and conventions for the tour, of which the first was the purchasing and reading of the text itself. They stipulated how, and when, visitors should arrive in Stratford, the acceptable duration of the trip, where and when they should go, and, perhaps most revealingly, how they should respond to their environment in terms of their behavior and emotions. In this way, the visit to Stratford and its clearly defined itinerary became ritualized, constituted by the repeated performances and acts that Balz Engler has argued were fundamental to the establishment of Stratford-upon-Avon as a site of pilgrimage.[22]

2. Take the Train

Like that other pilgrimage to Canterbury, the pilgrimage to Stratford should take place in April. This was the time, it was suggested, when the beauties of the English countryside could be seen at their best, and it also happened to be the month in which Shakespeare was born and died.[23] Unlike those pilgrims to Canterbury, however, pilgrims to Stratford were more likely to appreciate the landscape from the inside of a railway carriage as opposed to on foot. This modern mode of conducting a pilgrimage was mocked in a review of John Mounteney Jephson's book on Stratford: "The Rev. Mr Jephson, last autumn, made a *pilgrimage* (probably took the train to the nearest station!) to Shakespeare's Birthplace, home, and grave," sneered the critic.[24]

Even before the railway station was built in Stratford, the most convenient way of arriving in the town was by rail, the terminus at Leamington being the most common route. According to the auction catalogue of the Birthplace, this made it possible for visitors from London to make the journey there and back in a day.[25] Leamington thrived on its association with Stratford, with some guidebooks written expressly for the numerous visitors from the town.[26] In 1853 a bill was passed through Parliament to bring the railway network directly to Stratford. A local squib celebrated this development in a verse to be sung to the tune of "The King of the Cannibal Islands":

This is the age of progress, and
By steam we ride, o'er sea and land,
And now a great improvement's plann'd,
They call it the "Stratford Railway."

Yes! Shakspear's fame will last for aye,
While generations pass away;
And thousands now will gladly say—
We'll visit "Shakspeare's Birthplace."[27]

It went without saying, according to the *Illustrated London News*, that if Shakespeare had not been born in Stratford such a bill would never have been passed; the only guarantee of the success of the scheme was the circumstance of Stratford being a "Mecca" for the English-speaking world.[28] As the journalist remarked, "Shakspeare may be considered as 'patron' and originator of the project for giving his native town a railway."[29]

The convenience of the railways also brought its problems. When Harriet Beecher Stowe visited Stratford before the building of the train station, she predicted that the "railroad demon" would obliterate the character of the town: "Just think of that black little screeching imp rushing through these fields which have inspired so many fancies; how everything poetical will fly before it!" she wrote.[30] When the trains did eventually come, they impacted on more than Stratford's "poetical" associations, influencing not just how many tourists visited, but also the length of time they stayed there, no longer necessitating that the visit be for an extended duration. This had implications for the thriving commercial town that Stratford had become, and it was also a cause of more ethical concerns. Pilgrims to Canterbury would not have rushed around the cathedral, guidebooks in hands, with the aim of being back in London for dinner, yet this was precisely how tourists to Stratford were accused of behaving, with twenty minutes being the optimum time for parties from Leamington to see the whole of Stratford and its neighborhood, visiting the Birthplace, adding their names to the wall, helping to efface the curse on the tomb, and then hurrying back to the inn.[31]

This "railroad rate of traveling," as it was termed, was not solely the fault of the trains. Some writers blamed the guidebooks themselves, which prompted this mode of tour: with their snippets of history and criticism, extracts from poetry, sea-boat charges, and bills of fare, guidebooks like Murray's encouraged tourists to keep moving, meaning that they saw a lot but did not have time for reflection.[32] It was, predictably, Americans who were most severely criticized for their drive-by tours of Stratford (despite the fact that Washington Irving provided historical evidence for the longer tour). Some books advised American visitors to make Stratford an overnight stop, but only so that that they could have an early start the next morning to see all the places of Shakespearean interest before traveling on to London or Liverpool.[33] The Americans were "stop-watch excursionists," who apparently measured out the time they could devote to each site and rushed from place to place with "restless rapidity."[34] For them, it was argued, Stratford had become little more than part of a "grand tour" of England. As a commentator wrote, "too many of these transatlantic travellers merely visit a place like Stratford just to say they have been there; and people of that class are singularly unpleasant to meet."[35] One such American tourist, although of a more pleasant variety, appears in Richmal Crompton's story "William and the Lost Tourist" (1926); she is discovered by the protagonist weeping in her car because she cannot find her way to Stratford. When William fools her into believing that his village is the bard's town (they even visit "Anne Hathaway's cottage"—actually the home of the local crone), she is delighted that she is finally able to "tick off" Stratford and return to London for dinner.[36]

There were potential ways of controlling the length of time that visitors stayed in Stratford, however. In a letter addressed to the executive committee of the trustees of the Birthplace in 1880, Halliwell-Phillipps set out a plan for reducing the opening hours of the Birthplace:

> A reduction of the number of hours during which the Birth-Place could be inspected would probably result in a larger number of visitors making a more intelligent examination of the local memorials of Shakespeare than is now usual. In former days, there were few visitors who did not stay at least over one night, giving themselves time to gain some idea of the real interest attached to those memorials and to what remains in the town and neighbourhood of the Shakespearean period. Nowadays, the chief object of nearly all strangers is to rush through and "do" Stratford in as brief a time as possible. Any measure which would tend to arrest this mischievous tendency to merely useless and ignorant sight-seeing would surely in the long run be beneficial, and probably nothing

would tend to accomplish this object more than the proposed re-
duction in the hours of attendance. Visitors for the Birth-Place
who arrived in the town after four o'clock would have to remain
until the next morning, and do them good too.[37]

This letter takes its place alongside travel accounts and guidebooks that establish an etiquette for tourism, a conduct manual for how the visitor should behave. By controlling the opening hours of the Birthplace, Halliwell-Phillipps
intended to control the activities and reactions of the visitor, his language
suggesting a sharp and overtly moral divide between the "right" and "wrong"
kind of visit to Stratford: the right one being a thoughtful and intelligent pe-
rusal of the sites, with enough time for suitable contemplation, and the wrong
one being an ignorant visit to the prime locations, conducted in too much haste
to truly see and understand the attractions and thus to benefit from them.

3. Follow the Tourist Trail

Despite Halliwell-Phillipps's suggestions, the Birthplace remained open
from 9 A.M. to 6 P.M. in the summer and from 9 A.M. to dusk in winter, allowing tourists to continue to "do" Stratford in as brief a time as possible. With the
visit to Stratford becoming shorter, it was imperative to see the right things. The
guidebooks adapted themselves to this reduced tour, establishing fixed ideas
about what to see and what not to see. *Two Hours in Stratford-on-Avon* by the
Reverend Arbuthnot was intended specifically "to enable Visitors who have only
a few hours to spend in the Town, to see those sights which are worth seeing,
and to avoid wasting time over those which are not." Arbuthnot continues, "I
only pretend to show my Readers how to spend a short time here. I have written
upon the assumption that the Reader arrives by the Great Western Railway, but
should he come by the East and West Junction Line, he will find that he ought
just to reverse the order in which the different places of interest are visited."[38]
While the preferred method of transport for getting to Stratford was the
railway, once in the town the visitor was encouraged to walk, many of the
guidebooks taking the form of walking tours (although carriages offering trips
were waiting at the station for the less energetic tourist). After all, going on
foot was the proper way of performing a pilgrimage. As one travel guide states,
"We need scarcely observe, that the lover of a pedestrian ramble, which is the
true way of making a 'Pilgrimage,' will be able, as he pursues his way, to explore

many of the more sequestered beauties of this poetic region . . . far more en-
joyably than can be done by those who merely content themselves with being
carried along the main roads in a vehicle."[39] Walking around the town and its
vicinity had the added advantage of enhancing the visitor's connection with
Shakespeare, giving the sense that the tourist was walking in the poet's footsteps:

> These walks will ever derive their principal attraction for the
> thoughtful visitor from the conviction that they may each have been
> trodden by the feet of Shakspeare; that his eye must have rested
> on every hill and valley; that every turn of the classic river; every
> common flower that here takes root, was familiar to him; that he
> beheld the venerable Church as it now is, and in it joined in the
> public services of religion; and that he contemplated all these ob-
> jects in youth, when the divine fire was only yet struggling in his
> bosom, and again in after life, when his apprehension of all that he
> beheld may be said without exaggeration to have been more than
> mortal.[40]

What one actually saw on this walking tour of Stratford changed over the
course of the century. At the close of the eighteenth century, one visitor identified the main "curiosities" in the town as the Birthplace and its relics (including
the infamous chair) and the objects that had been carved out of the mulberry
tree.[41] The "curiosities" in the nineteenth century were rather different. The
mulberry tree, or its remains, did not hold the fascination that it had at the time
of Garrick, although the grounds of New Place where it once stood was a recognized tourist site that had been bought by the Birthplace Trust and turned
into gardens in 1862. Prior to the mid-nineteenth century, Holy Trinity Church
was the principal destination for the visitor. Writing in 1840, Howitt more or
less dismissed the Birthplace, commenting that Shakespeare's "birth there
was a mere accident, and the accidents of time have not added to the intrinsic
interest of the place."[42] However, the publicity surrounding the auction and restoration meant that by the 1860s it had become the main attraction on the recommended tourist trail, alongside the church, grammar school, New Place
gardens, and, following its opening in 1879, the Memorial Theatre. Visitors
were also directed to Charlecote Park and Anne Hathaway's cottage (there was
the occasional recommendation of a visit to Mary Arden's house at Wilmcote).[43]

Throughout the nineteenth century there was a growing interest in Anne Hathaway's cottage, which was located in Shottery, just outside Stratford-upon-Avon, and was the setting for Shakespeare's courtship and the place where, according to Howitt, he might have returned with his wife as an older man to indulge in reminiscences about the past (Figure 19).[44] The cottage had the advantage of being surrounded by beautiful English countryside (the inspiration, it was argued, for some of the plays), thus encouraging a connection between Shakespeare and the natural world. It was also said to be preserved in much the same character as it would have assumed in Shakespeare's day and was still occupied by descendants of the Hathaway family when it was purchased by the Birthplace Trust in 1892. In contrast to the Birthplace's sparsely furnished rooms, the interior of the cottage boasted an array of antique furniture and accessories, including an old clock, an ancient dresser, and a wooden

Figure 19. Ernest Edwards, "Ann Hathaway's Cottage, Shottery," from J. M. Jephson, *Shakespere: His Birthplace, Home, and Grave. A Pilgrimage to Stratford-on-Avon in the Autumn of 1863* (London: Lovell Reeve, 1864).

trencher. It was easy to imagine Shakespeare being at home there. One writer commented that it would hardly have astonished him if the poet had walked in through the door.[45]

Victorian visitors were encouraged to wander from Henley Street on a summer afternoon and take the footpath to Shottery, which Shakespeare must so often have walked "when his heart was beating high with love and hope."[46] For some tourists who followed this "Sacred Way of English literature" across the meadows, there were unexpected encounters, and not only with the ghostly specter of the bard.[47] Howitt bumps into the master of the local school and is introduced to one of his pupils, William Shakspeare Smith, who claims to be descended from Shakespeare's sister.[48] Howitt gives the boy a sixpence and issues an appeal to the public to support this impoverished family. Sanford R. Gifford described his visit to the cottage in a letter to his father: "In the evening of this day I walked through the fields to Shottery (a mile from here) to see Ann Hathaway's cottage. On the way I fell in with a not bad looking girl, who I found was a shop girl of Stratford taking her accustomed walk. She went with me to see the cottage (she had never seen it before) and accompanied me back in the twilight. She told me her little history, which I have not time now to repeat. She was certainly one of the most unsophisticated beings I ever met."[49] The lack of sophistication of the Stratford shop girl, while suggesting all sorts of intriguing possibilities about what might have happened or been said on Gifford's journey, is demonstrated by the fact that although she lives so close to Anne Hathaway's cottage, she has never visited it. But if the shop girl had not been lured into the cottage, then others certainly were, compelled to visit by stories of Shakespeare running through fields of flowers to meet his sweetheart, of the lovers sitting hand in hand in the garden and gazing up at the stars, and of Anne and William snuggling up together on the settle which was still in the house. A picture of the lovers sitting in the fireplace painted by Thomas Brooks hung on the wall beside this very hearth.

While tourists today still make their way to Anne Hathaway's cottage, Charlecote, one of the most popular Victorian destinations, is relatively forgotten. It was the site of the poaching incident which, tradition has it, led to Shakespeare being prosecuted by the owner of the deer park, Sir Thomas Lucy, and forced to leave the town. Many Victorian tourists traveled the four miles to visit the grounds of Charlecote, the interior being closed to the public, except on special occasions like the tercentenary festival. The deer-stealing episode was a highlight in the imaginative account of Shakespeare's youth; it also provided a convenient reason for Shakespeare's abandonment of his wife and children. Others argued against the story, unwilling to believe that Shakespeare could be responsible for any misdemeanor. Charles Holte Bracebridge, who provided the money for the completion of the restoration of the Birthplace, went to the lengths of writing a pamphlet arguing that Lucy's ownership of the deer park, which was not actually at Charlecote, was questionable, and that Shakespeare might have mistakenly assumed that he had as much right to the deer as Lucy himself.[50]

At times during the course of the century, these key tourist sites are supplemented with others. Arbuthnot heads straight for the Birthplace but draws the reader's attention to more unusual buildings along the way: the local hospital, which was erected thanks to Mr. and Miss Gibbins of Ettington, the national schools, the children's hospital, and the nursing home. To add to the thrills of this guided tour, Arbuthnot invites the thirsty reader to go to the Coffee Palace and Temperance Hotel on Bridge Street rather than frequenting one of the many public houses in the town.[51] Another guidebook recommends Victoria Spa, an elegant pump room, which had been conveniently erected about a mile from the town (the tranquility of Stratford, this guide states, is of great advantage to invalids when compared with Cheltenham or Leamington).[52]

But it was the main tourist sites outlined in contemporary travel accounts that seem to have formed the basis of actual visits to Stratford. When the Whitefriars Club in London made its "Pilgrimage to Shakespeare's Country" on Saturday, 23 June 1900, the members set out from Paddington at 9:40 and arrived at Warwick station at 11:57 where they took carriages to Charlecote Park.[53] They visited the Birthplace, Anne Hathaway's cottage, New Place, and Holy Trinity Church, their day ending with a tour of the Memorial Building and its theater, museum, picture gallery, and grounds. In travel narratives, details of these principal sites were often interwoven with biographical details of Shakespeare's life. Whether textual or actual, the tour usually followed the trajectory of the biography, starting at the Birthplace, moving through Shakespeare's youth with the grammar school and Anne Hathaway's cottage and concluding with New Place and the church. In the Whitefriars' party, the carriage of the principal members travels primarily according to this route.

For those who were in a hurry and risked being labeled as the ignorant sight-seers described by Halliwell-Phillipps, the most important destinations were the Birthplace, Anne Hathaway's cottage, and Holy Trinity Church.[54]

These were visited by Lucy M. Reynolds, who recorded the details of her day trip to Stratford in a scrapbook preserved in the collection of the Shakespeare Birthplace Trust (her signature appears in the Birthplace visitors' book on 29 July 1892).[55] Reynolds collected postcards, admission tickets, and photographs of the sites she visited and did a brass rubbing of the inscription on the tomb. Her trip, undertaken with two female companions, is recounted in a jaunty poem entitled "The Three Merry Pilgrims" and shares some striking similarities with modern tourist experiences, not least because the First Great Western train breaks down on the way back. Written on lined paper, the poem contains illustrative marginalia, including pencil drawings of the spire of Holy Trinity Church, Anne Hathaway's cottage, and the Stratford railway station.

Lucy Reynolds, like *Punch*'s Queen Victoria, visited the "right" places, but there were those who strayed from the path, although even these diversions were defined in terms of the proper tour and its established etiquette. When the creator of Peter Pan, J. M. Barrie, visited Stratford, he spent his time smoking "reverently" at the hotel door and lying down on the sofa (his companion accuses him of sleeping, but he protests that he was actually picturing to himself Shakespeare's boyhood).[56] Barrie's lethargy proves too much for his friend, who departs without him on a walking tour of Shakespeare country. Another promised trip that never takes place occurs in a travel account in *All the Year Round*. The article begins with the all too familiar references to Irving and other "pilgrims," but then takes a surprising detour: this particular visit, the writer comments, is for purely geographical reasons, the Avon at Stratford being the most convenient place to take the river to London in a rowboat: "I thought no more of the Birthplace of Shakespeare than of the Birthplace of Podgers," this tourist scandalously exclaims.[57] Visitors who flocked to the town on cheap rail days from Birmingham and Staffordshire might have been of the same opinion. On one such trip in 1864, a thousand people descended on Stratford. Of these, a little more than a hundred visited the Birthplace and around fifty went to look at the tomb. The rest of the visitors stood on the wharves for hours watching workmen clearing the canals of mud and applauding when an eel or another fish was captured; they were not even deterred by the pouring rain.[58]

4. Pay (for) a Visit to the Birthplace

If the tour of Stratford was subject to all sorts of regulations and conventions, then the Birthplace itself was more so. From the time when the house was purchased for the nation, visitors gained admittance from a custodian, who resided in a property on the grounds. But even this rule was often in danger of being broken, along with the knuckles of some eager visitors. In 1859 a native of Stratford wrote to the local newspaper complaining that some visitors, unable to find the custodian, were forced to walk away from the house without seeing the interior.[59] On several occasions he had been obliged to direct visitors to the custodian's cottage. He proposed that a sign be put up informing visitors where they were to go. It seems his advice was not followed because several weeks later a disgruntled visitor to Stratford told of his own experience: after knocking with some force on the door of the Birthplace, he was directed to a gate that was locked; eventually he ends up shouting so loudly that he wakes up the custodian along with most of the women and children in the neighborhood.[60] Unfortunately, this tourist's delay in entering the Birthplace prevents him from adding his verse to the visitors' book, which he includes, instead, in his letter to the newspaper:

> Shade of Avon's bard, sweet Will, knit not thy noble brow,
> Because, to gain admission here, I kicked up such a row.
> An humble pilgrim to thy shrine, I did not deem it right
> To leave unseen the room in which, 'tis said, you first saw light.[61]

It seems that this letter did the trick. A small placard was put on the side of the door of the Birthplace, informing visitors that ringing the bell would bring the custodian, who would show them around the house.

When a visitor was successfully past the first hurdle of gaining admittance to the Birthplace, there was the business of paying the admission fee, priced at sixpence from the 1860s, with a further sixpence payable by those who wanted to see the museum. The money was surrendered in the kitchen, in return for a ticket, which the visitor could keep as a souvenir. The fact that tourists were receiving something tangible in return for their cash, albeit an admission ticket, does not seem to have convinced many, some of whom, according to the text on the ticket itself, were "surprised" at the cost of the visit; it was justified in terms of the expenditure laid out on necessary repairs to the building and the staff needed to run it, including a librarian, two lady custodians, an assistant custodian, a doorkeeper, and a gardener.[62]

There were other ways to spend one's money within the house. Garrick's transformation of the birthroom into a bookshop seems to have continued well into the following century. Hawthorne recounts that during his visit in 1855 there were various prints, editions of Shakespeare's works, and local publications set on a table and chairs "all for sale, and from which, no doubt, this gentlewoman realizes a good deal of profit."[63] This arrangement is depicted in Henry Wallis's painting *The Room in Which Shakespeare Was Born*. Another American tourist in 1858 writes on notepaper that he has purchased from the custodian in the birthroom.[64] Even Halliwell reprinted Wheler's *Historical Account of the Birth-Place of Shakespeare* (1863) expressly to be sold at the house, although this was for the purpose of raising money for the Birthplace Trust.[65]

For the later Victorian visitor, attempts to quash the impression that Shakespeare's shrine was a shop took the form of a new regulation which specified that, apart from the sixpence to enter, no other money was to change hands. A clause to this effect was added to the top of the admission ticket in 1897: "The Committee request that no Gratuities be offered to the Attendants."[66] This ruling causes some problems for Morris Gedge, the fictional custodian in James's "The Birthplace," who feels decidedly uncomfortable when he is given a tip by a couple of American visitors, so much so that his confused fumbling almost sends the coin rolling to the floor.[67] Indeed, Gedge's relief that there "were no tips . . . at the Birthplace; there was the charged fee and nothing more; everything else was out of order," links this unnamed "Birthplace" even more securely with its Stratford counterpart.[68]

5. Get Excited

For their sixpences to enter the Birthplace, visitors were issued with a short written account and plan of the building printed on the ticket and were conducted on a tour of the house by the custodian, who directed tourists from room to room and recounted the official history of the building. William Winter writes with admiration of Caroline Chataway, one of the most celebrated custodians and possibly the inspiration for the great Miss Putchin, Gedge's predecessor, who, along with her sister, led tourists through the principal apartments and told them the story of the house in Shakespeare's days.[69] A resident of Stratford in the 1870s and 1880s refers to the propensity of the Chataway sisters to talk: "Both lived up very literally to their surname. How such fragile-looking people could talk so much and have enough breath left for a tour round with the next party of visitors, puzzled me."[70] The Chataways chatted away for seventeen years, retiring as custodians in 1889 when they were succeeded by the less talkative John Skipsey. Fortunately, applicants for the role of custodian do not seem to have had the same qualms about the role as Skipsey/Gedge: in June 1900, Mr. and Mrs. Rose of Erdington near Birmingham were chosen from 250 candidates for the job.

With the custodians acting as official guides and telling the official history, the visitor was encouraged, even if unconsciously, to react in the official way to the Birthplace, a reaction that had been determined by numerous accounts of previous tours. As one writer remarked, visitors to the Birthplace "tell us what they feel, as they stand in the upper room, or in the lower room, or in the coal-cellar of the house in Henley Street."[71] Ideally, what one felt in relation to the Birthplace should manifest itself even before one walked through the door. As early as 1795, Samuel Ireland recorded that a feeling "more elevated than that of mere curiosity" is experienced on entering Stratford and naturally directs the footsteps of the visitor to the Birthplace.[72] This "feeling" took on an added intensity in the Victorian period. When Fairholt first visits the Birthplace in 1839, his excitement gets the better of him about a mile from the town. Arriving in Stratford in the evening, he leaves his luggage with the waiter and ventures forth in the dark to find the "immortal house."[73] On discovering the building, he gazes at it through the darkness, crosses the road, and comes back again. Unable to concentrate or to leave the vicinity of Henley Street, he inquires of the owner whether he can see it there and then and is instructed, "Walk in, sir, and I'll fetch a light immediately." "No words ever sounded so delightfully," remarks Fairholt.[74]

Another visitor at the time of the tercentenary followed scores of pilgrims from the Great Western Railway, all the while preparing himself to feel that he was treading sacred ground and to be moved by everything he saw.[75] This pilgrim makes the mistake, however, of assuming that he will just come upon "the House" by some divine influence. Unwilling to rest for refreshment or to ask his way to the Birthplace in the same way that one would ask for directions to a post office or a bank, he finds himself in front of a yellow caravan exhibiting waxworks and a Scotch giant. When he eventually asks for directions, the person he enquires of does not know where the Birthplace is. With all hope lost, fireworks are set off in a neighboring field and he sees the building for the first time: "By the garish light of red and blue and green fires I saw a house which had been restored out of all its antiquity, which was trim, and neat, and angular, and varnished, and which, when the rockets exploded and rained down their spray of coloured fires, and the people shouted in the meadow, recalled a vision of Vauxhall."[76]

This account of anticipation and excitement, which eventually ends in disappointment, is an ironic comment on the unrealistic expectations of the pilgrim to Stratford that were generated by these textual narratives, a reminder that there might be a gap between the written and the actual tour. For other visitors, however, there seems to be no such disparity or disappointment, especially when they make it past the threshold of the house. So common was it to burst into tears, fall down, or kiss the floor, that the custodians no longer noticed these displays of affection for Shakespeare.[77] If the visitor to the Birthplace wanted even more communion with Shakespeare, he or she could always request to spend the night in the birthroom. An American visitor in the 1840s mentioned to a journalist from *Fraser's Magazine* that one of his party, a Mr. Jones from New Orleans, was so taken with Shakespeare that he had bribed the old woman in the mob-cap (Mrs. Court) to let him sleep in the room where Shakespeare was born and had hired a mattress for the purpose.[78] Another Mr. Jones, with whom the reader of this book is already familiar, had also made this request. In Cliffe's poem *The Pilgrim of Avon*, the pilgrim falls asleep in the birthroom, prompting a footnote from the author:

> The enthusiasm of the visitors, or, more properly speaking, PIL-GRIMS, to the birth-chamber of Shakspeare, has been evinced in so many different ways, that an interesting article might be written on the various effects which the power of his genius had over differently constituted minds. I shall, however, content myself with remarking that this incident is not one of ideality; for my valued and enthusiastic friend, Mr. George Jones, actually passed the night of the 25th of April 1835, on the oaken floor of the room in which the Bard was born; being, I believe, the first person that has ever done so since the room has been shewn as the poetical Loretto of Britain.[79]

If anyone could arrange a sleepover in Shakespeare's Birthplace, George Jones was the man.

Occasionally, however, there were tourists who, in defiance of these displays of affection, refused to get excited about the Birthplace at all. When the journalist Albert Smith accompanied Barnum on his tour of Stratford, he wrote that "We must confess—and it is, we know, only short of high treason to say so—that our enthusiasm was not in any way excited by entering the room, after ascending the flight of stairs from the dark back-parlour, in which 'le vieux Guillaume,' as Janin says, is reported to have uttered his first cry."[80] Hawthorne is similarly unimpressed. He describes the building as mean and dingy, concluding "I felt no emotion whatever in Shakspeare's house—not the slightest— nor any quickening of the imagination."[81] But perhaps Hawthorne's reaction, or lack of reaction, to the Birthplace is part of a wider politics. According to Tony Tanner, the "non-response" that Hawthorne displays "is in line with an habitual refusal of a number of American writers to be awed by the sacred places of the Old World."[82] This argument has been taken up more recently by Shirley Foster, who contends that such American visitors position themselves as "anti-tourists" in order to challenge the authority of British aesthetic heritage.[83] Certainly, when Henry James visits Warwickshire, he barely mentions Stratford and excuses himself when he does: "If I were to allude to Stratford, it would not be in connection with the fact that Shakespeare came into the world there. It would be rather to speak of a delightful old house near the Avon which struck me as the ideal home for a Shakespearean scholar."[84]

Even when they were not apparently motivated by a nationalist agenda, however, some visitors expressed a similar disenchantment with the house, particularly when they found themselves sharing the Birthplace experience with other (disagreeable) tourists. The painter, Benjamin Robert Haydon, makes a sharp exit when a squinting Cockney comes in,[85] while one unfortunate visitor at the tercentenary pays his sixpence only to find the birthroom occupied by two burly Warwickshire policemen in full uniform, whose presence is suggestive of a murder or robbery: "I could have been much impressed by those old worm-eaten boards, which Shakespeare's feet had trod, but who could adore a sacred spot with two policeman standing at his elbow, irreverently lounging against the walls, and blowing their noses like thunder in great sheets of red calico?"[86] From being "undesirables" themselves, policemen were sometimes called in to evict tourists from the Birthplace. One inhabitant of Stratford recounted how a constable was sent to pass through the house whenever "rough" visitors came from Birmingham and the Black Country.[87]

Reality, it seems, has a nasty habit of destroying the devotional experience, especially when it was the reality of the building itself. This was a particular problem before the restoration when, in the words of Edward Barry, the very appearance of the property caused the visitor "distress."[88] According to the *Illustrated London News*: "Of what it was in 1574, no notion can be gathered from what it is in 1847. There is something, indeed, most painful in the contrast of its present wretchedness, and our idea of its condition as the comfortable home of Shakespere's parents. The low, crazy frontage—the crippled hatch—the filthy remnant of a butcher's shamble, with its ghastly hook—on the outside; and the squalid forlornness of the rooms within, convey together such a sense of utter desolation as merges all those feelings of respect and awe which such a relic should inspire."[89] Garrick, it seems, had not exaggerated when he referred to Stratford as the "most dirty, unseemly, ill-paved wretched looking place in all Britain." One visitor in the 1840s described how, when walking down Henley Street, he saw a man cleaning the gutter in one of the houses. The smell was so offensive that he and his companions were induced to hurry on before they realized that the old tenement in front of them was the Birthplace.[90] They looked upon it with due reverence, but decided that "The people of Stratford are as dirty as ever."[91] Indeed, just months after £3,000 had been paid for the rundown remains of the Birthplace, the unsanitary and impoverished condition of the town was revealed in an inquiry by the Board of Health; sewers were eventually laid in 1855. Before these improvements there might, ironically, have been similarities between nineteenth-century Stratford and the Stratford of Shakespeare's time. After all, Shakespeare's father had been fined for making a dunghill on Henley Street.[92]

The worshipers of Shakespeare needed a fitting temple and it was this requirement that motivated the appeal to purchase and restore the property, enabling visitors to have the appropriate emotional response at the Birthplace that so many experienced at the grave. The strategy seems to have worked for the most part, a visitor commenting in 1884 that there is a holiness about the site that "is strong enough to defy the degradation of a thousand tourists and the exorcisms of a wilderness of guides."[93] Even informal "guides" were not immune to the effect of the Birthplace: an early twentieth-century writer described how the cabmen, who drove the tourists to the sites in Stratford, spoke of Shakespeare with tears in their eyes and a sentimental tone in their voices, with one particular driver so convinced of the virtues of the Birthplace that he showed passengers his own as well as Shakespeare's.[94]

6. Go to the Wall

For the tourist not permitted to sleep on the hallowed floor, there were other ways of displaying the proper emotional response to the Birthplace. A key component of the ritual of visiting the house was to sign one's name on the walls, ceilings, or windows. At times, a mere autograph would not do; many visitors wrote in verse, a tradition that was exploited by Mary Hornby before she was evicted from the Birthplace and decided to whitewash over the signatures. Hornby's collection of poems, some of which she penned herself, was published in 1817 under the title *Extemporary Verses, Written at the Birth Place of Shakspeare, at Stratford-on-Avon.*

Throughout the course of the century, the birthroom was transformed into a text, an inscription of the visitors who had been there before, from Walter Scott, Thackeray, Dickens, Byron, and Tennyson to various Russian and Austrian princes. Typically, it was the Americans who were said to be most fervent in this display of affection for Shakespeare, one commentator observing that "the names that were written in the largest characters and in the most conspicuous places, were those of ladies and gentlemen from the United States of America."[95] A verse written on a card that was hung up in the birthroom in 1851 describes the pressure to perform this ritual, even as it despairs at the state of the Birthplace:

> No intellect above the itch to scrawl,
> Lo! weak and strong alike went to the wall.
> The wall grown dark with marks, a loftier feeling
> Raised eyes and hands to scribble on the ceiling.
> For me, poor nameless bard, ah! sad disaster!
> No single inch remains of nameless plaster;
> Yet I thy pearls have trampled, and must sign
> My name among the other grateful swine
> Who come to make a sty of Shakspeare's shrine![96]

The occasional tourist did resist the pressure to sign the plaster. When the Scottish geologist and journalist Hugh Miller visited the Birthplace in 1845, he refused to add his name because his status as a writer made him acutely aware of his inferiority to Shakespeare:

> Messrs Wiggins and Tims, too, would have added *their* names; and all right. They might not exactly see for themselves what it was that rendered Shakspere so famous; but their admiration, entertained on trust, would be at least a legitimate *echo* of his renown;

and so their names would have quite a right to be there as representative of the outward halo—the *second* rainbow, if I may so express myself—of the poet's celebrity. But I was ashamed to add mine. I remembered that I was a *writer*; that it was my *business* to write—to cast, day after day, shavings from off my mind—the figure is Cowper's—that went rolling away, crisp and dry, among the vast heap already on the floor, and were never more heard of; and so I didn't add my name.[97]

Miller's refusal to add his autograph, while seeming to break with the accepted convention, actually suggests the ways in which he is enmeshed in the etiquette of the visit to Shakespeare's Birthplace: not signing his name is itself an act of reverence for the bard. For others, inscribing their names on the walls of the Birthplace marked an attempt to secure fame or even a sense of immortality, to place themselves alongside the great and good, whether they deserved it or not.[98] This desire was criticized by Hawthorne, who, after searching in vain for Walter Scott's signature, remarked, "Methinks it is strange that people do not strive to forget their forlorn little identities, in such situations, instead of thrusting them forward into the dazzle of a great renown, where, if noticed, they cannot but be deemed impertinent."[99]

With all of these autographs on display at the same time and competing for the same space, any sense of hierarchy, of the status of the persons to whom the names were attached, was lost. Some signatures, like those of the Americans, were bigger and bolder than others, but this did not necessarily mean that they were worthy of attention. Moreover, it was impossible to see or identify which of these signatures was worth looking at. It was no wonder that Hawthorne could not find Scott: Robert E. Hunter commented that Scott's signature "has been scribbled over by the impudent diamond of some snobbish nobody." Hunter goes on, "Many interesting autographs are effaced or cannot be traced from amongst others of less importance."[100]

The autographs were dangerously democratic: they broke down ranks, showing "the Peasant jostling with the Prince, poetical inspirations of one visitor, with the dull record of another."[101] There was even the danger that, with all of these famous names, Shakespeare would himself be eclipsed. When the American author Nathaniel Parker Willis visited the Birthplace (his signature appears in the visitors' book on 18 September 1835), he expressed his shock at the fact that the woman who showed him around (probably Mrs. Court) was more interested in the autographs on the wall than in Shakespeare: "She had worn out Shakspeare! She had told that story till she was tired of it! or (what perhaps is more probable) most people who go there fall to reading the names of the visitors so industriously, that she has grown to think some of Shakspeare's pilgrims greater than Shakspeare."[102]

The disorder that the signatures represented, both in the sense that they made the Birthplace look untidy and their suggestion of an anarchic confusion of rank, meant that the unspoken rule to add one's name to the wall was increasingly scorned upon. In Braddon's *Asphodel*, the days of signing the house are termed "unregenerate."[103] The writing was on the wall for the writing on the wall. By the 1860s tourists were encouraged to sign their names instead in the licensed and controlled space of the visitors' book, and this was an imperative by 1876 when there were apparently so many signatures that it was impossible to add another.[104] This new rule was made clear by a verse attached to the collection box in the Birthplace and written by "the Spirit of the room in which Shakspeare was born":

> In mercy, pilgrims, cease to lay
> The burden of your scrawls on me.
> Already am I so besmeared,
> I cannot point to those revered!
> Besides, be learned as you may,
> A fool can daub your lines away!
> For many here have courted fame,
> Who knew of Shakspeare but by name.
> This modest room, that once could own
> The loftiest mind the world has known,
> Can quite as well its gifts recall,
> Without your scribble on the wall.
> Whatever of me still remains,
> Pray let alone, for hallowed names,
> Inscribed by hands that still can raise
> No other tribute of their praise,
> Must force you to respect e'en those
> Whom no one cares for, no one knows.
> Nay, more—another token you can leave

> Of all the reverence you may have –
> Look round—that book has leaves to spare
> For every one that enters here.
> There write your name, and—if you're willing –
> For restorations add your shilling![105]

This verse, an appeal for money that addresses the many pilgrims who visit the Birthplace, suggests a community of visitors drawn together by the shared activity of writing their autographs, whether on the walls or in the visitors' book. By signing one's name, one entered into an implied relationship, a contract, with past and future tourists, who had performed or would perform the same ritual. It was a communion that was not always pleasing. When Tennyson saw the autographs on a visit to the Birthplace in 1840, he described how he was "seized with a sort of enthusiasm" and proceeded to add his signature to the others.[106] (Tennyson's name was, in fact, to become one of the most sought out by Victorian tourists.) Tennyson's enthusiasm, however, was short-lived, as the poet seemed to realize that any gesture of personal devotion to Shakespeare was subsumed under this collective act of signing: "I was a little ashamed of it afterwards: yet the feeling was genuine at the time, and I did homage with the rest."[107] Tennyson need not have worried: by 1889 his own signature had been obliterated "by the 'Jepherson P. Briggses' and the 'John Smiths.'"[108]

If the longing to sleep in the Birthplace suggests a desire to get closer to and commune with Shakespeare, the ritual of writing one's name on the wall or in the visitors' book in the Birthplace suggests a desire to commune with other tourists. This was reflected in the fact that some of the inscriptions were in dialogue with others. On the reverse of the card that was put up in 1851 describing the Birthplace with its numerous signatures as a "sty," someone commented on the fact that the original card had been stolen:

> How well our Shakspeare knew the human kind!
> How well he read ye mortals, minus mind!
> Ye pilfering fools, though past two hundred years,
> He saw your itching fingers, knew your poltroon fears;
> Ye steal from hallowed Birthplace, grave, nay, worse,
> Would steal his very bones but dread his curse![109]

The autograph provided proof that the tourist was walking not so much in the footsteps of Shakespeare as of other tourists. Today, we might have the same feeling when taking photographs of the Birthplace that have been taken thousands of time before, the sense that, even as we press the button, other visitors have engaged in exactly the same activity. This photographic ritual was beginning to manifest itself toward the end of the nineteenth century, but the most revealing signifier of a community of visitors was inscribed on the walls, ceilings, windows, and visitors' book in Shakespeare's Birthplace.

7. Admire Washington Irving's Poker

If the signatures inscribed in the Birthplace suggest a growing tendency to follow not so much in Shakespeare's footsteps as in those of other tourists, one of the most common footsteps belonged to Geoffrey Crayon, Gent., or, rather, Washington Irving, visitors to Stratford frequently conflating the narrator of *The Sketch Book* with the author. Americans, in particular, followed the tourist trail set out by Irving, and, as they did so, appropriated or laid claim to Stratford-upon-Avon, transforming this quintessentially English site of pilgrimage into a curiously American one. So established was the Irving tour of Stratford by the end of the nineteenth century that one American visitor was of the opinion that Irving had a great deal to do with the success of Stratford as a tourist destination.[110] While this visitor questioned the compulsion of fellow tourists to do the Irving tourist trail ("people shouldn't come here to see what *he* has seen"), he nevertheless planned to visit Charlecote "where *your* Shakspeare stole the deer, and where *our* Irving went."[111]

Another place where "*our* Irving went," and that formed the undoubted highlight of the Irving tour itinerary, was the Red Horse Inn on Bridge Street, where the fictional Geoffrey Crayon had stayed on his trip to Stratford. The parlor of the inn had a special appeal, Irving having described how the weary traveler kicks off his boots, puts on his slippers, and stretches himself out before the fire, the monarch of all he surveys: "The arm chair is his throne; the poker his sceptre, and the little parlour of some twelve feet square, his undisputed empire."[112] The hotel made its own way into the Stratford guidebooks where it was often pictured, and postcards of "Washington Irving's Parlour" could be purchased by visitors (Figure 20). In *Asphodel* Braddon describes summer as "the season of American tourists, doing Stratford and its environs,

Figure 20. Washington Irving's room in the Red Horse Inn, from H. Snowden Ward and Catherine Weed Ward, *Shakespeare's Town and Times* (London: Dawbarn & Ward, 1896).

guide-book in hand, and crowding in to The Red Horse parlour, after luncheon, to see the veritable chair in which Washington Irving used to sit."[113]

Some tourists were fortunate enough to stay in the Red Horse; unfortunately, the visitor who plans to visit Charlecote has to be accommodated at the White Lion because his party is too large for Irving's inn, while another group of American tourists, who could not get into the Red Horse, have to be satisfied with dinner in the adjacent bowling alley.[114] When Gifford arrives at this hotel he is informed by a pretty maid that he is occupying the very bedroom that Washington Irving once occupied. Gifford is thrilled when he sees the "throne" in the parlor and the poker in the corner of the grate, "the same that served for his sceptre."[115] Irving's poker, in fact, achieved cult status. Engraved with the inscription "Geoffrey Crayon's sceptre" and encased in a blue baize sheath embroidered with gold, one writer remarked that, following Irving's stirring of the fire, "it has been a holy poker ever since."[116] By the end of the nineteenth century, it was wrapped up in an American flag and only brought out on special occasions.

With the famous parlor where Crayon relaxed before the fireside, the chair in which he sat, the bedroom where he slept, and its "holy" relics, the Red Horse was a strange mirror image of the Birthplace itself. Visitors were even encouraged to autograph the walls. Gifford's excitement at discovering that he is staying at the very hotel where Irving stayed ("I could have hugged the maid (even if she had not been so very pretty) for the pleasure her announcement gave me")[117] recalls Fairholt's delight at being allowed to enter the Birthplace. Indeed, Gifford's language draws directly on the language of pilgrimage that was so commonly used to describe the house on Henley Street: "This bedroom from which I am now writing and that little parlor is a shrine at which all true Americans and many too (the walls tell me) of other nations bow with affectionate reverence."[118] The Red Horse had become a type of Birthplace, the ritualized activities of visitors to this "shrine" mimicking the conventions that defined the rituals of the house on Henley Street. The difference, though, was that whereas Shakespeare's Birthplace was frequently used to express notions of British (or, more accurately, English) national identity, Irving's Red Horse Inn was appropriated as a site that was specifically American.

And the Americans had apparently set their sights wider than the cozy parlor of the Red Horse Inn.[119] From the middle of the nineteenth century, tourists from the States were seen as taking over the whole town. Their presence in Stratford was marked by the erection in Market Square of the American Fountain (its official title was the Shakespeare Memorial Fountain and Clock Tower), which was presented by George W. Childs of Philadelphia in 1887, and the American window in Holy Trinity Church, unveiled in 1896, which depicts parallel images from American and British history. In the 1830s Nathaniel Parker Willis noted of the owner of the Birthplace (Mrs. Court) that it "seemed to bother her to comprehend why two-thirds of her visitors should be Americans."[120] But reports of Americans swarming to Stratford might have been largely exaggerated. Figures from the Birthplace Trust show that in 1902 there were 15,784 British visitors to the house and 7,580 Americans (along with one visitor from the Bahamas, six from the Sandwich Islands, and seventeen from Tasmania). Whether an accurate picture can be gained from these figures or not (they were compiled from an analysis of the signatures in the visitors' book), what is significant is the idea, even the fear, that Americans were colonizing the town.

If Mrs. Court could not comprehend why so many of her visitors were from the States, other commentators were at pains not only to identify the American "invasion"—and it was frequently described in such alarmist terms—but also to account for it in a way that would contain its threat. Thus, the phenomenon was explained in terms of the universal appeal of Shakespeare. When Thomas Carlyle gave his lectures on hero-worship in 1840, he suggested that in the not too distant future, England would contain only a small fraction of the English: "there will be a Saxondom covering great spaces of the Globe," he asserted, pointing, in particular, to the English expansion into America.[121] According to Carlyle, this global world with its nations of Englishmen will be united by Shakespeare, so that people from New York will be able to say that "this Shakspeare is ours."[122] Twenty or so years after Carlyle's lecture, commentators were still emphasizing Shakespeare's ability to unify people, but now it was in terms that reversed Carlyle's imagined migration: the American presence in Stratford was perceived as a testament to the power of Shakespeare to bring people from around the globe (back) to England: "[Shakespeare] continually calls these adventurous wanderers back to the very heart of their mother country. Many a 'passionate pilgrim' from the forests of Canada, and many devotees from amongst the Shakspeare-loving Americans, are irresistibly attracted to the room in Henley Street, in which our Poet was born three hundred years ago. In that room they meet wanderers from our Indian Empire, shepherds from the vast plains of Australia, and settlers from New Zealand and the Cape."[123] This passage, taken from a book commemorating the Shakespeare tercentenary, is not simply about the power of the bard, of course: it is about the power of the British Empire, an empire that, the language makes clear, owns Shakespeare (he is "our poet") in the same way that it owns countries ("our Indian Empire").[124] In this world view, the birthroom is the epicenter of the empire, and England, in the form of Stratford, is the "mother country" to which other countries submit.

But there was the possibility that America would not conform to this world view. Just as Barnum had been accused of wanting to take the Birthplace for himself, so American tourists were accused of being equally acquisitive in their appropriation of Shakespeare. The stereotypical American in this period had such knowledge of Shakespeare that it put the British to shame. In *Asphodel*, American tourists are described as "spectacled, waterproofed, hyperintelligent, and knowing a great deal more about Shakespeare's biography than is known to the duller remnant of the Anglo-Saxon race still extant on this side of the Atlantic."[125] Indeed, so knowledgeable were the Americans about Shakespeare that they could claim to be educating the English. In a review in the *New York Times* of James Leon Williams's *The Home and Haunts of Shakespeare* (1892), the critic remarked that the English knew little about Stratford until Irving introduced them to it and that Williams's book was further "evidence of this American mission to educate the Englishman in regard to memorable English things."[126]

If the British in Stratford felt outnumbered and outwitted by the Americans, there was no danger of being outclassed. In 1903 Marie Corelli drew up a list of commandments specifically for American tourists, which set out not so much what they should do, but what they should *not* do, when they visited Stratford:

Don't expect to buy picture postcards, photographs, or sweeties at Shakespeare's Birthplace. It is a Shrine—not a shop.

The "American Window" in the Holy Trinity Church, presented by "American Admirers" of Shakespeare, is not yet paid for. One Hundred and Ten Pounds are still owing. American millionaires, buck up!

Don't go into the confectioners' shops, fourteen at a time, and order two glasses of milk and one bun for the whole party, so that those who don't want to pay for a drop of the milk or a crumb of the bun, may ask for a glass of water gratis. This way of serving refreshments to the wealthy American makes Shakespeare's townspeople tired.

When driving from Leamington to Stratford in the inexpensive brake for the day, don't bring private paper parcels of lunch in pockets or baskets. Since so many trees have been cut down in the highways and byeways, and on the river banks, there is no corner left shady enough to cover up the business of cheap eating on the open highroad. The shameless act is seen by the whole town.

Don't go about grumbling at the prices of the hotels. They are moderation compared to what you all willingly pay at Monte

Carlo. Be thankful you are charged so little for the unique privilege of breathing a day or so in the same town where the Immortal Bard, whom you Americans love so much, lived and died. It is worth five guineas to any American to stand for five minutes on the Stratford soil. It's a thing he can't do in his own country.[127]

With these "rules" and Corelli's attack on Carnegie's library in the same publication, it is a wonder that the novelist, for all her promotion of the Stratford tourist industry, did not drive away Americans by the thousands. One can only assume that not many picked up a copy of *The Avon Star* when they visited Stratford in the summer of 1903. Corelli's attempts to curb the American visitor's behavior, then, might have gone largely unheeded, but there is also a sense in which these rules are not addressed solely to the American. Rather, they establish a stereotype that appeals to the British reader's affirmation and recognition, creating a comic idea of what American tourists signify and, in so doing, neutralizing any danger that they pose. Moreover, Corelli's commandments actually promote an etiquette of tourism for *all* visitors by stating, and in very stark terms, what is acceptable and unacceptable behavior on the pilgrimage to Stratford. The opposition established in this list is not only between the American and implied British tourist, but also between tourists and the native inhabitants of Stratford (of whom Corelli counts herself as one): it is the "townspeople" who serve in the confectioners' shops or watch visitors eating in public places, who have to endure the behavior of the tourists.

What is acceptable for all tourists is the spending of money, but only if this activity is carried out in the right places and on the right things. For Corelli, what marks out visitors from the States is that they are defined as vulgar consumers, unwilling to spend their cash in the restaurants and hotels of Stratford, but all too eager to purchase sweets and postcards in the Birthplace. In this way, the tension between shrine and shop that characterizes the Victorian history of the Birthplace is once again displaced onto the Americans. An even more questionable activity than purchasing the wrong sort of souvenirs and which fully betrays the Americans' vulgarity is the "shameless act" of picnicking in public. More correct behavior is evinced by the English "pilgrim," Lucy Reynolds, who adamantly refuses to eat in public, despite being pressured by her friend: "Joan said they there would eat their eggs,/But Lucy, she said 'Nay—' /To lunch in private she'd be glad,—but *not* on the highway!"[128] The verse is amusing, but it does suggest the stigma attached to the public

picnic, which for Corelli is an immoral act. Such vilification of American behavior, however, signifies more than a distaste for conspicuous consumption,
whether of souvenirs or of food. Rather, it suggests concerns about the ownership of Shakespeare and the question of national identity with which it is intertwined, the possibility that another emerging empire could lay claim to
Stratford and to Shakespeare. As one critic mused in the same year that
Corelli set forth her commandments, "What prompts the American to these
acts of devotion we do not know, unless it be the firm conviction . . . that
Shakespeare is the property not of England but of America."[129]

The stereotyping of American tourists was a way of invalidating this claim,
of suggesting their unworthiness to own Shakespeare, even if they were devoted to him and knew so much about him. Indeed, the depiction of the tourists from the States as knowledgeable (the spectacles and raincoats would
designate them as nerds today) served to fix and define them, to give the impression that the British reader understood these visitors and their behavior.[130]
Such stereotyping is at play even in the remarks of those who seem opposed to
the conventional idea of the American tourist to Stratford. When J. Harvey
Bloom replied to Corelli in *The Errors of the Avon Star* he defended Americans
by stating that he had spent many hours in the Birthplace and never heard a
request for candy or picture cards. As for Corelli's claims that these visitors try
to get drinking water for free, Bloom comments, "We didn't know the American
tourist was so temperate. We have heard of and tasted American drinks, 'short'
and 'long,' but water played no very great part in their manufacture."[131] Bloom,
then, only adds to Corelli's list of American character traits, although his remarks are not altogether negative. For one thing, a trip around Stratford with
the Americans promised to be livelier than a tour of the temperance hotels
with the Reverend Arbuthnot.

8. Take Home a Souvenir

At the time of Garrick, the most prized mementos of the trip to Stratford
were objects carved from the mulberry tree by the aptly named local carpenter
Thomas Sharp, including bowls, plates, and snuff boxes. (Among the items in
the collection of the Birthplace Trust are mulberry rosary beads and an ink
stand, while the Folger Shakespeare Library in Washington, D.C., contains sugar
tongs and a rolling pin.) So many of these items were produced, including a
rather large table, that questions began to be asked about whether they all

derived from the same source, Sharp swearing an affidavit on his deathbed that vouched for their authenticity.[132] Mulberry-tree relics were still changing hands, and for relatively high sums, in the Victorian period. In its tercentenary edition, the *Illustrated London News* published an engraving of an ornate box carved from the wood that had been presented to Garrick.

If the carvings had come to an end with Thomas Sharp's demise, other relics could be obtained, even if illicitly. Fairholt recounts how a large chunk had been cut out of the beam in the birthroom by a young lady while her friend kept Mrs. Court in conversation below.[133] Following this incident, Mrs. Court refused to leave visitors alone in the house.[134] (The injunction that "no Visitor, or Visitors, shall be left alone in any part of the Buildings" was expressly written into the regulations by 1906.)[135] Mrs. Court seems, however, to have turned a blind eye to the schoolboy pranks of George Gray, the brother of Effie Gray (later Millais), who wrote to his mother in 1844 that "the old woman that showed us it [the Birthplace] told us a story about some lady taking a large piece of wood in the room so I took a piece of the old plaster on the wood and put it in my pocket but she did not say anything she said she would not let many people take it."[136]

By the time William Howitt visited Stratford, the mulberry tree and relics from the fabric of the Birthplace, which claimed a direct and physical connection with Shakespeare, had largely been replaced by mass-produced commercial souvenirs. "Stratford appears now to live on the fame of Shakspeare," Howitt wrote, "You see mementos of the great native poet wherever you turn."[137] Wherever you turned, indeed, there were shops selling Shakespeare, busts of the bard staring out at passing tourists through gleaming glass. Nathaniel Parker Willis mourned the fact that the town was becoming clean and modern, with the latest fashion advertised in the shops. Stratford, he comments "should have been forbidden ground to builders, masons, shopkeepers, and generally to all people of thrift and whitewash."[138] By 1903, and despite her criticism of American consumerism, Corelli could offer a guide to where pretty things could be bought in Stratford, suggesting a visit to the jewelers on Bridge Street, where one could buy a dainty model of Shakespeare's chair or a copy of the signet ring.[139] There was also Quatremain on Church Street, which sold original watercolors of Stratford; Stanley, which sold fine photographs (and happened also to be the printer and publisher of Corelli's *Avon Star*); and the somewhat pricey Rathbone, which was directly opposite the Birthplace and sold antiques.

Corelli's shopping tips are intended to counteract what she regards as the common assumption that the only things for sale in Stratford were cheap busts of Shakespeare, picture postcards, and models of the Birthplace, which suggests, of course, that these were the principal items stocked in the gift shops.[140] The Birthplace itself proved highly marketable, new reproductive technologies allowing images of the building to be transferred onto egg cups, pocket handkerchiefs, and other household objects. Victorian souvenirs included: a cardboard model of the Birthplace set on a wooden base; a gold brooch, which showed the Birthplace behind the glass; the usual mugs, plates, and spoons with Shakespeare's head in the handles and the Birthplace in the bowls; silk bookmarks woven with pictures of Holy Trinity Church, the bust, and the Birthplace; Staffordshire pots and lids that depicted the birthroom; and a Mauchline ware souvenir egg timer in boxwood dating from the late nineteenth century decorated with a view of the Birthplace. Perhaps most revealing is the ceramic money box in the shape of the house from about 1862, which is inscribed with the words "Shakespeare Saving bank."[141]

Representations of the Birthplace, however diverse, were not enough for some tourists, who preferred natural rather than manufactured souvenirs. Numerous Victorian travel accounts tell of visitors plucking leaves from the trees in the churchyard or a rose from the garden of the Birthplace. One letter from J. Newman Hank of Washington, dated 6 September 1858 and written to his sister, is on headed notepaper that still shows the stitching where he attached an ivy leaf from the wall of the church.[142] The image of the leaf taken from Stratford and sent to relatives abroad (most commonly in America) also appears in several poems in the period which emphasize Shakespeare's status as the poet of nature. George Martin's sonnet "To G.I. at Stratford-on-Avon" begins with the lines "The leaf you plucked from Shakespeare's garden plot,/ And sent me, my most estimable friend,/The voyage of the salt sea injured not."[143]

Throughout the nineteenth century, the memento of Stratford became imbued with ideological as well as economic value. The acquisition of the souvenir served not only as a reminder of the trip, but also as part of the touristic ritual, an act that effectively conflated the worship of the bard with commercialism and exploited the Victorian desire to take home the home of Shakespeare, whether in the form of a flower from the garden, a piece of plaster, or a money box in the shape of the house on Henley Street.

These rituals formed part of an etiquette of the Victorian trip to Stratford that was created in writing, sometimes explicitly (as in Corelli), but often implicitly in the numerous descriptions of the tour that emphasized the myth of

Shakespeare which saturated the town and created the sense of pilgrimage and reverence. The rules, of course, did not go entirely unquestioned. With such expectations about the visit, it is not surprising that these expectations were sometimes ridiculed, satirized, and disappointed. But, above all, the guidelines were pervasive, generating notions of what one should do and how one should behave. It is no wonder that in James's "The Birthplace" the hundreds of visitors who flock into the house and lap up the stories told by the custodians are called "stupid."[144] Whether they were aware of it or not, Victorian visitors to Stratford were always on a guided tour.

Conclusion

The Place and the Plays

I did not set out to write a book about Shakespeare's Birthplace. The house crept up on me while I was undertaking research for another project. And once I had seen it, it would not go away. I opened illustrated editions of the plays and there it was, the dormer windows staring back at me under thick gabled eyebrows; I read works of criticism, newspapers, magazines, novels and poems, and there it was again, its insistent textual presence demanding a response. I eventually gave in and wrote this book. The Birthplace, as I have suggested, took on very different forms and meanings throughout the Victorian period, both in a material and an ideological sense, but it was strikingly ubiquitous and in some unexpected contexts.

As this book has shown, Shakespeare's Birthplace was essentially created by the Victorians, who inserted it into Shakespeare's biography, bought and restored it for the nation, authenticated it, and placed it at the center of the Stratford tourist trail. Following the momentary excitement of Garrick's Jubilee, it is possible that interest in Stratford would have waned and that tourism would have continued as an elitist rather than a popular activity. The Birthplace might even have remained in private hands, with only a blue plaque to mark its eminence. It was the auction of the property and its purchase for the nation that changed the course of the building's history and, with it, the fortunes of Stratford-upon-Avon. It also changed the fortunes of Shakespeare. Aaron Santesso has argued that the "Stratford model," which has come to dominate literary tourism today, is founded on the connection between the origins of an author and the work, with the Birthplace apparently enabling its visitors to understand the plays more fully.[1] It is a model, I would suggest, that is realized in the time period explored in this book. In conclusion, I want to suggest how the development of the Birthplace and the writings and activities surrounding it reflected, reproduced, and extended contemporary ideas and anxieties about Shakespeare and the plays.

The fascination with the Birthplace and the biographical construction of Shakespeare's young life that it encouraged added credibility to his construction as a domestic poet. It also helped domesticate the works themselves, which occupied an established and privileged position within the home. In the most humble of Victorian interiors, Shakespeare's works took their place beside the Bible. There were social and economic reasons for the frequent appearance of the plays on Victorian bookshelves: increases in population, literacy, and income occurred in this period, and the abolition of taxes on paper meant that editions became cheaper to produce. While these conditions affected the book-selling trade more generally, however, there seems to have been a specific demand for Shakespeare. Gary Taylor points out that while 65 editions of Shakespeare's works were published between 1709 and 1810, there were at least 162 between 1851 and 1860.[2] It was in the aftermath of the auction, then, that the trade in editions of Shakespeare's plays accelerated, as this particular event intensified the appetite for all things Shakespeare. Charles Knight's edition went through several formats following its initial publication a few years prior to the sale of the house: there was a Stratford Edition, Pictorial Edition, Cabinet Edition, National Edition, and an Imperial Edition, each one catering to a different sector of the market.[3]

Shakespeare's plays came increasingly to be regarded not just as texts to be performed in the theater but also as texts to be read in the home as books, even as novels, critics making explicit connections between Shakespeare and contemporary authors. In an address delivered in 1894 at the Shakespeare birthday dinner in London, for instance, Thomas Hall Caine labeled Shakespeare as the first English novelist.[4] The movement of the plays beyond the four walls of the theater to the four walls of the home is epitomized in a remarkable engraving that appeared in the *Eclectic Magazine*. The picture shows Shakespeare, presumably in the Henley Street house, reading *Hamlet* to his engrossed family (Figure 21).[5] Anne pauses in her sewing as her husband becomes particularly animated, while Shakespeare's doting daughters lean against him, and his son, Hamnet, stops to listen to the recital on his way out of the door. The older generations of the Shakespeare family are represented here, too, with an elderly gentleman, most likely John Shakespeare, sitting on

Figure 21. "Shakespeare and His Family," *Eclectic Magazine of Foreign Literature, Science, and Art,* January 1866.

a chair in the background and looking up from a book he has been reading. A claim is made in the accompanying text for the historical accuracy of the picture: "Without any positive knowledge on the subject," the editor writes, "we may believe the truth of the representation in the engraving. It is, moreover, quite possible that had some visible or invisible photographer been present to take an impression of the scene, this may have been the truthful one."[6] Such a claim might seem ludicrous to twenty-first-century eyes, but what was less obvious to its original viewers was the very Victorianness of the picture. Despite the Elizabethan costume and the odd lute, this is essentially a Victorian gathering in a Victorian parlor, with Shakespeare the Victorian patriarch reading aloud to his family.

In this engraving, Shakespeare is in every sense the family man, positioned within his Stratford home rather than a London playhouse. The home is also where the plays are located in the period: they exist as works to be read aloud within the confines of the domestic space. This activity had been encouraged earlier in the century with the publication of Bowdler's editions of Shakespeare's works which excised those parts of the text that should not be heard by sensitive ears. In the preface to *The Family Shakspeare* (1818), Thomas

Bowdler writes that "I can hardly imagine a more pleasing occupation for a winter's evening in the country, than for a father to read one of Shakspeare's plays to his family circle."[7] Bowdler's intention was to enable fathers to read aloud without raising a blush. This cleaned-up version of the plays was incredibly popular in the Victorian period; in 1847, the year of the auction, it had reached its ninth edition. No doubt the Victorian avatar of Shakespeare pictured in the *Eclectic Magazine* is also carefully regulating his reading of *Hamlet*.

It was this appropriation of Shakespeare as part of a family and the plays as suitable family reading that the interest in the Birthplace promoted. The focus on the boyhood of Shakespeare also went hand in hand with an emphasis on the girlhood of his heroines. Mary Cowden Clarke's *The Girlhood of Shakespeare's Heroines* (1850–52) is devoted to telling the stories of the childhood of Shakespeare's female characters, employing the same imaginative biographical register that was used to recreate Shakespeare's childhood in the Birthplace. Parallels had often been drawn between the figures from Shakespeare's early life and the female characters in the plays (Harriet Beecher Stowe, as I mentioned earlier, saw Mary Arden as a model for Desdemona's purity). Clarke's approach works to further domesticate these heroines in the same way that Shakespeare himself was domesticated by setting them within their early family environments. Indeed, the book is a curious example of Victorian child psychology, with the dysfunction of some of these families implicated in the subsequent actions and behavior of the figures in the plays: when her parents move to Paris, Ophelia is brought up by a nurse in the country and it is here that she learns the sexually explicit rhymes she recites when she goes mad; Desdemona has a jealous father with a violent temper; and little Gruoch, the future Lady Macbeth, is raised by a mother who desperately wanted a boy and, when she dies, by a father who is too indulgent.[8]

Paradoxically, it is the murderous Lady Macbeth who turns out to be one of the most domestic of Shakespeare's heroines in this period, for critics were eager to rehabilitate her by claiming that her ambition was only for her husband and not for herself. In many ways, Lady Macbeth was considered the ideal Victorian wife.[9] It is no surprise that the sleepwalking scene, where she attempts to rub the imaginary spots of blood from her hand, proved so fascinating—it suggested her conscience at work. Numerous paintings and illustrations depict this scene and it even becomes the inspiration for a comic advertisement in which her gentlewoman reassures Lady Macbeth that her hands will be made clean with a shilling bar of Pears' Soap.[10]

Lady Macbeth, clutching her hand, appears alongside Prince Hal, Falstaff, and Hamlet in Ronald Gower's monument to Shakespeare, which was erected in Stratford in October 1888 and can still be seen by tourists today (Figure 22). Looming above these figures is the sculpted image of Shakespeare himself. With his determined and contemplative stare across the Stratford landscape, Shakespeare is represented as a genius, set above mere mortals, but also poignantly human, as Gower manages successfully to capture those two intertwined elements of his identity. Shakespeare's absorbed gaze suggests that he has been caught in the act of imagining or actively creating his characters, which are made manifest beneath him yet immediately take on a life of their own. Set on separate plinths, they seem to be escaping their creator, an effect intensified by Gower's attempt to capture in an external form their inner lives and reality: Lady Macbeth is shown sleepwalking, Falstaff laughing, Hamlet gazing at a skull, and Prince Hal crowning himself.

Gower did not originally plan for the monument to be located in Stratford. When he began work on it, he had no idea where it would end up, but anticipated that it would probably be on the other side of the Atlantic.[11] Adrian Poole has suggested that the fact that these figures from the plays have been turned into "bodies with real appetites, desires and pains" makes the setting of the monument seem incongruous; its ethos, he comments, is more in keeping with Paris or Vienna than Stratford-upon-Avon.[12] In the case of the Shakespeare that this sculpture represents, however, late nineteenth-century Stratford was the perfect location. Gower's Shakespeare is the one who originates in the Birthplace, who possesses the same human reality and psychological richness and depth, who "dreams up" his characters. It is the young boy telling stories by the fireside in the house on Henley Street who grows into the creative genius. In Gower's monument, Shakespeare has come home.

The Birthplace forged a connection between Shakespeare, the plays, and a specific site that was far from natural or obvious. After all, what did the house in which William Shakespeare was born really have to do with the meanings of *Hamlet*? There is a sense in which the entire Stratford tourist industry emerged in the attempt to answer this question and to consolidate the union between the two, thereby establishing its own position and status. However appealing the anecdotes about little Will exploring the attic of the Birthplace were, they could not stand alone as justification of the importance of the house, or, indeed, of the other properties that the Birthplace Trust acquired. At the time of the auction, honoring (by visiting and buying) the house was

Figure 22. Ronald Gower's monument to Shakespeare, Stratford-upon-Avon, in its original position next to the theater, from John Leyland, *The Shakespeare Country Illustrated* (London: Offices of "Country Life Illustrated" and George Newnes, 1900).

presented as a way of directly paying tribute to Shakespeare since this material structure provided one of the only traces of his mortal existence. Following the purchase of the property, it was the association between the plays and the house that became the dominant reason for the Birthplace's cultural significance. Thus, Shakespeare learned the tools of his trade there, whether from a copy of Holinshed that he read by the fire, or from the Warwickshire countryside that surrounded the house.

The extent of this dialogue between plays and place was made manifest when the Hungarian statesman Lajos Kossuth visited Britain in 1853.

Kossuth's story of how he had learned English when imprisoned in a damp lonely cell with only a dictionary and Shakespeare's works to help him had been widely reported in the British press (the guards considered Shakespeare's plays nonpolitical, hence legitimate reading material), so it was only right to celebrate Kossuth's visit by presenting him with a sumptuous copy of Knight's edition of Shakespeare's works, which was superbly bound in mulberry-colored morocco and had been purchased by public subscription.[13] Such an edition needed a fitting home, and this home was no less than Shakespeare's, the volumes being encased in a model of the Birthplace, complete with timbers of black oak and walls of white holly to signify limewash. The plays could be accessed by opening the front of the house.

In addition to these public and political gestures, the Birthplace and the discourses surrounding it also influenced the critical reception and interpretation of Shakespeare's plays. It is telling that in 1849 George Henry Lewes opened his lengthy review of Shakespearean criticism in the *Edinburgh Review* with a reference not to the plays, but to the house on Henley Street, the durability of which he identified as a symbol of the durability of Shakespeare: while grander and newer houses have crumbled away and great literary names have risen and fallen, the Birthplace and Shakespeare remain.[14]

The Birthplace had certainly endured throughout the nineteenth century, but this was largely the result of its substantial restoration. Indeed, the attempt to physically recreate the house and bring the past to life had parallels with how Shakespeare was represented on the stage in this period and the vogue for historically accurate performances.[15] It calls to mind a similar attempt at documentary truth in the Victorian art world, where the Pre-Raphaelite Brotherhood, which was founded in 1848, frequently looked to Shakespearean subject matter. The artists went to extraordinary lengths to ensure that scenes looked authentic, including almost freezing to death Elizabeth Siddal, the model for John Everett Millais's *Ophelia* (1851–52), when she posed in a bathtub full of cold water.[16]

Editions of Shakespeare's plays, like Knight's, similarly gave a historical and thus "factual" context for the plays, while the editorial process itself was often described in way that was markedly similar to the language used to define, and criticize, the restoration of the Birthplace. One angry critic of an edition by Charles and Mary Cowden Clarke, for example, referred to the "numberless alterations, mutilations, corruptions, or whatever we may choose to call them, which deface these noble dramas."[17] By following Bowdler's example and making the texts more palatable for the Victorian audience, editors threatened to "improve" Shakespeare's plays, with all the derogatory meanings that this term implied. As one critic notes, "In the course of another century, the alterations necessary to adapt these plays to prudish tastes will perhaps be twice as numerous;—other and bolder editors will arise, and will make still wider havoc;—and so on until Shakespeare's text be gradually "improved off the face of the earth.'"[18] Knight appealed for a return to the "original" texts. In the introductory notice for his Stratford Edition of the *Works*, he discusses the practice of editing, commenting that "our confidence in the original copies has been suddenly disturbed by 'Emendations' of a more sweeping character than have been ventured upon since the days of Rowe."[19] Knight's aim is "to uphold the authority of the ancient text of Shakspere—purified, by the labours of successive commentators, of unquestionable errors, and made as correct as we can possibly make it, by a careful comparison of the early editions."[20]

Significantly, "restoration" is a term that is frequently employed in these discussions.[21] Quoting from his earlier Library Edition, Knight remarks that "In restoring even an ancient reading, upon full conviction, an Editor must give very satisfactory reasons for the rejection of the supposed improvement."[22] Later in the text, he asserts that "The altered language of Shakspere cannot be implicitly received as the restored language. . . . It would be easy to make the thirty-seven dramas, which are the glory of English literature, more popular and intelligible; but this is not to 'restore' Shakspere, even if he needed restoration, which we take leave to doubt."[23] For Knight, "restoration" does not necessarily mean a return to the "original"; on the contrary, it is often a synonym for "improvement" and "substitution." And this was also true in the case of the restoration of the Birthplace.

Perhaps it is not surprising that dealings with the Birthplace in this period mirrored so closely dealings with the plays because it was the leading Shakespearean scholars, including Charles Knight, John Payne Collier and J. O. Halliwell(-Phillipps), who were involved with the purchase and development of the house. At the time that Halliwell-Phillipps was working in the library of the Birthplace Museum, he was also a member of the New Shakspere Society. This was founded in 1873 under the auspices of Frederick James Furnivall, who pioneered the statistical analysis and measurement of Shakespeare's meter and rhyme. Such a method of interpreting Shakespeare's plays took Victorian scientism to extremes, but its underlying impetus stemmed from the focus on Shakespeare's biography and a connection with Stratford that had been central to the way that the Birthplace was represented in the decades leading up to the founding of this society. As Furnivall argued (and he frequently did argue, with Halliwell-Phillipps and almost everyone else he came into contact with), the close study of the metrical characteristics of Shakespeare's verse would allow the chronology of the plays to be discovered and provide an insight into the workings and evolution of Shakespeare's mind. This evolution was explicitly identified by Furnivall in terms of Shakespeare's move from Stratford to London and back again, the early comedies tinged "with the recollection of all his greenwood life and his pleasant youth at Stratford," followed by his articulation of the concerns of the Elizabethan era at the London court, and his eventual return to the town of his birth: "and then at last to the poet's peaceful and quiet home-life again in Stratford, where he ends with his Prospero and Miranda, his Leontes finding again his wife and daughter in Hermione and Perdita; in whom we may fancy that the Stratford both of his early and late days lives again, and that the daughters he saw there, the sweet English maidens, the pleasant country scenes around him, passt as it were again into his plays."[24]

The reading of the plays that Furnivall undertakes is, of course, influenced by the general interest in Shakespeare's biography that had gathered momentum from the eighteenth century, but it is more specific than this. Stratford features everywhere in Furnivall's analysis and in the aims and objectives of his project: it inspires Shakespeare's language, plots, characters, even in the case of those plays that, as Furnivall acknowledges, were clearly written in London. The bond between plays and place on which this depends is characteristic of how Stratford was defined, and how it defined itself, in the years surrounding the purchase of the Birthplace and its incursion into the public consciousness.

In the Victorian period, then, Stratford and the Birthplace were portals not only to the life of Shakespeare but also to the plays themselves. So effective was the consolidation of this connection that by the last decade of the nineteenth century Stratford finally became home to a Shakespeare theater. This was a significant development considering that at the beginning of Victoria's reign Shakespeare's plays could only be performed legally in a handful of London theaters.[25] The plan to build a theater in the town derived from the failed monument scheme that had been part of the tercentenary festival. Its champion was Charles Flower, a brewer and wealthy resident of Stratford. The plan received some resistance, especially from the London-based press, which failed to see how a theater could thrive outside the capital: "What must be the inevitable fate of a theatre at a place to which it will not only be necessary to send actors to play, but audiences to see them playing?" asked one commentator.[26]

A cartoon showed the production of the plays before an audience of a handful of cowherds.[27] Despite the malicious nature of such jibes, the Shakespeare Memorial Theatre opened its doors on 19 April 1879 and marked the culmination of the tendency to associate Shakespeare with Stratford (as opposed to London) that had been signaled at the time of the auction and again at the tercentenary. This was made explicit in the choice of the first production in the new theater: *As You Like It*, which is set in an imaginary version of Warwickshire's Forest of Arden. The correlation between Shakespeare's play and the Stratford environs was rendered even more obvious when, to great applause from the audience, two hounds from the Charlecote estate and a deer, which had been shot specifically for the occasion, were brought on stage by the Charlecote gamekeeper dressed up as a forester.[28]

Without the acquisition and growing significance of the Birthplace, it is unlikely that the scheme to bring a world-class theater to Stratford would ever have been proposed, much less come to fruition. Critics of the project were mistaken in assuming that it would be a struggle to find an audience. The theater did take a while to establish itself, but by the beginning of the twentieth century W. B. Yeats, on his own trip to see Shakespeare's plays in Stratford, could confidently proclaim that people from all parts of England, Scotland, Ireland, and America were willing to travel to this theater.[29] This successful venture, on which so much Shakespearean tourism now depends, was a direct result of the purchase of the Birthplace and its prominent position in Victorian texts and images.

With the acquisition of the properties and building of the playhouse, Stratford was intertwined with Shakespeare, but there were problems with this intimacy, and these revolved around the very location of Shakespeare's birth and upbringing. How was it, doubters asked, that someone from such humble and rustic origins could have written these plays? This market town, it seemed, could not possibly have provided Shakespeare with the education and training necessary to compose such extraordinary texts, however much reading he had done as a boy on Henley Street. Questions about Shakespeare's authorship of the plays began in earnest in 1857 with Delia Bacon's contention that they had been written by a group of men, among them Francis Bacon. By 1884 the authorship dispute had spread to America, France, Germany, and India, resulting in the publication of over 250 books, pamphlets, and articles.[30] Maurizio Ascari has recently suggested that there is a connection between the controversy surrounding the authorship of Shakespeare's plays and the nineteenth-century pilgrimage to the Birthplace. He points out that while the Birthplace seems to stand as proof of Shakespeare's existence and authorship, there were frequently doubts expressed about its status, most notably by American authors like Washington Irving, Nathaniel Hawthorne, and Henry James.[31] I would go further and suggest an even closer proximity: that the authorship controversy was, in fact, a reaction to the mid-nineteenth-century appropriation of the Birthplace and the interconnection between plays and place that it instigated. It is revealing that those who questioned Shakespeare's authorship were defined specifically as "anti-Stratfordians." Even the terms of the debate (the provincial Shakespeare versus the metropolitan Francis Bacon, or numerous other contenders) bear an uncanny resemblance to the rivalry between Stratford and London that features so prominently in the Victorian history of the house.

This hostility toward the Birthplace and all it stood for, however, was ultimately recuperated as another of its authentication strategies. In his discussion of authenticity in museums and art galleries, David Phillips contends that the authentic is characterized not so much by the abstract values that are attached to it, but by what it is not: the fake, the forgery, the false, and so on.[32] This seems to be true (or perhaps not true) of the authenticity of the Birthplace, which was validated by the very opposition of the so-called anti-Stratfordians, the critics who followed Delia Bacon in undermining Shakespeare's authorship of the plays. By setting themselves up against "Stratford," they actually helped to promote the town and the Birthplace as an accepted "truth" that needed to be debunked. It was almost too remarkable, the anti-Stratfordians frequently pointed out, that so little was known about Shakespeare's life; the Birthplace conveniently filled in the gaps. Such was the contention of Francis E. C. Habgood and R. L. Eagle in an essay originally published in *Baconiana* in 1940, which opened with the revelation that "the property in Henley Street, Stratford-upon-Avon, which is now shown for one shilling each to about 90,000 people every year as the Birthplace of William Shakespeare, has no claim whatever to this honour, except a very doubtful traditional one."[33] Despite Habgood's and Eagle's assertion, it appears that by 1940 the validity of the Birthplace was established, so much so that their opening sentence is intended to shock even the cynical Baconians.

From tumble-down terraced cottage to respectable residence, from the object of derision to veneration, the nineteenth-century history of the Birthplace is one of change and adaptation. The Birthplace trustees sought to provide what its visitors needed, and this is as much in evidence today as it was in the

Victorian period. I remember my first visit to the house on Henley Street. I was eleven years old and on a camping vacation with my parents. I hated camping. How I longed, if I had only known the reference then, for the comfortable parlor of the Red Horse Inn, where the weary tourist could put on his or her slippers and meditate in front of the fire on a day spent visiting the sites. Instead of a roaring fire, we had a gas stove, and rather than slippers I had Wellington boots for nocturnal treks across muddy fields to the bathroom. Despite the accommodation, I loved Stratford. There was something almost magical about seeing the antique buildings that Shakespeare might have seen, of walking across countryside that he, too, might have strolled along. As a child, I happily bought into the myth. Geoffrey Crayon was right: believing was pleasant, enjoyable, desirable.

My father's was the voice of reason. When we were wandering around the Birthplace, he remarked, in an embarrassingly loud aside that attracted a caustic glance from the guide, that there was probably nothing "original" there, that even the walls, ceilings, and floorboards had most likely been replaced at some time or another. His words shattered the illusion. Almost. In writing this book, I have felt a little bit like my father. The Birthplace, I argue, was a product of the nineteenth century. This was the period in which the walls, ceilings, and floorboards were quite literally replaced. This was also a period in which the meanings and values of the building were created, along with the very idea that there was an illusion to be shattered. But, as much as it is indebted to the father's urge to unmask the myth, this book has also been driven by the child's recognition of the power of the story.

This power is still present in the rooms of the Birthplace, although the bare interior that characterized the Victorian rendition of the house is now fully furnished: there are linens on the beds, cooking utensils in the kitchen, and even a glover's workshop where Shakespeare's father might have made his wares. Imagining Shakespeare at home as a young boy (at the age of ten, according to the historically accurate interior) might not require the creative energies it once did, but there is still a cultural need to situate Shakespeare as a real, historical being within this domestic environment.

The reconstruction of the Birthplace as a Tudor abode serves an instructive as well as an aesthetic purpose. The modern Birthplace does not inspire much awe for Shakespeare (indeed, for the parties of schoolchildren who frequently congregate on the bank of the Avon, reverence seems to have been replaced by revelry). The house is less a site of pilgrimage than a site of pedagogy, as the information for tourists describes the visit as an opportunity to learn about Shakespeare, his life, and the Elizabethan period. No prior knowledge is required, not even for those waterproofed tourists from the States. For the contemporary visitor, the Birthplace is more of an educational rather than an emotional experience.

In a sense, though, the house on Henley Street today provides an even closer intimacy between the place and the plays than the ideological link on which meanings of the building came to depend in the Victorian period. Twenty-first century tourists to Stratford can view the Birthplace from an entirely different perspective. The colossal statue of Shakespeare, through the eyes of which the sites of London could be seen, never materialized, but Stratford now has its own, admittedly less ostentatious, viewing platform: a tower built onto the Royal Shakespeare Theatre, which enables tourists to see across Stratford and the adjoining countryside. The tower connects the auditorium of the theater with the trajectory of Shakespeare's life. From here, visitors can see the Birthplace, Holy Trinity Church, and the other Shakespearean properties alongside Snitterfield, where Shakespeare's father was born, as well as Wilmcote, the location of Mary Arden's house, and Charlecote. For those who prefer to keep their feet on the ground, a recent initiative has situated actors in the house and grounds of the Birthplace. Bursting into verse at appropriate moments, they give the tourist the chance to discover Titania in a bower of flowers in the garden or to bump into the witches brewing up some evil concoction in the kitchen. Such participatory strategies are intended, according to Kate Rumbold, "to heighten visitors' sense of connection with 'Shakespeare'"; they provide a doorway into Shakespeare's writing, a unique point of access into the bard's imagination.[34]

As the number of visitors attests, the appeal of the house on Henley Street still endures, although for me it has another allure. The specter of Shakespeare might haunt the house, but there are other ghosts who also occupy this hallowed space: Halliwell-Phillipps, who pores over his documents; George Jones, who snores away on the floor of the birthroom; and those anonymous gentlemen in top hats and ladies in crinolines who pose, uneasily, for their photographs. The heritage of the Birthplace is as much a Victorian legacy as a Tudor one. The Victorians "invented" the Birthplace and Stratford, but they also invented a history, a narrative, which is in process and that still has the power to attract different types of pilgrims today. As a recent publicity leaflet claims, Shakespeare's Birthplace is "so much more than the house itself."[35] For the Victorians, it always was.

Notes

Introduction

Note to epigraph: J. Hollingshead, "A Startling Confession," *Train: A First-Class Magazine* 4:21 (September 1857): 138.

1. Hollingshead, "A Startling Confession," p. 139.
2. Hollingshead, "A Startling Confession," p. 139.
3. Hollingshead, "A Startling Confession," p. 140.
4. A model of Shakespeare's Birthplace, which was made by J. Powell of Trentham, Newcastle-under-Lyme, and on display in the Great Exhibition, was said to have been repeatedly visited by Queen Victoria. Edmund Kirby, a Manchester architect, designed two semi-detached cottages for William Hesketh Lever in 1896 as reproductions of Shakespeare's Birthplace. They were situated in "Poet's Corner" in Port Sunlight, the village that Lever designed for the workers in his factory. The houses were demolished in 1938.
5. For the establishment of the Trust, see Levi Fox, *The Shakespeare Birthplace Trust: A Personal Memoir* (Norwich: Shakespeare Birthplace Trust in association with Jarrold Publishing, 1997), pp. 24–27.
6. See Aaron Santesso, "The Birth of the Birthplace: Bread Street and Literary Tourism Before Stratford," *ELH* 71:2 (Summer 2004): 377–403.
7. See Nicola J. Watson, *The Literary Tourist: Readers and Places in Romantic and Victorian Britain* (Basingstoke: Palgrave Macmillan, 2006), pp. 58–59.
8. Advertisement dated 23 November 1866, *A Collection of Pamphlets, Posters &c, Relating to the Shakespeare Tercentenary Festival at Stratford-upon-Avon*. In the collection of the British Library, London.
9. Roger Pringle, "The Rise of Stratford as Shakespeare's Town," in *The History of an English Borough: Stratford-upon-Avon 1196–1996*, ed. Robert Bearman (Gloucestershire: Sutton in association with the Shakespeare Birthplace Trust, 1997), p. 162.
10. Sanford R. Gifford to his father, 13 July 1855, Sanford Robinson Gifford Papers, Archives of American Art, Smithsonian Institution, Washington D.C.
11. Numerous studies have focused on the "making" of Shakespeare and his reputation, particularly in relation to the eighteenth and nineteenth centuries. See, for example, Robert Witbeck Babcock, *The Genesis of Shakespeare Idolatry, 1766–1799* (Chapel Hill: University of North Carolina Press, 1931), Jonathan Bate, *Shakespearean Constitutions: Politics, Theatre,*

Criticism, 1730–1830 (Oxford: Clarendon, 1989), Michael Dobson, *The Making of the National Poet: Shakespeare, Adaptation, and Authorship, 1660–1769* (Oxford: Clarendon, 1992), Louis Marder, *His Exits and His Entrances: The Story of Shakespeare's Reputation* (London: John Murray, 1963), Gary Taylor, *Reinventing Shakespeare: A Cultural History from the Restoration to the Present* (London: Hogarth, 1990).

12. "To Chalfont and Milton's Cottage," *All the Year Round*, 6 May 1893, p. 416.

13. Adrian Poole, *Shakespeare and the Victorians* (London: Thomson Learning, 2004), p. 2.

14. Ivor Brown and George Fearon, *The Shakespeares and the Birthplace* (Stratford-on-Avon: Edward Fox and Son, 1939), p. 228. See also A. K. Chesterton, *Brave Enterprise: A History of the Shakespeare Memorial Theatre, Stratford-upon-Avon* (London: J. Miles and Co., 1934).

15. Fox, *The Shakespeare Birthplace Trust*. See also Levi Fox, "The Heritage of Shakespeare's Birthplace," in *Shakespeare Survey* I, ed. Allardyce Nicoll (Cambridge: Cambridge University Press, 1948), pp. 79–88.

16. Other historically based accounts of the Birthplace can be found in Henry C. Shelley, *Shakespeare and Stratford* (London: Simpkin, Marshall Hamilton, Kent and Co., 1913), Ivor Brown and George Fearon, *Amazing Monument: A Short History of the Shakespeare Industry* (London: William Heinemann, 1939), and, more recently, Pringle, "The Rise of Stratford as Shakespeare's Town."

17. See Brown and Fearon, *Amazing Monument*, Graham Holderness, "Bardolatry: or, The Cultural Materialist's Guide to Stratford-upon-Avon," in *The Shakespeare Myth*, ed. Graham Holderness (Manchester: Manchester University Press, 1988), pp. 2–15, Marder, *His Exits and His Entrances*, pp. 237–47, Nicola J. Watson, "Shakespeare on the Tourist Trail," in *The Cambridge Companion to Shakespeare and Popular Culture*, ed. Robert Shaughnessy (Cambridge: Cambridge University Press, 2007), pp. 199–226.

18. See, for example, the approach of Norman Scarfe, in "Shakespeare: Stratford-Upon-Avon and Warwickshire," in *Shakespeare: A Celebration 1564–1964*, ed. T. J. B. Spencer (London: Penguin, 1964), pp. 15–29.

19. See, for example, Barbara Hodgdon's account of the Shakespeare industry in contemporary Stratford in *The Shakespeare Trade: Performances and Appropriations* (Philadelphia: University of Pennsylvania Press, 1998), pp. 191–240. Douglas Lanier refers to the Birthplace in the context of tourism and festivals in *Shakespeare and Modern Popular Culture* (Oxford: Oxford University Press, 2002), pp. 143–67.

20. See, in particular, Harald Hendrix, ed., *Writers' Houses and the Making of Memory* (New York: Routledge, 2008), Santesso, "The Birth of the Birthplace," Watson, *The Literary Tourist*, and Watson, ed., *Literary Tourism and Nineteenth-Century Culture* (Basingstoke: Palgrave Macmillan, 2009). An account of the Birthplace also appears in Ian Ousby, *The Englishman's England: Taste, Travel and the Rise of Tourism* (Cambridge: Cambridge University Press, 1990), pp. 45–57. Michael Rosenthal discusses tourism to Stratford in "Shakespeare's Birthplace at Stratford: Bardolatry Reconsidered," in Hendrix, ed., *Writers' Houses and the Making of Memory*, pp. 31–44.

21. The Birthplace was clearly in Stopford Brooke's mind when he was negotiating the purchase of Wordsworth's home. In a letter discussing the possibility of establishing a Wordsworth Museum in Dove Cottage, Brooke comments on the fact that Shakespeare's Birthplace makes £650 a year in admissions. Stopford Augustus Brooke to W. A. Knight, 21

January 1890. In the Knight Collection, Morgan Library and Museum, New York. See also Polly Atkin, who refers to Brooke's pamphlet, which set out his plans and revealed his debt to the Shakespeare Birthplace Trust. Polly Atkin, "Ghosting Grasmere: The Musealisation of Dove Cottage," in Watson, ed., *Literary Tourism and Nineteenth-Century Culture*, pp. 84–94.

22. This connection is discussed at some length in Watson, *The Literary Tourist*, pp. 56–89.

23. Balz Engler, "Stratford and the Canonization of Shakespeare," *European Journal of English Studies* 1:3 (1997): 354–66.

24. This book is situated in criticism that explores the complex ways in which Shakespeare was appropriated in the nineteenth century. See Richard Foulkes, *Performing Shakespeare in the Age of Empire* (Cambridge: Cambridge University Press, 2002), Gail Marshall, *Shakespeare and Victorian Women* (Cambridge: Cambridge University Press, 2009), Marshall and Poole, eds., *Victorian Shakespeare, Volume 1: Theatre, Drama and Performance* and *Volume 2: Literature and Culture* (Basingstoke: Palgrave Macmillan, 2003), Andrew Murphy, *Shakespeare for the People: Working-Class Readers, 1800–1900* (Cambridge: Cambridge University Press, 2008), Marianne Novy, *Engaging with Shakespeare: Responses of George Eliot and Other Women Novelists* (Athens: University of Georgia Press, 1994), Poole, *Shakespeare and the Victorians*, Linda Rozmovits, *Shakespeare and the Politics of Culture in Late-Victorian England* (Baltimore: Johns Hopkins University Press, 1998).

25. Harald Hendrix, "Writers' Houses as Media of Expression and Remembrance: From Self-Fashioning to Cultural Memory," in *Writers' Houses and the Making of Memory*, p. 5.

26. [George Linnaeus Banks], *All About Shakespeare: Profusely Illustrated with Wood Engravings by Thomas Gilks, Drawn by H. Fitzcook. In Commemoration of the Ter-Centenary* (London: Henry Lea, 1864).

27. For a description of the graphotype, see Geoffrey Wakeman, *Victorian Book Illustration: The Technical Revolution* (Detroit: Gale Research Co., 1973), pp. 95–98.

28. This pictorial plagiarism can also be seen in an "original drawing" of the Birthplace by James Pyne that appeared in Charles Knight's biography of Shakespeare, which was actually based on a sketch made by Henry Edridge. Charles Knight, *William Shakspere: A Biography*. Revised and augmented (London: J. S. Virtue and Co., 1865), p. 32.

29. Hollingshead, "A Startling Confession," p. 139.

30. Mackenzie Bell, "Shakespeare at Stratford-on-Avon," *The Poems of Mackenzie Bell* (London: James Clarke and Co., 1909), p. 41.

31. Caroline Arscott, "Victorian Development and Images of the Past," *The Imagined Past: History and Nostalgia*, ed. Christopher Shaw and Malcolm Chase (Manchester: Manchester University Press, 1989), pp. 58–60.

32. Michael Hunter, ed., *Preserving the Past: The Rise of Heritage in Modern Britain* (Gloucestershire: Alan Sutton, 1996), p. 5.

33. Shaw and Chase, eds., *The Imagined Past: History and Nostalgia*, p. 4.

34. Shaw and Chase, eds., *The Imagined Past: History and Nostalgia*, p. 4.

Chapter 1. The Birth of "Shakespeare"

1. [Francis Lloyd], "Hoax of the Shakspeare Birth-House; and Relic Trade at Stratford-on-Avon. By a Warwickshire Man," *Bentley's Miscellany*, 23 (March 1848): 286–87.

2. "Shakspere's House, Stratford-upon-Avon," *Reynolds's Miscellany of Romance, General Literature, Science, and Art* 18:453 (March 1857): 105.

3. "Men and Places," *Chambers's Journal of Popular Literature, Science, and Art*, 6 October 1888, 626.

4. Nicola J. Watson, *The Literary Tourist: Readers and Places in Romantic and Victorian Britain* (Basingstoke: Palgrave Macmillan, 2006).

5. Michel Foucault, "What Is an Author?" in *Language, Counter-Memory, Practice: Selected Essays and Interviews*, ed. Donald F. Bouchard, trans. Donald F. Bouchard and Sherry Simon (Oxford: Basil Blackwell, 1977), p. 122.

6. William Dugdale, *The Antiquities of Warwickshire Illustrated; From records, leiger books, manuscripts, charters, evidences, tombes and armes: beautified with maps, prospects and portraictures* (London: Thomas Warren, 1656), p. 523.

7. Samuel Winter, plan of Stratford on Avon. In the collection of the Shakespeare Birthplace Trust, Stratford-upon-Avon.

8. For discussions of Garrick's Jubilee, see Christian Deelman, *The Great Shakespeare Jubilee* (London: Michael Joseph, 1964), Johanne M. Stochholm, *Garrick's Folly: The Shakespeare Jubilee of 1769 at Stratford and Drury Lane* (London: Methuen, 1964), Levi Fox, *A Splendid Occasion: The Stratford Jubilee of 1769*, Dugdale Society Occasional Papers no. 20 (Oxford: printed for the Dugdale Society by Vivian Ridler, 1973).

9. Nicola J. Watson, "Shakespeare on the Tourist Trail," in *The Cambridge Companion to Shakespeare and Popular Culture*, ed. Robert Shaughnessy (Cambridge: Cambridge University Press, 2007), p. 205.

10. F. E. Halliday, *The Cult of Shakespeare* (London: Gerald Duckworth, 1957), p. 67. See also Deelman, *The Great Shakespeare Jubilee*, p. 21. The designation of this room has an interesting history: labeled the "birthroom" by Garrick, it became known as the "First Bedchamber" when the house was refurbished in 2000 and was referred to as "Shakespeare's birthroom" (in quotation marks) in the official guidebook to the Shakespeare properties published in 2009.

11. "When dying clouds contend with growing light." William Shakespeare, *The Third Part of King Henry the Sixth* 2.5.2, *The Complete Works of Shakespeare*, ed. Peter Alexander (London: Collins, 1951).

12. Deelman, *The Great Shakespeare Jubilee*, pp. 188–89.

13. This is described by Samuel Ireland in *Picturesque Views on the Upper, or Warwickshire Avon, from its Source at Naseby to its Junction with the Severn at Tewkesbury: With Observations on the Public Buildings, and other Works of Art in its Vicinity* (London: R. Faulder, 1795), p. 223.

14. David Garrick, "The Mulberry Tree," in *The Jubilee Concert: or, The Warwickshire Lad. Being a Collection of Songs Performed at the Jubilee, in Honour of Shakespear, at Stratford upon Avon, and at the Theatre Royal, Drury-Lane* (London, 1769).

15. Qtd. in Ivor Brown and George Fearon, *Amazing Monument: A Short History of the Shakespeare Industry* (London: William Heinemann, 1939), p. 85.

16. Brown and Fearon, *Amazing Monument*, p. 87.

17. Brown and Fearon, *Amazing Monument*, p. 77. The first biographer of Garrick, Thomas Davies, comments that the lower-class Stratford locals, who viewed Garrick as a magician, saw the rain as the vengeance of heaven for their engagement in activities such as exhibitions, fireworks, and masquerades. Thomas Davies, *Memoirs of the Life of David*

Garrick, Esq. interspersed with characters and anecdotes of his theatrical contemporaries. The whole forming a history of the stage, which includes a period of thirty-six years, vol. II (London: printed for the author, 1780), pp. 226–27.

18. Qtd. in Brown and Fearon, *Amazing Monument*, p. 92.

19. Thomas Davies calls Stratford a "rude and uncivilized spot." There is a sense of relief in his account of the Jubilee when the events transfer from Stratford to London. Davies, *Memoirs of the Life of David Garrick*, pp. 227–28.

20. The performance is described by Arthur Murphy in *The Life of David Garrick, Esq.*, vol. II (London: J. Wright, 1801), p. 72.

21. David Garrick, "Ode on Dedicating a Building—and Erecting a Statue to Shakespeare, at Stratford Upon Avon," in Murphy, *The Life of David Garrick*, p. 316.

22. See, for example, George Romney's paintings *The Infant Shakespeare Attended by Nature and the Passions* (c. 1791–92) and *The Infant Shakespeare Nursed by Tragedy and Comedy* (1790).

23. W. T. Moncrieff, *Excursion to Stratford upon Avon: With Historical and Descriptive Notices of the Town, Church, Shakspeare's House, and other Remarkable Buildings; Together with a Compendious Life of Shakspeare, Being by far more complete than any hitherto published. Copious Extracts from The Shakspearian Album; Account of the Far-Famed Jubilee; Catalogue of the Shakspeare Relics; With the Controversy on their Authenticity, And an Analysis of the Proceedings of the Proposed National Monument to the Memory of the Immortal Bard* (Leamington: Elliston, 1824), p. 16.

24. F. W. Fairholt, unpublished autograph account of his visit to Shakespeare's Birthplace, 29 August 1839. In the collection of the Folger Shakespeare Library, Washington, D.C.

25. Walter Savage Landor, "The Sale of Shakespeare's House. To the Editor of The Examiner," *Examiner*, 24 July 1847.

26. For more information on this painting, see William L. Pressly, *A Catalogue of Paintings in the Folger Shakespeare Library* (New Haven: Yale University Press, 1993), pp. 349–52.

27. Charles LaPorte, "The Bard, The Bible, and the Victorian Shakespeare Question," *ELH* 74 (2007): 609–28. For the blurring of the secular and religious in the development of the cult of Shakespeare worship, see Péter Dávidházi, *The Romantic Cult of Shakespeare: Literary Reception in Anthropological Perspective* (Basingstoke: Macmillan, 1998).

28. Qtd. in C.V.G. [Charles Vaughan Grinfield], *A Pilgrimage to Stratford-upon-Avon, The Birthplace of Shakspeare* (London: Longman, Brown and Co.; Coventry: John Merridew, 1850), p. 28.

29. See John R. Gillis, *Youth and History: Tradition and Change in European Age Relations, 1770–Present* (New York: Academic Press, 1981).

30. Washington Irving, *The Sketch Book of Geoffrey Crayon, Gent.*, ed. Haskell Springer, in *The Complete Works of Washington Irving*, ed. Richard Dilworth Rust, vol. 8 (1819–20; Boston: Twayne, 1978), p. 210.

31. Irving, *The Sketch Book*, p. 210.

32. Leigh Cliffe, *The Pilgrim of Avon* (London: Simpkin and Marshall; Stratford-upon-Avon: J. Ward, 1836), p. iii.

33. [Peter Cunningham], "A Fine Day at Stratford-upon-Avon," *Fraser's Magazine for Town and Country* (November 1844): 505.

34. Cliffe, *The Pilgrim of Avon*, pp. 17–18.

35. Charles Whibley, "The Limits of Biography," *Nineteenth Century: A Monthly Review* 41:241 (March 1897): 433.

36. S. Schoenbaum, *Shakespeare's Lives* (Oxford: Clarendon, 1970), p. 383.

37. Schoenbaum, *Shakespeare's Lives*, p. 383. Popular fictional accounts of the life of Shakespeare included the novels about his youth written by Robert Folkestone Williams between 1838 and 1844, Emma Severn's *Anne Hathaway; Or, Shakspeare in Love* (1845), Henry Curling's *The Forest Youth: Or, Shakspere as he Lived* (1853), and *The Merry Wags of Warwickshire. Or the Early Days of Shakspere* (1854).

38. Walter Bagehot, "Shakespeare," *Prospective Review* 9 (1853): 401. This article was published in 1901 as *Shakespeare the Man*.

39. C. Roach Smith, *Remarks on Shakespeare, his Birth-Place, etc. Suggested by a Visit to Stratford-upon-Avon, in the Autumn of 1868* (London, 1868–69), p. 1.

40. "Notes Drawn on the Avon Bank for General Circulation," *London Society* 5:30 (May 1864): 414.

41. See, for example, an article in *Fraser's Magazine*, where Shakespeare and his works are read in the light of the Warwickshire countryside, dialect and belief in fairies. J.W., "Shakspeare and His Native County," *Fraser's Magazine for Town and Country* (October 1856): 446–56.

42. Charles Knight, "Advertisement," *William Shakspere; A Biography* (London: C. Knight and Co., 1843).

43. Knight, *William Shakspere*, pp. 111–12.

44. Charles Knight, *Passages of a Working Life During Half a Century: With a Prelude of Early Reminiscences*, vol. 2 (London: Bradbury and Evans, 1864), p. 303.

45. Ireland, *Picturesque Views on the Upper, or Warwickshire Avon*, facing p. 189.

46. J. M. Jephson, *Shakespere: His Birthplace, Home, and Grave: A Pilgrimage to Stratford-on-Avon in the Autumn of 1863* (London: Lovell Reeve, 1864), p. 37.

47. *A Shakespeare Memorial* (London: S. O. Beeton, 1864), p. 2.

48. [John Dick], *Here and There in England; Including a Pilgrimage to Stratford-upon-Avon* (London: John Russell Smith, 1871), pp. 172–73.

49. See, for example, Shaw's *The Tourist's Picturesque Guide to Leamington and the Surrounding District* (London: Simpkin, Marshall and Co., 1872).

50. Catherine Belsey, *Why Shakespeare?* (Basingstoke: Palgrave Macmillan, 2007), p. 17.

51. Knight, *William Shakspere*, pp. 111–15.

52. Charles Wordsworth, *Man's Excellency A Cause of Praise and Thankfulness to God. A Sermon Preached at Stratford-Upon-Avon on Sunday, April 24, 1864* (London: Smith, Elder & Co., 1864), p. 14.

53. Wordsworth, *Man's Excellency*, p. 25.

54. Wordsworth, *Man's Excellency*, p. 20.

55. Wordsworth, *Man's Excellency*, p. 15.

56. C. W. Frederickson, "To the Editor," in J. F. and W. W. Sabin, *Shakespeare's Home; Visited and Described by Washington Irving and F. W. Fairholt . . . With Etchings by J. F. and W. W. Sabin* (New York: J. Sabin and Sons, 1877), p. 2.

57. Nathaniel Hawthorne, *The English Notebooks 1853–1856*, ed. Thomas Woodson and Bill Ellis, in *The Centenary Edition of the Works of Nathaniel Hawthorne*, vol. 21 (Columbus: Ohio State University Press, 1997), p. 199.

58. Nathaniel Hawthorne, *Our Old Home: A Series of English Sketches*, in *The Centenary Edition of the Works of Nathaniel Hawthorne*, vol. 5 (Columbus: Ohio State University Press, 1970), p. 97.

59. Harriet Beecher Stowe, *Sunny Memories of Foreign Lands* (London: Sampson Low, Son and Co., 1854), p. 148.

60. Stowe, *Sunny Memories*, pp. 149, 150.

61. While unidentified, the signature on this image seems to be that of Thomas Brooks, who painted a number of Shakespearean scenes throughout his career, including *Shakespeare Before Sir Thomas Lucy* (1855) and *The Courtship of Shakespeare* (1857). Brooks was also well known for his genre scenes of mothers and children. *The Courtship of Shakespeare* was painted in Anne Hathaway's cottage, so it is possible that Brooks painted the image of Mary Arden in the Birthplace itself. The attention to the detail of the room would certainly suggest this.

62. George H. Calvert, *Shakespeare: A Biographic Aesthetic Study* (Boston: Lee and Shepard, 1879), p. 9.

63. See, for example, Harriet Beecher Stowe, who regards Anne Hathaway as a "rustic beauty, entirely incapable either of appreciating or adapting herself to that wide and wonderful mind in its full development." Stowe, *Sunny Memories*, p. 155.

64. James Leon Williams, *The Home and Haunts of Shakespeare* (London: Sampson Low, Marston and Co., 1892), section II.

65. Emma Marshall, *Shakespeare and his Birthplace* (London: E. Nister, 1890).

66. Stowe, *Sunny Memories*, p. 149.

67. Charles Knight described the Shakespeares as "frugal and orderly in all their household arrangements." Knight, *Passages of a Working Life*, p. 299.

68. Gaston Bachelard, *The Poetics of Space*, trans. Maria Jolas (1958; Boston: Beacon Press, 1964).

69. Harald Hendrix, ed., *Writers' Houses and the Making of Memory* (New York: Routledge, 2008).

70. Pierre Nora, *Realms of Memory*, trans. Arthur Goldhammer, vol. 1 (1992; New York: Columbia University Press, 1996).

71. Nora, *Realms of Memory*, p. 7.

72. Mary Elizabeth Braddon, *Asphodel: A Novel*, vol. 2 (Leipzig: Bernhard Tauchnitz, 1881), pp. 41–42. *Asphodel* was originally serialized in *All the Year Round* between July 1880 and March 1881.

73. C. M. Ingleby, *Shakespeare's Bones: the proposal to disinter them, considered in relation to their possible bearing on his portraiture: illustrated by instances of visits of the living to the dead* (London: Trübner and Co, 1883).

74. Sigmund Freud, "Address Delivered in the Goethe House at Frankfurt," in *The Standard Edition of the Complete Psychological Works of Sigmund Freud*, trans. James Strachey, vol. 21 (London: Hogarth Press and the Institute of Psycho-Analysis, 1964), p. 212.

75. Hawthorne, *The English Notebooks*, p. 200.

76. Hawthorne, *Our Old Home*, p. 100.

77. John R. Wise, *Shakspere: His Birthplace and Its Neighbourhood* (London: Smith, Elder and Co., 1861), p. 1.

78. Wise, *Shakspere*, p. 2.

79. For a discussion of this story in the light of James's participation in the homes and haunts tradition, see Alison Booth, "The Real Right Place of Henry James: Homes and Haunts," *Henry James Review* 25:3 (Fall 2004): 216–27.

80. Henry James, "The Birthplace," *The Better Sort* (London: Methuen, 1903), p. 216.

81. Timothy Stevens, "John Thomas," *Oxford Dictionary of National Biography*, http://www.oxforddnb.com.

82. Sidney Lee, "The Commemoration of Shakespeare," *Nineteenth Century and After: A Monthly Review* 57:338 (April 1905): 586.

83. Qtd. in Lee, "The Commemoration of Shakespeare," p. 585. For more on Mathews's proposal and its failure, see Louis Marder, *His Exits and His Entrances: The Story of Shakespeare's Reputation* (London: John Murray, 1963), pp. 34–36.

84. Victor Hugo, *William Shakespeare*, trans. A. Baillot (London: Hurst and Blackett, 1864), p. 307.

85. For a description of this statue, see "Colossal Monument to Shakspeare," *Art-Journal* (August 1854): 260.

86. "Colossal Monument to Shakspeare," p. 260.

87. From John Milton, "On Shakespear," *Poems* (1632). In the early years of the twentieth century when the idea of a Shakespeare monument was once again discussed, Alfred Austin, the Poet Laureate, engaged with Milton's verse, asking "Why should we lodge in marble or in bronze / Spirits more vast than earth, or sea, or sky?" His answer, predictably, was that "Gods for themselves are monuments enough." Alfred Austin, "A Shakespeare Memorial," *Sacred and Profane Love, and other Poems* (London: Macmillan, 1908).

88. Robert E. Hunter, *Shakespeare and Stratford-upon-Avon, A "Chronicle of the Time:" Comprising the Salient Facts and Traditions, Biographical, Topographical, and Historical, Connected with the Poet and his Birth-Place; Together with a Full Record of the Tercentenary Celebration* (London: Whittaker and Co.; Stratford: Edward Adams, 1864), p. 97.

89. Qtd. in Hunter, *Shakespeare and Stratford-upon-Avon*, p. 98.

90. John Ruskin to E. S. Dallas, 10 February 1864, *Letters of Ruskin, The Works of John Ruskin*, ed. E. T. Cook and Alexander Wedderburn, vol. 36 (London: George Allen, 1903–12), p. 466.

91. Ruskin to E. S. Dallas, p. 466.

92. Anthony Trollope to Kate Field, 11 April 1878, *The Letters of Anthony Trollope*, ed. N. John Hall, vol. 2 (Stanford: Stanford University Press, 1983), p. 770.

93. *Illustrated London News*, 11 July 1863, p. 30.

94. "Shakespearean Monuments," *The Times*, 20 January 1864, p. 6.

95. *Illustrated London News*, 30 April 1864, p. 422.

96. *Illustrated London News*, 30 April 1864, p. 422. These nationalist politics took a different turn when the meeting on Primrose Hill became a protest about Giuseppe Garibaldi, a prominent figure in the unification of Italy, who had unexpectedly cut short his visit to England that morning in a way that looked as if he had been expelled. See Richard Foulkes, *The Shakespeare Tercentenary of 1864* (London: Society for Theatre Research, 1984), pp. 43–44.

97. *Illustrated London News*, 30 April 1864, p. 422.

98. Hunter, *Shakespeare and Stratford-upon-Avon*, pp. 95–96.

99. Lee, "The Commemoration of Shakespeare," p. 588.

100. William Howitt, *Homes and Haunts of the Most Eminent British Poets*, vol. 1 (London: Richard Bentley, 1847), p. 48.

101. Douglas Jerrold, "Shakespeare's House. (1847)," in *The Wit and Opinions of Douglas Jerrold. Collected and Arranged by his Son, Blanchard Jerrold* (London: W. Kent and Co., 1859), p. 240.

Chapter 2. Bidding for the Bard

1. "Surrey Zoological Gardens," *Illustrated London News*, 31 July 1847, p. 78.

2. Poster for Surrey Zoological Gardens, in Theodosius Purland, *Boke of Scraps Relating to Shakspere his House* (title page dated 14 September 1847; printed half-title, 1857). Unpublished scrapbook. In the collection of the Shakespeare Birthplace Trust, Stratford-upon-Avon.

3. Poster for Surrey Zoological Gardens.

4. Ivor Brown and George Fearon, *Amazing Monument: A Short History of the Shakespeare Industry* (London: William Heinemann, 1939).

5. Barbara Hodgdon, *The Shakespeare Trade: Performances and Appropriations* (Philadelphia: University of Pennsylvania Press, 1998), p. 191.

6. Douglas Jerrold, "Shakespeare's House. (1847.)," in *The Wit and Opinions of Douglas Jerrold. Collected and Arranged by his Son, Blanchard Jerrold* (London: W. Kent and Co., 1859), p. 241.

7. [Francis Lloyd], "Hoax of the Shakspeare Birth-House; and Relic Trade at Stratford-on-Avon," *Bentley's Miscellany* 23 (March 1848): 283.

8. Figures for Admissions to Shakespeare's Birthplace. In the collection of the Shakespeare Birthplace Trust, Stratford-upon-Avon.

9. Purland, *Boke of Scraps*.

10. *Art-Union*, 1 September 1847, p. 355. I have not been able to locate an 1845 edition of Fairholt's book, but it is mentioned in the preface to Samuel Neil, *The Home of Shakespeare described by Samuel Neil and illustrated in thirty-three engravings by the late F. W. Fairholt* (Warwick: Henry T. Cooke and Son, 1871).

11. "Our Library Table," *Athenaeum*, 7 August 1847, p. 837.

12. Purland, *Boke of Scraps*.

13. Purland, *Boke of Scraps*.

14. "Shakspeare's House," *The Times*, 20 July 1847, p. 8. The anxiety about the Birthplace turning into a "common show" continued into the twentieth century. One journalist, writing in 1903, complained that the guide showing visitors around the house "imparts even to the room in which Shakespeare was born the appearance of a peepshow." [Charles Whibley], "Musings Without Method," *Blackwood's Edinburgh Magazine* 174 (September 1903): 385.

15. [Thomas Kibble Hervey], "Our Weekly Gossip," *Athenaeum*, 28 August 1847, p. 914.

16. John Stuart Mill describes the reasons for this crisis in *Principles of Political Economy with Some of their Applications to Social Philosophy*, Book III (1848; London: Longmans, Green and Co., 1900), p. 320.

17. Frederick Engels, "The Commercial Crisis in England.—The Chartist Movement.—Ireland," Karl Marx and Frederick Engels, *Collected Works*, vol. 6 (London: Lawrence and Wishart, 1976), p. 307. First published in *La Réforme* 26 October 1847.

18. J. O. Halliwell, *Collectanea Respecting the Birth-Place of Shakespeare at Stratford-on-Avon, Copied from the Manuscript Collections of the Late R. B. Wheler. With a few additions by J. O. Halliwell* (1862; London: Thomas Richards, 1865), p. 25.

19. Charles Knight, *William Shakspere; A Biography* (London: C. Knight and Co., 1843), p. 31.

20. "Shakspeare's Birthday," *The Times*, 25 April 1846, p. 7.

21. "Shakspeare's House," *The Times*, 26 April 1847, p. 8.

22. For Dickens's involvement with the campaign, see Harland Nelson, "Dickens and the Shakespeare Birthplace Trust: 'What a Jolly Summer!'" in *A Humanist's Legacy: Essays in Honor of John Christian Bale* ed. Dennis M. Jones (Decorah, Iowa: Luther College, 1990), pp. 72–80.

23. "A Warwickshire Man to the Editor of *The Times*," *The Times*, 11 September 1847, p. 6.

24. "Shakspeare's House," *The Times*, 20 July 1847, p. 8.

25. "Sale of Shakespere's House," *Illustrated London News*, 25 September 1847, p. 208.

26. "Sale of Shakspeare's House," *Morning Chronicle*, 17 September 1847.

27. Levi Fox, *The Shakespeare Birthplace Trust: A Personal Memoir* (Norwich: Shakespeare Birthplace Trust in association with Jarrold Publishing, 1997), p. 8.

28. "A Prologue Written for the Occasion by Mr. Charles Knight, and Spoken by Mr. Phelps," in *The Shakespeare Night, in Aid of the Fund for the Purchase and Preservation of Shakespeare's House. Tuesday 7 December 1847, at the Royal Italian Opera, Covent Garden*, p. 8.

29. *Daily News*, 27 August 1847.

30. [Thomas Kibble Hervey], "Our Weekly Gossip," *Athenaeum*, 24 July 1847, p. 791.

31. *Daily News*, 27 August 1847.

32. *Daily News*, 27 August 1847.

33. Harriet Martineau, "Shakespere's House.—To The People," *Manchester Times and Gazette*, 3 August 1847.

34. Douglas Jerrold, "Shakespeare's Home Preserved to the People," in *The Wit and Opinions of Douglas Jerrold*, p. 243.

35. *The Times*, 21 July 1847, p. 5.

36. "Shakspere's House," *Musical World* 22:33 (August 1847): 524.

37. [Thomas Kibble Hervey], "Shakspeare's House," *Athenaeum*, 7 August 1847, p. 840.

38. "The House Where Shakspeare Was Born," *Sharpe's London Magazine*, 4 September 1847, pp. 302–3.

39. *Royal Leamington Spa Courier and Warwickshire Standard*, 31 July 1847.

40. [Hervey], "Shakspeare's House," p. 840.

41. "The Birth-place of Shakspeare," *Athenaeum*, 17 July 1847, p. 769.

42. [Hervey], "Shakspeare's House," p. 840.

43. "The Birth-place of Shakspere," *Morning Herald*. Reprinted in the *Glasgow Herald*, 2 August 1847.

44. [Douglas Jerrold], "Shakspeare's House," *Punch, or the London Charivari* 12, 29 May 1847, p. 220.

45. [Hervey], "Shakspeare's House" p. 840. A similar concern was expressed when an appeal was made to purchase the gardens of New Place in 1861: there was the danger, *The Times* warned, that the gardens would be destroyed and a "'Shakspeare-crescent' of the red

brick of Warwickshire erected on the site." "Shakspeare's Garden," *The Times*, 21 October 1861, p. 4.

46. Letter to Theodosius Purland, *Boke of Scraps*.

47. The so-called "Poet of Moses" was something of a celebrity in the period. The *Man in the Moon* jocularly referred to him as "the Tennyson of tailors—the Monckton Milnes of the Minories—the Patmore of puffers—the Babington Macaulay of bad manufactures." "Homes and Haunts of the British Poets," *Man in the Moon* 1, no. 4 (April 1846): 242.

48. *Shakspere Newspaper*, no. 1 (London, 1847), p. 8.

49. Louis Marder, "The Birthplace Auction—1847," *The Shakespeare Newsletter* 15, no. 4 (September 1965): 32.

50. Purland, *Boke of Scraps*.

51. "The Drama," *Daily News*, 27 August 1847.

52. Purland, *Boke of Scraps*.

53. [Percival Leigh], "A Fast Man's Opinions on Shakspeare," *Punch, or the London Charivari* 13, 21 August 1847, p. 64.

54. "The Dwellings of Genius," *Illustrated London News*, 21 August 1847.

55. "The Dwellings of Genius."

56. *Royal Leamington Spa Courier and Warwickshire Standard*, 31 July 1847. This was reprinted from the *Literary Gazette*.

57. Walter Savage Landor, "The Sale of Shakespeare's House. To the Editor of The *Examiner*," *Examiner*, 24 July 1847.

58. "Letter to the Editor from 'An Admirer of Shakespeare,'" *Royal Leamington Spa Courier and Warwickshire Standard*, 9 September 1847.

59. J. G. Jackson to Theodosius Purland, *Boke of Scraps*.

60. "Letter to the Editor from 'An Admirer of Shakespeare,'" *Royal Leamington Spa Courier*.

61. [Hervey], "Shakspeare's House," p. 840.

62. [Thomas Kibble Hervey], "Our Weekly Gossip," *Athenaeum*, 28 August 1847, p. 914.

63. This opinion was expressed at the initial meeting of the London committee. Purland, *Boke of Scraps*.

64. "Shakspeare's House," *Daily News*, 27 August 1847.

65. "Shakspere's House," *Musical World*, p. 524.

66. "The Dwellings of Genius," *Illustrated London News*, 21 August 1847.

67. Halliwell adopted the name "Phillipps," his wife's family name, when his father-in-law died in 1872. Throughout this book, I have used "Halliwell" for his publications prior to 1872 and "Halliwell-Phillipps" for publications after this date.

68. Martineau, "Shakespere's House.—To The People."

69. [Hervey], "Our Weekly Gossip," *Athenaeum*, 31 July 1847, p. 817.

70. [Hervey], "Our Weekly Gossip," p. 817.

71. See Andrew Murphy, *Shakespeare for the People: Working-Class Readers, 1800–1900* (Cambridge: Cambridge University Press, 2008).

72. *Evening Sun*, 17 September 1847.

73. [Douglas Jerrold], "Purchase of Shakspeare's House," *Punch, or the London Charivari* 13, 23 October 1847, p. 152.

74. [Jerrold], "Purchase of Shakspeare's House."

75. The house was actually referred to as a "national monument" in the first meeting of the London Committee on 26 August, *London Committee for the Purchase of Shakespeare's House* (London, 1847), p. 3.

76. "The Shakspeare Album," *Bentley's Miscellany* 21 (1847): 50.

77. "Shakespere's House; and Thou Art Gone From My Gaze" (E. M. Hodges, n.d.). In the collection of the Folger Shakespeare Library, Washington, D.C.

78. "Shakspeare's House," *The Times*, 15 June 1847, p. 7.

79. "Speculators on the Alert," *Shakspere Newspaper* no. 1 (London, 1847), p. 3.

80. *The Times*, 21 July 1847, p. 5.

81. Yvonne Shafer describes George Jones's theatrical career in America, where audiences laughed and threw pennies at him during performances. Yvonne Shafer, *The Changing American Theatre: Mainstream and Marginal, Past and Present* (Valencia: University of Valencia, 2002), pp. 19–27.

82. Leigh Cliffe, *The Pilgrim of Avon* (London: Simpkin and Marshall; Stratford-upon-Avon: J. Ward, 1836), dedication. Many library catalogues indentify "Leigh Cliffe" as the pseudonym for George Jones himself.

83. [Tom Taylor], "Shakspeare and Mr. George Jones," *Punch, or the London Charivari* 13, 4 September 1847, p. 84.

84. Purland, *Boke of Scraps*.

85. Advertisement for George Jones's People's Committee (1847), Purland, *Boke of Scraps*.

86. Advertisement for George Jones's People's Committee. Some of these objectives were later taken up by the organizers of the tercentenary celebrations.

87. This idea was also mooted in several magazines. See "Shakspeare's House," *Punch, or the London Charivari* 12, 29 May 1847, p. 220. It was at the centre of the campaign in the *Athenaeum* from the outset. See [Thomas Kibble Hervey], "Our Weekly Gossip," *Athenaeum*, 24 July 1847, p. 791.

88. Dickens organized and performed in plays to this end in 1848. He wrote to Miss Burdett Coutts that "I have set my heart on seeing Sheridan Knowles installed at Stratford on Avon, as the Curator of Shakespeare's House—the only and the best resource I know for him." Charles Dickens to Miss Burdett Coutts, 24 May 1848, *The Letters of Charles Dickens*, ed. Graham Storey and K. J. Fielding, vol. 5 (Oxford: Clarendon, 1981), p. 317. For more on Dickens and the campaign to purchase the Birthplace, see Nelson, "Dickens and the Shakespeare Birthplace Trust."

89. "Shakspeare's Habitation," *Daily News*, 14 August 1847.

90. *Daily News*, 27 August 1847.

91. Qtd. in Henry C. Shelley, *Shakespeare and Stratford* (London: Simpkin, Marshall Hamilton, Kent and Co., 1913), p. 43.

92. [Douglas Jerrold], "Shakspeare's House.—Mulberry College," *Punch, or the London Charivari* 13, 2 October 1847, p. 121.

93. Ironically, Shafer has argued that in America, Jones was vilified for being pro-European and Anti-American. Shafer, *The Changing American Theatre*, p. 24.

94. [Jerrold], "Shakspeare's House.—Mulberry college."

95. J. Stirling Coyne, *This House to Be Sold; (The Property of the Late William Shakspeare.) Inquire Within.* (London: National Acting Drama Office, 1847), p. 4.

96. Richard W. Schoch, *Not Shakespeare: Bardolatry and Burlesque in the Nineteenth Century* (Cambridge: Cambridge: University Press, 2002), p. 78.

97. Unidentified newspaper cutting, 18 February 1865, Purland, *Boke of Scraps*.

98. Unidentified newspaper cutting, Purland, *Boke of Scraps*.

99. *Annual Register* 1847, p. 124. These rumors certainly stuck. At the end of the century, stories were still told of how the Birthplace might have been shipped to the United States. When one young lady visits Stratford in 1892, she writes a poem referring to this legend: "Some say they'd like it in the States,—but all of us say "Nay," –/We'll keep it safe in England here for all that they may say!" Lucy M. Reynolds, "The Three Merry Pilgrims," *Shakespeariana*. Unpublished scrapbook. In the collection of the Shakespeare Birthplace Trust, Stratford-upon-Avon.

100. "Shakspeare's House to be Sold," *Punch, or the London Charivari* 12, 15 May 1847, p. 198.

101. "The House Where Shakspeare Was Born," p. 303.

102. "The House Where Shakspeare Was Born," p. 303.

103. P. T. Barnum, *The Autobiography of P. T. Barnum: Clerk, Merchant, Editor, and Showman* (London: Ward and Lock, 1855), pp. 104–6.

104. Albert Smith, "A Go-A-Head Day with Barnum," *Bentley's Miscellany* 21 (1847): 525–26.

105. Smith, "A Go-A-Head Day with Barnum," p. 524.

106. The fact that Haydon had noted the attendance of 133 (and a half) visitors at his own exhibition and 12,000 visitors to see Tom Thumb was recorded at the coroner's inquest into his death. "Melancholy Suicide of the Late Mr. R. B. Haydon," *The Times*, 25 June 1846, p. 8.

107. [Thomas Kibble Hervey], "Our Weekly Gossip," *Athenaeum*, 18 September 1847, p. 985.

108. "Interesting Sale," *Man in the Moon* 2, no. 10 (October 1847): 206. The replica birthplace did not, in fact, disappear after the auction. Nathaniel Hawthorne reported seeing one at the Liverpool Zoological Gardens. Nathaniel Hawthorne, *The English Notebooks 1853–1856*, ed. Thomas Woodson and Bill Ellis, in *The Centenary Edition of the Works of Nathaniel Hawthorne*, vol. 21 (Columbus: Ohio State University Press, 1997), p. 198. In the celebrations for the tercentenary in 1864, a replica house was installed in the central transept of the Crystal Palace. See *Illustrated London News*, 30 April 1864, p. 423.

Chapter 3. Bringing Down the House

1. *Particulars of Shakspeare's House at Stratford on Avon, For Sale by Auction by Mr. Robins* (London, 1847).

2. This plan is mentioned in Harriet Martineau, "Shakspere's House.—To The People," *Manchester Times and Gazette*, 3 August 1847.

3. W. O. Hunt, Correspondence: Hunt Papers, May 1856–January 1860. In the collection of the Shakespeare Birthplace Trust, Stratford-upon-Avon.

4. W. O. Hunt, Correspondence: Hunt Papers.

5. This information about John Shakespear appears in his obituary in the *Royal Leamington Spa Courier and Warwickshire Standard*, 3 July 1858.

6. "Stratford-on-Avon. Vice-Chancellor's Court," *Royal Leamington Spa Courier and Warwickshire Standard*, 24 December 1859.

7. "Stratford-Upon-Avon. Court of Chancery," *Royal Leamington Spa Courier and Warwickshire Standard*, 4 February 1860.

8. Levi Fox, *The Shakespeare Birthplace Trust: A Personal Memoir* (Norwich: Shakespeare Birthplace Trust in association with Jarrold Publishing, 1997), p. 13.

9. Shakspearean Club, *A Circular Relative to the Restoration and Preservation of the Bust and Monument of Shakspeare* (Stratford upon Avon, 1835).

10. Douglas Jerrold, "Shakespeare's House. (1847.)," in *The Wit and Opinions of Douglas Jerrold. Collected and Arranged by his Son, Blanchard Jerrold* (London: W. Kent and Co., 1859), p. 242.

11. John Payne Collier to Dr. Thomas Thomson, 9 September 1856. In the collection of the Shakespeare Birthplace Trust, Stratford-upon-Avon.

12. John Payne Collier to Thomas Thomson, 17 October 1856. In the collection of the Shakespeare Birthplace Trust, Stratford-upon-Avon.

13. John Ruskin, *The Seven Lamps of Architecture, The Works of John Ruskin*, ed. E. T. Cook and Alexander Wedderburn, vol. 8 (London: George Allen, 1903–12), p. 242.

14. Ruskin, *The Seven Lamps of Architecture*, p. 244.

15. John Ruskin, "A Letter to Count Zorzi," *Works*, vol. 24, pp. 410–11.

16. Rev. W. Heather, *Church Restoration: A Paper Read Before the Herefordshire Philosophical, Literary, and Antiquarian Society, November 15 1864* (Hereford: R. Redman, 1864), p. 8.

17. Heather, *Church Restoration*, p. 9.

18. John Ruskin, *The Opening of the Crystal Palace Considered in Some of its Relations to the Prospects of Art, Works*, vol. 12, p. 431.

19. For more on the Society for the Protection of Ancient Buildings, see Chris Miele, "The First Conservation Militants: William Morris and the Society for the Protection of Ancient Buildings," in *Preserving the Past: The Rise of Heritage in Modern Britain*, ed. Michael Hunter (Gloucestershire: Alan Sutton, 1996), pp. 17–37.

20. William Morris, "Society for the Protection of Ancient Monuments," *Athenaeum*, 10 March 1877, p. 326.

21. Report to Dr. Thomson from Edward M. Barry, 29 June 1857. In the collection of the Shakespeare Birthplace Trust, Stratford-upon-Avon.

22. Report to Dr. Thomson from Edward M. Barry.

23. W. O. Hunt, Correspondence: Hunt Papers.

24. [John Payne Collier], "Our Weekly Gosssip," *Athenaeum*, 14 March 1857, p. 345.

25. Thirty years later, in his lectures to the Royal Academy, Barry observed that "between maintenance and restoration the boundary is narrow." Edward M. Barry, *Lectures on Architecture Delivered at the Royal Academy*, ed. Alfred Barry (London: John Murray, 1881), p. 147.

26. *Royal Leamington Spa Courier and Warwickshire Standard*, 7 March 1857.

27. The Cambridge Camden Society, also known as the Ecclesiological Society, was founded in 1839 by undergraduates at Cambridge University and went on to boast over seven hundred members, Pugin himself sharing the society's taste for the Gothic.

28. Edward Barry was compelled to write to the *Athenaeum* when it erroneously referred to the report on the Birthplace as having been written by Charles Barry. [William Hepworth Dixon], "Our Weekly Gossip," *Athenaeum*, 25 July 1857, p. 945.

29. W. O. Hunt to C. F. Skirrow, solicitor to Mr John Shakespear, 14 June 1856. In the collection of the Shakespeare Birthplace Trust, Stratford-upon-Avon.

30. *Royal Leamington Spa Courier and Warwickshire Standard*, 3 October 1857.

31. W. O. Hunt to Lord Carlisle. Unpublished draft letter. In the collection of the Shakespeare Birthplace Trust, Stratford-upon-Avon.

32. *Gentleman's Magazine*, July 1769, p. 345.

33. For information about Richard Greene, see Arthur Sherbo, "Richard Greene," *Oxford Dictionary of National Biography*, http://www.oxforddnb.com.

34. Lucy Peltz, "Aestheticizing the Ancestral City: Antiquarianism, Topography and the Representation of London in the Long Eighteenth Century," in *The Metropolis and Its Image: Constructing Identities for London, c. 1750–1950*, ed. Dana Arnold (Oxford: Blackwell, 1999), p. 12.

35. This interest in prints is in evidence in Greene's correspondence. See Levi Fox, ed., *Correspondence of the Reverend Joseph Greene* (London: HMSO, 1965), pp. 17–18.

36. Peltz identifies this imaginary perspective as a convention. Peltz, "Aestheticizing the Ancestral City," p. 16.

37. W. O. Hunt, Correspondence: Hunt Papers.

38. Minutes of the proceedings of the Trustees acting under a Deed of Gift by John Shakespear, 6 July 1857. In the collection of the Shakespeare Birthplace Trust, Stratford-upon-Avon.

39. *Royal Leamington Spa Courier and Warwickshire Standard*, 24 April 1858.

40. Fox, *The Shakespeare Birthplace Trust*, p. 51.

41. "Covent-Garden Theatre. Shakspeare's House," *The Times*, 8 December 1847, p. 5.

42. J. P. Collier to Thomas Thomson, 17 October 1856. In the collection of the Shakespeare Birthplace Trust, Stratford-upon-Avon.

43. This preoccupation is in evidence as far back as Samuel Ireland, who muses on the fact that John Shakespeare is a gentleman yet lives in a humble home. Samuel Ireland, *Picturesque Views on the Upper, or Warwickshire Avon, from its Source at Naseby to its Junction with the Severn at Tewkesbury: with Observations on the Public Buildings, and other Works of Art in its Vicinity* (London: R. Faulder, 1795), pp. 194–95.

44. Charles Knight, *Passages of a Working Life During Half a Century: With a Prelude of Early Reminiscences*, vol. 2 (London: Bradbury and Evans, 1864), pp. 298–99.

45. Victor Hugo, *William Shakespeare*, trans. A. Baillot (London: Hurst and Blackett, 1864), p. 8.

46. *A Shakspeare Memorial* (London: S. O. Beeton, 1864), p. 3.

47. *Royal Leamington Spa Courier and Warwickshire Standard*, 20 October 1860.

48. Nathaniel Hawthorne, *The English Notebooks, 1853–1856*, ed. Thomas Woodson and Bill Ellis, in *The Centenary Edition of the Works of Nathaniel Hawthorne*, vol. 21 (Columbus: Ohio State University Press, 1997), p. 199.

49. Grace Greenwood, "Notes from Over the Sea," *New York Times*, 30 June 1875.

50. John R. Wise, *Shakspere: His Birthplace and Its Neighbourhood* (London: Smith, Elder and Co., 1861), p. 15.

51. Wise, *Shakspere*, p. 15.

52. Ireland, *Picturesque Views on the Upper, or Warwickshire Avon*, facing p. 189.

53. [Thomas Kibble Hervey], "Our Weekly Gossip," *Athenaeum*, 31 July 1847, p. 817.

54. Detailed information about this work is given in *Edward Gibbs Holtom of Stratford*. In the collection of the Shakespeare Birthplace Trust, Stratford-upon-Avon.

55. The idea of converting the house into a museum had been raised following the auction of the house. On 1 October 1847, the *Art-Union* suggested that such a museum

should contain every edition of Shakespeare's works and engravings of the plays. *Art-Union*, 1 October 1847, p. 361.

56. Mary Elizabeth Braddon, *Asphodel: A Novel*, vol. 3 (Leipzig: Bernhard Tauchnitz, 1881), p. 24.

57. James Hakewill, *An Attempt to Determine the Exact Character of Elizabethan Architecture* (London, 1835), p. 20.

58. George Fildes, *On Elizabethan Furniture* (London: F. W. Calder, 1844), p. 5.

59. Robert Blatchford, *Merrie England* (London: Clarion Office, 1894).

60. Blatchford, *Merrie England*, pp. 43–44.

61. F. W. Fairholt, unpublished autograph account of his visit to Shakespeare's Birthplace, 29 August 1839. In the collection of the Folger Shakespeare Library, Washington, D.C.

62. W. O. Hunt to the Earl of Warwick, 12 February 1857. In the collection of the Shakespeare Birthplace Trust, Stratford-upon-Avon.

63. Earl of Warwick to W. O. Hunt, 19 February 1857. In the collection of the Shakespeare Birthplace Trust, Stratford-upon-Avon.

64. Edward Gibbs, report to the trustees under the deed and gift of John Shakespear, 23 April 1858. In the collection of the Shakespeare Birthplace Trust, Stratford-upon-Avon.

65. *Royal Leamington Spa Courier and Warwickshire Standard*, 6 April 1861.

66. This house was built for Robert Dudley, earl of Leicester, around 1575 and originally called Leicester House. It was inherited by the earl of Essex and renamed in 1588 and demolished in the 1670s.

67. *Royal Leamington Spa Courier and Warwickshire Standard*, 12 October 1861.

68. Unpublished letter, 26 June 1861. In the collection of the Shakespeare Birthplace Trust, Stratford-upon-Avon.

69. J. M. Jephson, *Shakespere: His Birthplace, Home, and Grave. A Pilgrimage to Stratford-on-Avon in the Autumn of 1863* (London: Lovell Reeve, 1864), pp. 36–37.

70. [Charles Whibley], "Musings Without Method," *Blackwood's Edinburgh Magazine* 174 (September 1903): 383.

71. See, for example, Samuel Neil, who praises the care and accuracy of the restoration in *The Home of Shakespeare described by Samuel Neil and illustrated in thirty-three engravings by the late F. W. Fairholt* (Warwick: Henry T. Cooke and Son, 1871), p. 17.

72. *A Shakspeare Memorial*, p. 15.

73. J. O. Halliwell, preface, R. B. Wheler, *An Historical Account of the Birth-Place of Shakespeare . . . reprinted from the edition of 1824 with a few prefatory remarks by J. O. Halliwell* (Stratford-on-Avon, 1863), pp. 6–7.

74. *Royal Leamington Spa Courier and Warwickshire Standard*, 9 March 1861.

75. "His Birth, Birthplace, Life, and Writings," *Chambers's Journal of Popular Literature, Science and Art*, Shakspeare Tercentenary Number (23 April 1864): 3.

76. Edgar Flower, *Shakespeare's Birthplace. Important Statement by Mr. Edgar Flower.* Reprinted from the *Stratford-upon-Avon Herald*, 8 May 1903, p. 1.

77. Flower, *Shakespeare's Birthplace*, p. 2.

78. An account of these events can be found in Sidney Lee, *The Alleged Vandalism at Stratford-on-Avon* (London: Archibald Constable, 1903).

79. Joseph Hill qtd. in Marie Corelli, ed., *The Avon Star: A Literary Manual for the Stratford-on-Avon Season of 1903* (Stratford-on-Avon: A. J. Stanley, 1903), p. 77.

80. Lee, *The Alleged Vandalism at Stratford-on-Avon*, pp. 14–15.

81. See Joseph Hill qtd. in Corelli, *The Avon Star*, p. 78.

82. See Flower, *Shakespeare's Birthplace*, p. 3.

83. Theodore Martin to Trustees of Shakespeare's Birthplace, 28 October 1904. Reprinted from the *Stratford-upon-Avon Herald*. In the collection of the Shakespeare Birthplace Trust, Stratford-upon-Avon.

84. Marie Corelli, "An Open Letter to the Mayor and Corporation of Stratford-on-Avon," *The Avon Star*, p. 140.

85. Lee, *The Alleged Vandalism at Stratford-on-Avon*, p. 19.

86. Corelli, "The Spoliation of Henley Street," *The Avon Star*, p. 74.

87. Marie Corelli, qtd. in Lee, *The Alleged Vandalism at Stratford-on-Avon*, p. 45.

88. Qtd. in Lee, *The Alleged Vandalism at Stratford-on-Avon*, p. 46 n2.

89. Lady Colin Campbell qtd. in Corelli, "The Spoliation of Henley Street," *The Avon Star*, p. 76.

90. Richard T. Randle Milliken, qtd. in Corelli, "The Spoliation of Henley Street," *The Avon Star*, p. 88.

91. Qtd. in Lee, *The Alleged Vandalism at Stratford-on-Avon*, p. 28.

92. Corelli qtd. in Lee, *The Alleged Vandalism at Stratford-on-Avon*, pp. 18–19.

93. Corelli, "Murmurings of the Avon," *The Avon Star*, p. 4.

94. J. Harvey Bloom, ed., "The Gurglings of the Brook," *The Errors of the Avon Star: Another Literary Manual for the Stratford-on-Avon Season of 1903* (Stratford-on-Avon: John Morgan, 1903), p. 4. This house is now the home of the Shakespeare Institute.

95. Bloom, "The Gurglings of the Brook," *The Errors of the Avon Star*, p. 5.

96. Milliken qtd. in Corelli, "The Spoliation of Henley Street," *The Avon Star*, p. 88.

97. *Vanity Fair* qtd. in Corelli, "The Spoliation of Henley Street," *The Avon Star*, p. 70.

98. Lee, *The Alleged Vandalism at Stratford-on-Avon*, p. 16.

99. Lee, *The Alleged Vandalism at Stratford-on-Avon*, p. 17.

100. Lee, *The Alleged Vandalism at Stratford-on-Avon*, p. 32.

101. Likewise, one local guide book published in 1860 had nothing but praise for the demolition of Middle Row, a cluster of buildings in Bridge Street, which allowed for the opening up of the prospect on the approach to the town from the Clopton Bridge, calling it the "greatest improvement which has taken place in this town for many years." *Hand Book for Visitors to Stratford-upon-Avon* (Stratford: Edward Adams, 1860), p. 7.

102. "His Birth, Birthplace, Life, and Writings," *Chambers's Journal of Popular Literature, Science and Art*, Shakspeare Tercentenary Number (23 April 1864): 3. This view is also expressed in *From St. Paul's in London, to St. Peter's in Manchester, on Foot and Alone; with Rough Notes of What I saw, Heard, and Thought, What I Liked and Disliked on the Way. Being a Diary of Eleven-Days' Travel, Through Seven English Counties, in the Leafy Month of June, 1876.* Unpublished diary of a walking tour. In the collection of the Shakespeare Birthplace Trust, Stratford-upon-Avon.

103. As F. E. Halliday writes, "the present Elizabethan appearance of Stratford is a post-festival phenomenon." F. E. Halliday, *The Cult of Shakespeare* (London: Gerald Duckworth, 1957), p. 158.

104. Corelli, "The Spoliation of Henley Street," *The Avon Star*, p. 69.

105. Qtd. in "The Old Tudor House, Stratford-on-Avon, A. J. Stanley, Proprietor" (Stratford-upon Avon, n.d.). Advertisement. In the collection of the Shakespeare Birthplace Trust Stratford-upon-Avon.

106. Corelli, "Murmurings of the Avon," *The Avon Star*, p. 4.

107. Corelli, "Murmurings of the Avon," *The Avon Star*, p. 5.

108. Lee, *The Alleged Vandalism at Stratford-on-Avon*, p. 38.

109. Lee, *The Alleged Vandalism at Stratford-on-Avon*, p. 64.

110. *New Liberal Review* qtd. in Lee, *The Alleged Vandalism at Stratford-on-Avon*, p. 47.

111. Corelli, "The Spoliation of Henley Street," *The Avon Star*, p. 71.

112. Albert H. Smyth, "The Alleged Vandalism at Shakespeare's Home" (Philadelphia, 1903).

113. Corelli, "Murmurings of the Avon," *The Avon Star*, p. 8.

114. Bloom, "The Gurglings of the Brook," *The Errors of the Avon Star*, p. 3.

Chapter 4. Real Estate?

1. *Royal Leamington Spa Courier and Warwickshire Standard*, 24 April 1858.

2. Edward M. Barry, *Lectures on Architecture Delivered at the Royal Academy*, ed. Alfred Barry (London: John Murray, 1881), p. 154.

3. This is how the Birthplace was recently described on the Shakespeare Birthplace Trust website. http://houses.shakespeare.org.uk/shakespeares-Birthplace.html.

4. J. Hollingshead, "A Startling Confession," *Train: A First-Class Magazine* 4:21 (September 1857): 143.

5. George Wilkins, "Shakspeare's House. To the Editor of the *Examiner*," *Examiner*, 7 August 1847.

6. "The Shakspeare Night at Covent Garden Theatre," *Man in the Moon* 3:13 (December 1847): 26.

7. "Sale of Shakespere's House," *Illustrated London News*, 18 September 1847, pp. 189–90.

8. For a discussion of the problems of authenticity in the space of the museum, see David Phillips, *Exhibiting Authenticity* (Manchester: Manchester University Press, 1997).

9. S. Schoenbaum, *Shakespeare's Lives* (Oxford: Clarendon, 1970), p. 408.

10. J. O. Halliwell, preface, in R. B. Wheler, *An Historical Account of the Birth-Place of Shakespeare . . . reprinted from the edition of 1824 with a few prefatory remarks by J. O. Halliwell* (Stratford-on-Avon, 1863), pp. 11–13.

11. Jordan's drawing of Brook House appeared in the *Gentleman's Magazine* in April 1808 and a retaliatory letter by Wheler was published in August 1808.

12. John Jordan qtd. in J. O. Halliwell, *Collectanea Respecting the Birth-Place of Shakespeare at Stratford-on-Avon, Copied from the Manuscript Collections of the Late R. B. Wheler. With a few additions by J. O. Halliwell* (1862; London: Thomas Richards, 1865), p. 5.

13. Halliwell, *Collectanea*, p. 5.

14. John Jordan, *Original Memoirs and Historical Accounts of the Families of Shakespeare and Hart, deduced from an early period and continued down to this present year 1790. With drawings of their dwelling-houses and coats of arms*, ed. J. O. Halliwell (London, 1865).

15. See Schoenbaum, *Shakespeare's Lives*, pp. 122–24.

16. Halliwell, preface, Wheler, *An Historical Account*, p. 3.

17. This evidence is outlined in Halliwell, preface, Wheler, *An Historical Account*, p. 5.

18. Halliwell, preface, Wheler, *An Historical Account*, p. 6.

19. Halliwell, preface, Wheler, *An Historical Account*, p. 7.

20. *Scrapboxes of J. O. Halliwell-Phillipps*. In the collection of the Folger Shakespeare Library, Washington, D.C.

21. Sidney Lee, *A Life of William Shakespeare* (1898; London: Smith, Elder, and Co., 1908), p. 9.

22. There are numerous sketches of the cellar in the Halliwell-Phillipps collection in the Folger Shakespeare Library, Washington, D.C.

23. Schoenbaum, *Shakespeare's Lives*, p. 405.

24. This evidence is revealed in Joseph Hunter, *New Illustrations of the Life, Studies, and Writings of Shakespeare*, vol. 1 (London: J. B. Nichols and Son, 1845), p. 18.

25. Schoenbaum, *Shakespeare's Lives*, p. 346.

26. Stephen Orgel, *Imagining Shakespeare: A History of Texts and Visions* (Basingstoke: Palgrave Macmillan, 2003), p. 79.

27. Sigmund Freud, "Address Delivered in the Goethe House at Frankfurt," in *The Standard Edition of the Complete Psychological Works of Sigmund Freud* trans. James Strachey, vol. 21 (London: Hogarth Press and the Institute of Psycho-Analysis, 1964), p. 211.

28. Schoenbaum, *Shakespeare's Lives*, pp. 192–93. This story is also recounted in James Payn's novel, *The Talk of the Town*.

29. John R. Wise, *Shakspere: His Birthplace and Its Neighbourhood* (London: Smith, Elder and Co., 1861), p. 14.

30. C. Roach Smith, *Remarks on Shakespeare, His Birth-Place, etc. Suggested by a Visit to Stratford-upon-Avon, in the Autumn of 1868* (London, 1868–69), p. 2.

31. Halliwell, preface, Wheler, *An Historical Account*, p. 4.

32. R. B. Wheler, *A Guide to Stratford-upon-Avon* (Stratford: J. Ward; London: Longman, 1814), p. 11.

33. J. O. Halliwell-Phillipps, *New Evidences in Confirmation of the Traditional Recognition of Shakespeare's Birth-Room, A.D 1769–A.D. 1777* (Brighton, 1888), p. 5.

34. Halliwell-Phillipps, *New Evidences*, p. 19.

35. Washington Irving, *The Sketch Book of Geoffrey Crayon, Gent.*, ed. Haskell Springer, in *The Complete Works of Washington Irving*, ed. Richard Dilworth Rust, vol. 8 (1819–20; Boston: Twayne, 1978), pp. 210–11.

36. Irving, *The Sketch Book*, p. 212.

37. Charles Knight, *William Shakspere: A Biography*, revised and augmented edition (London: J. S. Virtue and Co., 1865), pp. 31–33.

38. Rev. George Wilkins qtd. in [Francis Lloyd], "Hoax of the Shakspeare Birth-House; and Relic Trade at Stratford-on-Avon," *Bentley's Miscellany* 23 (March 1848): 287.

39. James Orchard Halliwell, *The Life of William Shakespeare* (London: John Russell Smith; Warwick: H. T. Cooke, 1848), pp. 38–39.

40. F. W. Fairholt, *The Home of Shakspere Illustrated and Described* (London: Chapman and Hall, 1847), p. 3.

41. Irving, *The Sketch Book*, p. 210.

42. Irving, *The Sketch Book*, p. 210.

43. Revealingly, William Henry Ireland's forgeries included his own Shakespearean "relics," such as a love letter to Anne Hathaway.

44. Samuel Ireland, *Picturesque Views on the Upper, or Warwickshire Avon, from its Source at Naseby to its Junction with the Severn at Tewkesbury: with Observations on the Public Buildings, and other Works of Art in its Vicinity* (London: R. Faulder, 1795), pp. 189–90.

45. Wheler, *An Historical Account*, pp. 18–19.

46. W. T. Moncrieff, *Excursion to Stratford upon Avon: With Historical and Descriptive Notices of the Town, Church, Shakspeare's House, and other Remarkable Buildings; Together with a Compendious Life of Shakspeare, Being by far more complete than any hitherto published. Copious Extracts from The Shakspearian Album; Account of the Far-Famed Jubilee; Catalogue of the Shakspeare Relics; With the Controversy on their Authenticity, And an Analysis of the Proceedings of the Proposed National Monument to the Memory of the Immortal Bard* (Leamington: Elliston, 1824), pp. 15–16. A visitor to the Birthplace in 1819 records other relics, including the glass out of which Shakespeare drank without rising in his last illness, his wife's shoe, his pencil case and his christening bowl. See Henry C. Shelley, *Shakespeare and Stratford* (London: Simpkin, Marshall Hamilton, Kent and Co., 1913), pp. 30–31.

47. Qtd. in Ivor Brown and George Fearon, *Amazing Monument: A Short History of the Shakespeare Industry* (London: William Heinemann, 1939), p. 151.

48. For an account of these disputes, see F. E. Halliday, *The Cult of Shakespeare* pp. 120–24.

49. Thomas Hart died, leaving the Birthplace to his son, John Shakespeare Hart, who let the house to Thomas and Mary Hornby. On the death of John Shakespeare Hart, the whole property was sold to Thomas Court. The Courts lived in the Swan and Maidenhead, while the Hornbys remained in the "Birthplace" (the butcher's shop) as tenants.

50. Qtd. in Halliday, *The Cult of Shakespeare*, p. 124.

51. [Lloyd], "Hoax of the Shakspeare Birth-House," p. 282.

52. [Lloyd], "Hoax of the Shakspeare Birth-House," p. 285.

53. [Lloyd], "Hoax of the Shakspeare Birth-House," p. 285.

54. "Shakspeare Packing up his Goods," *Man in the Moon* 2:9 (September 1847): 177.

55. *Particulars of Shakspeare's House at Stratford on Avon, For Sale by Auction by Mr Robins* (London, 1847), pp. 14–16.

56. Richard Savage and William Salt Brassington, eds., *Stratford-Upon-Avon From "The Sketch Book" of Washington Irving. With Notes and Original Illustrations* (Stratford-upon-Avon: Edward Fox, 1900), p. 115.

57. J. O. Halliwell-Phillipps, *A Brief Report on the Interchange of Books, Relics, &c., Between The New Place and The Birthplace Museum, and on the Re-Arrangement of The Library; Drawn up in Pursuance of Directions Given by the Trustees, May 5th, 1881. And Now Submitted to the Consideration of the Executive Committee* (Brighton, 1881), pp. 5–7.

58. Halliwell-Phillipps, *A Brief Report on the Interchange of Books*, p. 5.

59. J. Cuming Walters, "The Shakespeare Relics at Stratford," *The Times*, 8 September 1903, p. 5.

60. J. Cuming Walters, "Pseudo-Shakespeare Relics at Stratford," *The Times*, 18 September 1903, p. 8.

61. "The Visitors to Shakespeare's Birthplace," *Pall Mall Gazette*, 6 June 1889.

62. Grace Greenwood, "Notes from Over the Sea," *New York Times*, 30 June 1875.

63. Halliwell also believed that there was little doubt that this ring belonged to Shakespeare, arguing that he had lost it shortly before his death and in between the drafting and the execution of the will. This, he asserted, explained the last clause of the will, where the word "hand" was substituted for "seal" ("In witness whereof I have hereunto put my *hand* the daie and yeare first above written") as if Shakespeare had lost his ring seal. See *A Shakspeare Memorial* (London: S. O. Beeton, 1864), p. 16.

64. H. Snowden Ward, "Shakespeare Relics at Stratford," *The Times*, 23 September 1903, p. 6. Ward and his wife were responsible for the photographically illustrated book of Stratford, *Shakespeare's Town and Times*, published in 1896.

65. Joseph Skipsey qtd. in Walters, "The Shakespeare Relics at Stratford," p. 5.

66. Tony Tanner has pointed out James's own obsession with Shakespeare the man, while Andrea Zemgulys has argued that the story is critical of those doubters of the Birthplace, the skeptical American tourists, who sympathize with Gedge's position. Tony Tanner, "The Birthplace," *Henry James: The Shorter Fiction: Reassessments*, ed. N. H. Reeve (Basingstoke: Macmillan, 1997) p. 90. Andrea Zemgulys, "Henry James in a Victorian Crowd: 'The Birthplace' in Context," *Henry James Review* 29:3 (Fall 2008): 245–56.

67. Skipsey qtd. in Walters, "The Shakespeare Relics at Stratford," p. 5.

68. Elsewhere, Skipsey apparently complained that "the Birthplace itself was a matter of grave doubt." Qtd. in Ian Ousby, *The Englishman's England: Taste, Travel, and the Rise of Tourism* (Cambridge: Cambridge University Press, 1990), p. 55.

69. Robert Spence Watson, *Joseph Skipsey: His Life and Work* (London: T. Fisher Unwin, 1909), p. 74.

70. Ernest Rhys, *Everyman Remembers* (New York: Cosmopolitan Book Corp., 1931), p. 211.

71. Walters, "Pseudo-Shakespeare Relics at Stratford," p. 8.

72. Sidney Lee, "Shakespeare Relics at Stratford," *The Times*, 23 September 1903, p. 6.

73. Sanford R. Gifford to his father, 13 July 1855. Sanford Robinson Gifford Papers. Archives of American Art, Smithsonian Institution.

74. *A Shakspeare Memorial*, p. 2.

75. Underwood and Underwood, the main producer of stereographs from 1890 to 1910, had a series on Stratford, which included the Birthplace and its rooms. I am grateful to John Plunkett for this reference.

76. Artemus Ward [Charles Farrar Browne], *Artemus Ward in London, and Other Papers* (New York: G. W. Carleton and Co., 1867), p. 37.

77. Walter Benjamin, "The Work of Art in the Age of Mechanical Reproduction," *Illuminations*, ed. Hannah Arendt, trans. Harry Zohn (1955; London: Fontana, 1992), pp. 211–44.

78. Charles Knight, *Passages of a Working Life During Half a Century: With a Prelude of Early Reminiscences*, vol. 2 (London: Bradbury and Evans, 1864), p. 303.

79. F. W. Fairholt to R. B. Wheler, 28 July 1847. In the collection of the Shakespeare Birthplace Trust, Stratford-upon-Avon.

80. F. W. Fairholt to R. B. Wheler, 5 August 1847. In the collection of the Shakespeare Birthplace Trust, Stratford-upon-Avon.

81. Fairholt, *The Home of Shakspere*, p. 2.

82. "Reviews," *Art-Union*, 1 September 1847, p. 335.

83. Halliwell, *The Life of William Shakespeare*, pp. xiii–xiv.

84. "Shakespere and Stratford-upon-Avon," *Illustrated London News*, 18 September 1847, p. 179.

85. Justin H. McCarthy, "A Pilgrimage to Stratford-upon-Avon," *Belgravia: A London Magazine* 52:207 (January 1884): 349.

86. Halliwell, preface, Wheler, *An Historical Account*, p. 6.

87. *A Catalogue of Books, Pamphlets, Etc. Illustrating the Life and Writings of Shakespeare* (London: John Russell Smith, 1864), p. 35.

88. Roland Barthes, *Camera Lucida: Reflections on Photography*, trans. Richard Howard (1981; London: Vintage, 1993), p. 87. Carol Armstrong has recently argued that Barthes's analysis of photography comes closest to the Victorian sense of the genre. Carol Armstrong, *Scenes in a Library: Reading the Photograph in the Book, 1843–1875* (Cambridge, Mass.: MIT Press, 1998), pp. 5–17.

89. Barthes, *Camera Lucida*, p. 6.

90. Armstrong, *Scenes in a Library*, p. 167.

91. Armstrong, *Scenes in a Library*, p. 277.

92. Helen Groth, *Victorian Photography and Literary Nostalgia* (Oxford: Oxford University Press, 2003), p. 36.

93. [Elizabeth Eastlake], "Photography," *Quarterly Review* (April 1857): 466.

94. See, for example, Howard Staunton, *Memorials of Shakspeare* (London, 1864).

95. *A Collection of Pamphlets, Posters &c, Relating to the Shakespeare Tercentenary Festival at Stratford-upon-Avon*. In the collection of the British Library, London.

96. H. Snowden Ward and Catharine Weed Ward, *Shakespeare's Town and Times* (London: Dawbarn and Ward, 1896).

97. George Wood Clapp, *The Life and Work of James Leon Williams* (New York: Dental Digest, 1925), p. 250.

98. Clapp, *The Life and Work of James Leon Williams*, p. 250.

99. Horace Howard Furness, "Introduction," in James Leon Williams, *The Home and Haunts of Shakespeare*, section I (London: Sampson Low, Marston and Co., 1892), p. vii.

100. Jennifer Green-Lewis, *Framing the Victorians: Photography and the Culture of Realism* (Ithaca, N.Y.: Cornell University Press, 1996), p. 4.

101. *A Short Descriptive Guide to the East and West Junction Railway, Being the Shortest and Most Direct Route from London to Stratford-on-Avon via London and North Western Railway* (London: Macfarlane and Co., 1886), advertisement.

102. This regulation was amended in 1907 to include not only photographs but also sketches and paintings. Shakespeare Birthplace Trust, *Regulations for the Management of Shakespeare's Birthplace, &c., Trust, Comprising Shakespeare's Birthplace, Anne Hathaway's Cottage, and New Place* (Stratford-upon-Avon, 1904). In the collection of the Shakespeare Birthplace Trust, Stratford-upon-Avon. I am grateful to Helen Rees for this reference.

Chapter 5. Eight Things to Do in Stratford-upon-Avon

1. [Douglas Jerrold], "Royal Visit to Stratford on Avon," *Punch, or the London Charivari*, 8 May 1847, p. 188.

2. [Jerrold], "Royal Visit to Stratford on Avon," p. 188.

3. [Jerrold], "Royal Visit to Stratford on Avon," p. 188.

4. See Richard Foulkes, who outlines Victoria's involvement with the theater, in *Performing Shakespeare in the Age of Empire* (Cambridge: Cambridge University Press, 2002).

5. Nicholas Fogg, ed., *Victorian Stratford-upon-Avon in Old Photographs* (Gloucestershire: Alan Sutton, 1990), pp. 10–11.

6. P. T. Barnum, *The Autobiography of P. T. Barnum: Clerk, Merchant, Editor, and Showman* (London: Ward and Lock, 1855), p. 104.

7. Winter's "bright little volumes are in the hands of the majority of pilgrims." [F. T. Graham], "Graeme's Wanderings. Stratford-on-Avon," article from the *Metropolitan*

mounted in a booklet with a letter from F. T. Graham of Chicago to Richard Savage, 22 October 1896. In the collection of the Shakespeare Birthplace Trust, Stratford-upon-Avon. Winter himself is recorded as a donor to the Shakespeare Memorial Theatre, library and picture gallery for the year ending 31 March 1892.

8. [Peter Cunningham], "A Fine Day at Stratford-upon-Avon," *Fraser's Magazine for Town and Country* (November 1844): 505–6.

9. "Shakspere's House, Stratford-upon-Avon," *Reynolds's Miscellany of Romance, General Literature, Science, and Art* 18:453 (March 1857): 105–6.

10. W. W. Fenn, "The Pilgrims of the Avon—and Their Devotions," *London Society* 67:400 (April 1895): 357–72.

11. John R. Wise, *Shakspere: His Birthplace and Its Neighbourhood* (London: Smith, Elder and Co., 1861), p. 15.

12. Abel Heywood, *A Guide to Stratford-on-Avon; Its Church and Vicinity* (Manchester: Abel Heywood and Son; London: F. Pitman, 1892), p. 7.

13. Letter from F. W. Fairholt to James Orchard Halliwell, in J. O. Halliwell, *A New Boke About Shakespeare and Stratford-on-Avon* (London, 1850).

14. *Illustrated London News*, 14 August 1847, p. 106.

15. "The Birthplace of Shakespeare," *The Times*, 26 October 1868, p. 5.

16. *Guide to Stratford-upon-Avon* (Stratford-upon-Avon: John Smith, n.d.).

17. George May, *A Guide to the Birth-Town of Shakspere and the Poet's Rural Haunts* (Evesham: George May, 1847), p. 15.

18. Artemus Ward [Charles Farrar Browne], *Artemus Ward in London, and Other Papers* (New York: G. W. Carleton and Co., 1867), p. 40.

19. Nathaniel Hawthorne, *The English Notebooks, 1853–1856*, ed. Thomas Woodson and Bill Ellis, in *The Centenary Edition of the Works of Nathaniel Hawthorne*, vol. 21 (Columbus: Ohio State University Press, 1997), p. 201.

20. *A Brief Guide for Strangers Who Are Visiting Stratford-on-Avon for the First Time, and Who Are Staying in the Town Merely for a Few Hours* (London, 1869).

21. Justin H. McCarthy, "A Pilgrimage to Stratford-upon-Avon," *Belgravia: A London Magazine* 52:207 (January 1884): 349.

22. Balz Engler, "Stratford and the Canonization of Shakespeare," *European Journal of English Studies* 1:3 (1997): 354–66.

23. "By the Avon in April," *All the Year Round*, 22 April 1893, p. 367.

24. "Current History of Literary and Scientific Events," *Rose, the Shamrock and the Thistle* 5:25 (May 1864): 106.

25. *Particulars of Shakspeare's House at Stratford on Avon, For Sale by Auction by Mr Robins* (London, 1847).

26. See C.V.G. [Charles Vaughan Grinfield], *A Pilgrimage to Stratford-upon-Avon, The Birthplace of Shakspeare* (London: Longman, Brown and Co.; Coventry: John Merridew, 1850). A letter in a copy of this book in the collection of the Shakespeare Birthplace Trust states that one of the booksellers in Leamington asked Grinfield to write a guide to Stratford.

27. "The Stratford Railway." In the collection of the Shakespeare Birthplace Trust, Stratford-upon-Avon.

28. "Commemoration of the Birth of Shakspeare," *Illustrated London News*, 7 May 1853, p. 345.

29. "Commemoration of the Birth of Shakspeare," p. 345.

30. Harriet Beecher Stowe, *Sunny Memories of Foreign Lands* (London: Sampson Low, Son and Co., 1854), p. 145.

31. [Peter Cunningham], "Another Day at Stratford," *Fraser's Magazine for Town and Country* (December 1844): 719.

32. [Cunningham], "Another Day at Stratford," p. 719.

33. *A Short Descriptive Guide to the East and West Junction Railway, Being the Shortest and Most Direct Route from London to Stratford-on-Avon via London and North Western Railway* (London: Macfarlane and Co., 1886), p. 5.

34. "The Visitors to Shakespeare's Birthplace," *Pall Mall Gazette*, 6 June 1889.

35. C. [Mortimer Collins], "Towns on the Avon," *Temple Bar* (August 1864): 202.

36. Richmal Crompton, "William and the Lost Tourist," *William–The Conqueror*, illustrated by Thomas Henry (London: George Newnes, 1926), pp. 78–96. I am grateful to Paul Young for this reference.

37. J. O. Halliwell-Phillipps, "A Letter Addressed to the Executive Committee of the Trustees of the Birth-Place of Shakespeare at Stratford-on-Avon, 31st May, 1880," (Brighton, 1880), pp. 6–7.

38. George Arbuthnot, *Morgan's Penny Guide. Two Hours in Stratford-on-Avon. An Itinerarium, By the Rev. G. Arbuthnot* (Stratford-on-Avon: J. Morgan, 1889).

39. C.V.G., *A Pilgrimage to Stratford-upon-Avon*, p. 7.

40. *The Hand Book for Visitors to Stratford-upon-Avon* (Stratford-upon-Avon: F. & E. Ward, 1851), p. 40.

41. Edward Daniel Clarke, *A Tour Through the South of England, Wales, and Part of Ireland, made during the summer of 1791* (London, 1793), pp. 380–82.

42. William Howitt, *Visits to Remarkable Places: Old Halls, Battle-Fields, and Scenes Illustrative of Striking Passages in English History and Poetry* (1840; London: Longman, Brown, Green, Longmans and Roberts, 1856), p. 91.

43. See *A Short and Plain Pocket Guide with Map, to Stratford-on-Avon* (Stratford-on-Avon: W. Stanton, 1894) and Heywood, *Guide to Stratford-on-Avon*, p. 8.

44. Howitt, *Visits to Remarkable Places* p. 92.

45. "Anne Hathaway's Cottage," *All the Year Round*, 30 April 1892, p. 418.

46. *Ward and Lock's Illustrated Guide to and Popular History of Stratford-upon-Avon* (London: Ward and Lock, 1881), pp. 21–22.

47. Mary Elizabeth Braddon, *Asphodel: A Novel*, vol. 2 (Leipzig: Bernhard Tauchnitz, 1881), p. 51.

48. Howitt, *Visits to Remarkable Places*, pp. 98–103.

49. Sanford R. Gifford to his father, 13 July 1855. Sanford Robinson Gifford papers. Archives of American Art, Smithsonian Institution.

50. Charles Holte Bracebridge, *Shakespeare No Deerstealer, or, A short account of Fulbroke Park, near Stratford-on-Avon* (London: Harrison and Sons, 1862).

51. Arbuthnot, *Two Hours in Stratford-on-Avon*, pp. 6–7. Arbuthnot's personal commitment to the Temperance Movement is described in Freda Kitcher, *A Parson and His Parish: the Work of the Reverend George Arbuthnot Vicar of Stratford-on-Avon 1879–1908* (Wallingford: Gem Publishing, 2006), pp. 82–98. The vicar's comment in his guidebook that it was unfortunate that Shakespeare had not been a total abstainer was angrily rebuffed by Eric Mackay of the Falcon Hotel in Stratford, who wrote a letter to the

Stratford-upon-Avon Herald arguing that in the sixteenth century a man who did not drink was not considered a gentleman. Eric Mackay, "An Insult to Shakespeare. To the Editor of the *Stratford-upon-Avon Herald*," 29 May 1890.

52. *The Hand Book for Visitors to Stratford-upon-Avon* (Stratford-upon-Avon: F. & E. Ward, 1851), p. 33.

53. Whitefriars Club, London, printed program for a "Pilgrimage to Shakespeare's Country," 23 June 1900. In the collection of the Shakespeare Birthplace Trust, Stratford-upon-Avon.

54. See, for example, Heywood, *Guide to Stratford-on-Avon*, p. 8.

55. Lucy M. Reynolds, *Shakespeariana*. Unpublished scrapbook. In the collection of the Shakespeare Birthplace Trust, Stratford-upon-Avon.

56. J. M. Barrie, *My Lady Nicotine* (London: Hodder and Stoughton, 1890), p. 46. I am grateful to Leonée Ormond for this reference.

57. "From Stratford to London," *All the Year Round*, 9 April 1887, p. 279.

58. "Notes Drawn on the Avon Bank for General Circulation," *London Society* 5:30 (May 1864): 415.

59. "Shakspeare's House.—To the Editor," *Royal Leamington Spa Courier and Warwickshire Standard*, 19 March 1859.

60. "Shakspeare's Birthplace.—To the Editor of the *Leamington Courier*," *Royal Leamington Spa Courier and Warwickshire Standard*, 2 April 1859.

61. "Shakspeare's Birthplace.—To the Editor of the *Leamington Courier*."

62. Admission ticket to the Birthplace, dated 3 July 1897. In the collection of the Shakespeare Birthplace Trust, Stratford-Upon-Avon.

63. Hawthorne, *The English Notebooks*, p. 200.

64. J. Newman Hank to "Dear Sister Havenner," 6 September 1858. In the collection of the Shakespeare Birthplace Trust, Stratford-upon-Avon.

65. R. B. Wheler, *An Historical Account of the Birth-Place of Shakespeare . . . reprinted from the edition of 1824 with a few prefatory remarks by J. O. Halliwell* (Stratford-on-Avon, 1863).

66. Admission ticket to the Birthplace, dated 3 July 1897.

67. Henry James, "The Birthplace," *The Better Sort* (London: Methuen, 1903), p. 201.

68. James, "The Birthplace," p. 201.

69. William Winter, *Old Shrines and Ivy* (Edinburgh: David Douglas, 1892), p. 43.

70. Fanny D. Rowley, *Stratford-upon-Avon in the Seventies*, section 8, (c. 1950), p. 3. Unpublished manuscript. In the collection of the Shakespeare Birthplace Trust, Stratford-upon-Avon.

71. "From Stratford to London," p. 278.

72. Samuel Ireland, *Picturesque Views on the Upper, or Warwickshire Avon, from its Source at Naseby to its Junction with the Severn at Tewkesbury: with Observations on the Public Buildings, and other Works of Art in its Vicinity* (London: R. Faulder, 1795), p. 186.

73. F. W. Fairholt, unpublished autograph account of his visit to Shakespeare's Birthplace, 29 August 1839. In the collection of the Folger Shakespeare Library, Washington, D.C.

74. Fairholt, unpublished autograph account.

75. [Andrew Halliday], "Shakespeare-Mad," *All the Year Round*, 21 May 1864, p. 347.

76. [Halliday], "Shakespeare-Mad," p. 348.

77. F. W. Fairholt, *The Home of Shakspere Illustrated and Described* (London: Chapman and Hall, 1847), p. 8.

78. [Cunningham], "Another Day at Stratford," p. 718.

79. Leigh Cliffe, *The Pilgrim of Avon* (London: Simpkin and Marshall; Stratford-upon-Avon: J. Ward, 1836), p. 19n. Nathaniel Parker Willis, who visited Stratford in 1835, also seems to allude to Jones's sleepover at the Birthplace, recounting how the woman who showed him the house "commenced a long story of an American, who had lately taken the whim to sleep in Shakspeare's birth-chamber." Nathaniel Parker Willis, *Romance of Travel, Comprising Tales of Five Lands* (New York: S. Colman, 1840), p. 283.

80. Albert Smith, "A Go-Ahead Day with Barnum," *Bentley's Miscellany* 21 (1847): 525.

81. Hawthorne, *The English Notebooks*, p. 200.

82. Tony Tanner, "The Birthplace," *Henry James: The Shorter Fiction: Reassessments*, ed. N. H. Reeve (Basingstoke: Macmillan, 1997), p. 94n.

83. Shirley Foster, "Americans and Anti-Tourism," in *Literary Tourism and Nineteenth-Century Culture* ed. Nicola J. Watson (Basingstoke: Palgrave Macmillan, 2009), pp. 175–83.

84. Henry James, "In Warwickshire," *Portraits of Places* (London: Macmillan, 1883), p. 261.

85. Benjamin Robert Haydon, *The Autobiography and Memoirs of Benjamin Robert Haydon*, ed. Tom Taylor, vol. 2 (London: Peter Davies, 1926), p. 446.

86. [Halliday], "Shakespeare-Mad," p. 348.

87. Rowley, *Stratford-upon-Avon in the Seventies*, section 8, p. 4.

88. Report to Dr. Thomson from Edward M. Barry, 29 June 1857. In the collection of the Shakespeare Birthplace Trust, Stratford-upon-Avon.

89. "Shakespere and Stratford-upon-Avon," *Illustrated London News*, 18 September 1847, p. 11.

90. [Cunningham], "A Fine Day at Stratford-upon-Avon," p. 509.

91. [Cunningham], "A Fine Day at Stratford-upon-Avon," p. 509.

92. Sigmund Freud refers to this dunghill and its incompatibility with the idea of "civilization": "We do not think highly of the cultural level of an English country town in Shakespeare's time when we read that there was a big dung-heap in front of his father's house in Stratford." Sigmund Freud, "Civilization and its Discontents," *The Standard Edition of the Complete Psychological Works of Sigmund Freud*, trans. James Strachey, vol. 21 (London: Hogarth Press and the Institute of Psycho-Analysis, 1964), p. 93.

93. Justin H. McCarthy, "A Pilgrimage to Stratford-upon-Avon," *Belgravia: A London Magazine* (January 1884): 350.

94. [Charles Whibley], "Musings Without Method," *Blackwood's Edinburgh Magazine* 174 (September 1903): 384.

95. [Halliday], "Shakespeare-Mad," p. 349.

96. *Chambers's Journal of Popular Literature, Science and Art, Shakspeare Tercentenary Number*, 23 April 1864, p. 4.

97. Hugh Miller, *First Impressions of England and its People* (1847; Edinburgh: William P. Nimmo, 1873), pp. 230–31.

98. This "childish fancy" is referred to in Mary Elizabeth Braddon, *Asphodel: A Novel*, vol. 3 (Leipzig: Bernhard Tauchnitz, 1881), p. 25.

99. Nathaniel Hawthorne, *Our Old Home: A Series of English Sketches*, in *The Centenary Edition of the Works of Nathaniel Hawthorne*, vol. 5 (Columbus: Ohio State University Press, 1970), p. 98.

100. Robert E. Hunter, *Shakespeare and Stratford-upon-Avon, A "Chronicle of the Time": Comprising the Salient Facts and Traditions, Biographical, Topographical, and Historical, Connected with the Poet and his Birth-Place; Together with a Full Record of the Tercentenary Celebration* (London: Whittaker and Co., Stratford: Edward Adams, 1864), p. 68.

101. *Particulars of Shakspeare's House at Stratford on Avon, For Sale by Auction by Mr Robins* (London, 1847).

102. Willis, *Romance of Travel*, p. 282.

103. Braddon, *Asphodel*, vol. 3, p. 25

104. *From St Paul's in London, to St Peter's in Manchester, on Foot and Alone; with Rough Notes of What I saw, Heard, and Thought, What I Liked and Disliked on the Way. Being a Diary of Eleven-Days' Travel, Through Seven English Counties, in the Leafy Month of June, 1876.* Unpublished diary of a walking tour. In the collection of the Shakespeare Birthplace Trust, Stratford-upon-Avon.

105. *Chambers's Journal of Popular Literature, Science and Art, Shakspeare Tercentenary Number*, 23 April 1864, p. 4.

106. Alfred Tennyson to Emily Sellwood, c. 8 June 1840, *The Letters of Alfred Lord Tennyson* ed. Cecil Y. Lang and Edgar F. Shannon, Jr., vol. 1 (Oxford: Clarendon, 1982), p. 182.

107. Tennyson to Emily Sellwood, p. 182.

108. "The Visitors to Shakespeare's Birthplace," *Pall Mall Gazette*, 6 June 1889.

109. *Chambers's Journal of Popular Literature, Science and Art, Shakspeare Tercentenary Number*, 23 April 1864, p. 4.

110. [Cunningham], "Another Day at Stratford," p. 718.

111. [Cunningham], "Another Day at Stratford," p. 718.

112. Washington Irving, *The Sketch Book of Geoffrey Crayon, Gent.*, ed. Haskell Springer, in *The Complete Works of Washington Irving* ed. Richard Dilworth Rust, vol. 8 (1819–20; Boston: Twayne, 1978), p. 209.

113. Braddon, *Asphodel*, vol. 2, p. 39.

114. Allison Lockwood, *Passionate Pilgrims: The American Traveler in Great Britain, 1800–1914* (New York: Cornwall, 1981), p. 316.

115. Gifford to his father, 13 July 1855. Typescript copy of a letter. In the collection of the Shakespeare Birthplace Trust, Stratford-upon-Avon.

116. [Halliday], "Shakespeare-Mad," p. 350.

117. Gifford to his father, 13 July 1855.

118. Gifford to his father, 13 July 1855.

119. For an extensive account of American tourism in Britain during this period, see Lockwood, *Passionate Pilgrims*.

120. Willis, *Romance of Travel*, p. 283.

121. Thomas Carlyle, "The Hero as Poet. Dante: Shakspeare," *The Works of Thomas Carlyle*, vol. 1 (1840; London: Chesterfield Society, n.d.), p. 340.

122. Carlyle, "The Hero as Poet," p. 340.

123. *A Shakspeare Memorial* (London: S. O. Beeton, 1864), p. 2.

124. Carlyle commented that, faced with the question "Will you give up your Indian Empire or your Shakspeare?" the empire should go. Carlyle, "The Hero as Poet," p. 340.

125. Braddon, *Asphodel*, vol. 1, p. 213.

126. "Shakespeare's Home," *New York Times*, 21 December 1891.

127. Marie Corelli, ed., "Hints to American Trippers," *The Avon Star: A Literary Manual for the Stratford-on-Avon Season of 1903* (Stratford-on-Avon: A. J. Stanley, 1903), pp. 124–25.

128. Lucy M. Reynolds, "The Three Merry Pilgrims," *Shakespeariana*. Unpublished scrapbook. In the collection of the Shakespeare Birthplace Trust, Stratford-upon-Avon.

129. [Charles Whibley], "Musings Without Method," *Blackwood's Edinburgh Magazine* 174 (September 1903): 385.

130. In this way, the Americans were caught up in the practices that Stuart Hall has identified with stereotyping. According to Hall, power is not simply conceived in economic or physical terms, but as "the power to represent someone or something in a certain way—within a certain 'regime of representation.'" Stuart Hall, ed., *Representation: Cultural Representations and Signifying Practices* (London: Sage in association with the Open University, 1997), p. 259.

131. J. Harvey Bloom, ed., "Hints to American Trippers," *The Errors of the Avon Star: Another Literary Manual for the Stratford-on-Avon Season of 1903* (Stratford-on-Avon: John Morgan, 1903), pp. 33–34.

132. This affidavit, dated 14 October 1799, is in the collection of the Shakespeare Birthplace Trust, Stratford-upon-Avon.

133. Fairholt, *The Home of Shakspere*, p. 8.

134. Fairholt, *The Home of Shakspere*, p. 8.

135. Shakespeare Birthplace Trust, *Regulations for the Management of Shakespeare's Birthplace, &c., Trust, Comprising Shakespeare's Birthplace, Anne Hathaway's Cottage, and New Place* (Stratford-upon-Avon, 1904). In the collection of the Shakespeare Birthplace Trust, Stratford-upon-Avon.

136. George Gray Jr. to his mother, May 1844. In the collection of the Morgan Library and Museum, New York.

137. Howitt, *Visits to Remarkable Places*, p. 82.

138. Willis, *Romance of Travel*, p. 280.

139. Corelli, "Where to Buy Pretty Things in Stratford," *The Avon Star*, pp. 126–28.

140. Corelli, "Where to Buy Pretty Things in Stratford," p. 126.

141. These objects are in the collection of the Shakespeare Birthplace Trust, Stratford-upon-Avon.

142. J. Newman Hank to "Dear Sister Havenner," 6 September 1858. In the collection of the Shakespeare Birthplace Trust, Stratford-upon-Avon.

143. George Martin, "To G.I. at Stratford-on-Avon," *Marguerite; or, the Isle of Demons and Other Poems* (Montreal: Dawson Brothers, 1887), p. 279.

144. Henry James, "The Birthplace," *The Better Sort* (London: Methuen, 1903), p. 187.

Conclusion

1. Aaron Santesso, "The Birth of the Birthplace: Bread Street and Literary Tourism Before Stratford," *ELH* 71:2 (Summer 2004): 385, *passim*.

2. Gary Taylor, *Reinventing Shakespeare: A Cultural History from the Restoration to the Present* (London: Hogarth, 1990), p. 184.

3. As Andrew Murphy notes, Knight intended his "Stratford Shakespeare" (1854–56) for "The People." Andrew Murphy, *Shakespeare in Print: A History and Chronology of Shakespeare Publishing* (Cambridge: Cambridge University Press, 2003), p. 181.

4. Thomas Hall Caine, "The Novelist in Shakspeare," *New Review* 11:63 (August 1894): 121.

5. The engraving is after a painting by Edouard Hamman (1819–1888), a copy of which is in the Folger Shakespeare Library. The presence of all the family suggests that the setting is intended to be the Henley Street property since Shakespeare did not purchase New Place until 1597, a year after Hamnet's death. The imaginative re-creation of the scene, however, indicates that the artist was not overly concerned with historical accuracy. The *Eclectic* simply states that the picture shows "Shakespeare and his family at their home at Stratford-upon-Avon." [W. H. Bidwell], "Shakespeare and His Family: A Sketch by the Editor," *Eclectic Magazine of Foreign Literature, Science, and Art* (January 1866): 128.

6. [Bidwell], "Shakespeare and His Family," p. 128.

7. Thomas Bowdler, ed., *The Family Shakspeare, In Ten Volumes; in which nothing is added to the original text; but those words and expressions are omitted with cannot with propriety be read aloud in a family*, vol. I (London: Longman, Hurst, Rees, Orme, and Brown, 1818), p. x.

8. Mary Cowden Clarke, *The Girlhood of Shakespeare's Heroines; in a series of fifteen tales* (London: W. H. Smith and Son; Simpkin, Marshall and Co., 1850–52).

9. For a discussion of this phenomenon, see Georgianna Ziegler, "Accommodating the Virago: Nineteenth-Century Representations of Lady Macbeth," in *Shakespeare and Appropriation*, ed. Christy Desmet and Robert Sawyer (London: Routledge, 1999), pp. 119–41.

10. This appeared as an advertisement in *Punch* on 26 January 1889.

11. Lord Ronald Gower, "A Monument to Shakespeare," *Art Journal* (November 1881): 329.

12. Adrian Poole, *Shakespeare and the Victorians* (London: Thomson Learning, 2004), p. 78.

13. "Presentation of the Shakspeare Testimonial to Kossuth," *Illustrated London News*, 14 May 1853, pp. 373–74.

14. [G. H. Lewes], "Shakspeare's Critics: English and Foreign," *Edinburgh Review* 90:181 (July 1849): 39.

15. For the historical accuracy of the Victorian stage, see Poole, *Shakespeare and the Victorians*, pp. 24–25.

16. See Leslie Parris, ed., *The Pre-Raphaelites* (London: Tate Gallery, 1984), p. 98.

17. Jaques, "Modern Corruptions of Shakespeare's Text: A Letter to a Friend on the Subject of 'Cassell's Illustrated Shakespeare'" (London: printed for private circulation, 1869), pp. 3–4.

18. Jaques, "Modern Corruptions of Shakespeare's Text," p. 5.

19. Charles Knight, *Old Lamps, or New? A Plea for the Original Editions of the Text of Shakspere: Forming an Introductory Notice to the Stratford Shakspere, Edited by Charles Knight* (London, 1853).

20. Knight, *Old Lamps, or New?* p. xxxiii.

21. See, for example, C. M. Ingleby, who set out his views on legitimate emendation in *The Still Lion: An Essay Towards the Restoration of Shakespeare's Text*, first published in Germany in 1867.

22. Knight, *Old Lamps, or New?* p. xxxix.

23. Knight, *Old Lamps, or New?* p. xli.

24. F. J. Furnivall qtd. in *New Shakspere Society's Transactions* (London: Trübner and Co., 1874), p. vi. Charles Cattermole (1832–1900) depicted Shakespeare's return to Stratford, with Henley Street as the setting, as one of the final images in his *Life of Shakespeare*, a series of thirteen watercolors, which were frequently reproduced as prints and postcards in the period.

25. See Richard Foulkes, *Performing Shakespeare in the Age of Empire* (Cambridge: Cambridge University Press, 2002), pp. 7–10.

26. "The Man in the Street," *Funny Folks*, 1 March 1879, p. 66.

27. A. K. Chesterton, *Brave Enterprise: A History of the Shakespeare Memorial Theatre Stratford-upon-Avon* (London: J. Miles and Co., 1934), p. 10.

28. Mary Elizabeth Lucy, *Mistress of Charlecote: The Memoirs of Mary Elizabeth Lucy, 1803–1889*, introduced by Alice Fairfax-Lucy, ed. Elsie Burch Donald (London: Orion Books, 1983), p. 155.

29. W. B. Yeats, "At Stratford-on-Avon," *Ideas of Good and Evil* (London: A. H. Bullen, 1903), p. 146.

30. S. Schoenbaum, *Shakespeare's Lives* (Oxford: Clarendon, 1970), p. 554.

31. Maurizio Ascari, "Pilgrims and Heretics at the Shrine: Reassessing the History of Shakespeare's Birthplace," in *The Cultural Reconstruction of Places*, ed. Ástráður Eysteinsson (Reykjavík: University of Iceland Press, 2006), pp. 11–21.

32. David Phillips, *Exhibiting Authenticity* (Manchester: Manchester University Press, 1997), p. 5.

33. Francis E. C. Habgood and R. L. Eagle, *The Stratford Birthplace* (London: Bacon Society, 1940), unpaginated.

34. Farah Karim-Cooper and Kate Rumbold, "Literary Heritage: Stratford and the Globe," in *Authors at Work: The Creative Environment*, ed. Ceri Sullivan and Graeme Harper, *Essays and Studies 2009* (Cambridge: D. S. Brewer for the English Association, 2009), p. 149.

35. "Shakespeare's Houses and Gardens" (Stratford: Shakespeare Birthplace Trust, 2009).

Bibliography

Arbuthnot, George. *A Guide to Stratford-on-Avon.* Stratford-on-Avon: J. Morgan, 1893.

Armstrong, Carol. *Scenes in a Library: Reading the Photograph in the Book, 1843–1875.* Cambridge, Mass.: MIT Press, 1998.

Arscott, Caroline. "Victorian Development and Images of the Past," in *The Imagined Past: History and Nostalgia.* Ed. Christopher Shaw and Malcolm Chase. Manchester: Manchester University Press, 1989. 47–67.

Ascari, Maurizio. "Pilgrims and Heretics at the Shrine: Reassessing the History of Shakespeare's Birthplace," in *The Cultural Reconstruction of Places.* Ed. Ástráður Eysteinsson. Reykjavík: University of Iceland Press, 2006. 11–21.

Atkin, Polly. "Ghosting Grasmere: The Musealisation of Dove Cottage," in *Literary Tourism and Nineteenth-Century Culture.* Ed. Nicola J. Watson. Hampshire: Palgrave Macmillan, 2009. 84–94.

Austin, Alfred. "A Shakespeare Memorial," in *Sacred and Profane Love, and Other Poems.* London: Macmillan, 1908.

Babcock, Robert Witbeck. *The Genesis of Shakespeare Idolatry, 1766–1799.* Chapel Hill: University of North Carolina Press, 1931.

Bachelard, Gaston. *The Poetics of Space.* Trans. Maria Jolas. 1958. Boston: Beacon Press, 1964.

[Banks, George Linnaeus]. *All About Shakespeare: Profusely Illustrated with Wood Engravings by Thomas Gilks, Drawn by H. Fitzcook. In Commemoration of the Ter-Centenary.* London: Henry Lea, 1864.

Barnum, P. T. *The Autobiography of P. T. Barnum: Clerk, Merchant, Editor, and Showman.* London: Ward and Lock, 1855.

Barrie, J. M. *My Lady Nicotine.* London: Hodder and Stoughton, 1890.

Barry, Edward M. *Lectures on Architecture Delivered at the Royal Academy.* Ed. Alfred Barry. London: John Murray, 1881.

Barthes, Roland. *Camera Lucida: Reflections on Photography.* Trans. Richard Howard. London: Vintage, 1993.

Bate, Jonathan. *Shakespearean Constitutions: Politics, Theatre, Criticism 1730–1830.* Oxford: Clarendon, 1989.

Bell, Mackenzie "Shakespeare at Stratford-on-Avon," in *The Poems of Mackenzie Bell.* London: James Clarke and Co., 1909. 41.

Belsey, Catherine. *Why Shakespeare?* Basingstoke: Palgrave Macmillan, 2007.

Benjamin, Walter. "The Work of Art in the Age of Mechanical Reproduction," in *Illuminations*. Ed. Hannah Arendt. Trans. Harry Zohn. 1955. London: Fontana, 1992. 211–44.

Black, Adam and Charles. *Black's Picturesque Guide to Warwickshire*. Edinburgh: Adam and Charles Black, 1857.

Blatchford, Robert. *Merrie England*. London: Clarion Office, 1894.

Bloom, J. Harvey, ed. *The Errors of the Avon Star: Another Literary Manual for the Stratford-on-Avon Season of 1903*. Stratford-on-Avon: John Morgan, 1903.

Booth, Alison. "The Real Right Place of Henry James: Homes and Haunts." *Henry James Review* 25:3 (Fall 2004). 216–27.

Bowdler, Thomas, ed. *The Family Shakspeare, in Ten Volumes; in which nothing is added to the original text; but those words and expressions are omitted with cannot with propriety be read aloud in a family*. Vol. I. London: Longman, Hurst, Rees, Orme, and Brown, 1818.

Bracebridge, Charles Holte. *Shakespeare No Deerstealer, or, A short account of Fulbroke Park, near Stratford-on-Avon*. London: Harrison and Sons, 1862.

Braddon, Mary Elizabeth. *Asphodel: A Novel*. 3 vols. Leipzig: Bernhard Tauchnitz, 1881.

A Brief Guide for Strangers Who Are Visiting Stratford-on-Avon for the First Time, and Who are Staying in the Town Merely for a Few Hours. London, 1869.

Brooke, Stopford Augustus to W. A. Knight. 21 January 1890. Knight Collection, Morgan Library and Museum, New York.

Brown, Ivor. *The Shakespeares and the Birthplace*. Stratford-on-Avon: Edward Fox and Son, 1939.

Brown, Ivor and George Fearon. *Amazing Monument: A Short History of the Shakespeare Industry*. London: William Heinemann, 1939.

C.V.G. [Charles Vaughan Grinfield]. *A Pilgrimage to Stratford-upon-Avon, The Birthplace of Shakspeare*. London: Longman, Brown and Co.; Coventry: John Merridew, 1850.

Calvert, George H. *Shakespeare: A Biographic Aesthetic Study*. Boston: Lee and Shepard, 1879.

Carlyle, Thomas. "The Hero as Poet. Dante: Shakspeare," in *The Works of Thomas Carlyle*. Vol. 1. 1840. London: Chesterfield Society, n.d.

A Catalogue of Books, Pamphlets, Etc. Illustrating the Life and Writings of Shakespeare. London: John Russell Smith, 1864.

Chesterton, A. K. *Brave Enterprise: A History of the Shakespeare Memorial Theatre Stratford-upon-Avon*. London: J. Miles and Co., 1934.

Clapp, George Wood. *The Life and Work of James Leon Williams*. New York: Dental Digest, 1925.

Clarke, Edward Daniel. *A Tour Through the South of England, Wales, and Part of Ireland, made during the summer of 1791*. London, 1793.

Clarke, Mary Cowden. *The Girlhood of Shakespeare's Heroines; in a series of fifteen tales*. London: W. H. Smith and Son; Simpkin, Marshall and Co., 1850–52.

Cliffe, Leigh. *The Pilgrim of Avon*. London: Simpkin and Marshall; Stratford-upon-Avon: J. Ward, 1836.

A Collection of Pamphlets, Posters &c, Relating to the Shakespeare Tercentenary Festival at Stratford-upon-Avon. Collection of the British Library. London. 1864.

Corelli, Marie, ed. *The Avon Star: A Literary Manual for the Stratford-on-Avon Season of 1903*. Stratford-on-Avon: A. J. Stanley, 1903.

Coyne, J. Stirling. *This House to Be Sold; (The Property of the Late William Shakspeare.) Inquire Within*. London: National Acting Drama Office, 1847.

Crompton, Richmal. "William and the Lost Tourist," in *William—The Conqueror*. Illus. Thomas Henry. London: George Newnes, 1926. 78–96.

Dávidházi, Péter. *The Romantic Cult of Shakespeare: Literary Reception in Anthropological Perspective*. Basingstoke: Macmillan, 1998.

Davies, Thomas. *Memoirs of the Life of David Garrick, Esq. interspersed with characters and anecdotes of his theatrical contemporaries. The whole forming a history of the stage, which includes a period of thirty-six years*. London: printed for the author, 1780.

Deelman, Christian. *The Great Shakespeare Jubilee*. London: Michael Joseph, 1964.

[Dick, John]. *Here and There in England; Including a Pilgrimage to Stratford-upon-Avon*. London: John Russell Smith, 1871.

Dickens, Charles. *The Letters of Charles Dickens*. Ed. Graham Storey and K. J. Fielding. Vol. 5. Oxford: Clarendon, 1981.

Dobson, Michael. *The Making of the National Poet: Shakespeare, Adaptation, and Authorship, 1660–1769*. Oxford: Clarendon, 1992.

Dugdale, William. *The Antiquities of Warwickshire Illustrated; from records, leiger books, manuscripts, charters, evidences, tombes and armes: beautified with maps, prospects and portraictures*. London: Thomas Warren, 1656.

Engels, Frederick. "The Commercial Crisis in England.—The Chartist Movement. — Ireland," in Karl Marx and Frederick Engels, *Collected Works*. Vol. 6. London: Lawrence and Wishart, 1976.

Engler, Balz. "Stratford and the Canonization of Shakespeare." *European Journal of English Studies* 1:3 (1997). 354–66.

Fairholt, Frederick W. Autograph account of his visit to Shakespeare's Birthplace. 29 August 1839. Collection of the Folger Shakespeare Library, Washington, D.C.

——. *The Home of Shakspere Illustrated and Described*. London: Chapman and Hall, 1847.

Fildes, George. *On Elizabethan Furniture*. London: F. W. Calder, 1844.

Flower, Edgar. *Shakespeare's Birthplace. Important Statement by Mr. Edgar Flower*. Reprinted from the *Stratford-upon-Avon Herald*. 8 May 1903.

Fogg, Nicholas, ed. *Victorian Stratford-upon-Avon in Old Photographs*. Gloucestershire: Alan Sutton, 1990.

Foster, Shirley. "Americans and Anti-Tourism," in *Literary Tourism and Nineteenth-Century Culture*. Ed. Nicola J. Watson. Hampshire: Palgrave Macmillan, 2009. 175–83.

Foucault, Michel. "What Is an Author?" in *Language, Counter-Memory, Practice: Selected Essays and Interviews*. Ed. Donald F. Bouchard. Trans. Donald F. Bouchard and Sherry Simon. Oxford: Basil Blackwell, 1977. 113–38.

Foulkes, Richard. *Performing Shakespeare in the Age of Empire*. Cambridge: Cambridge University Press, 2002.

——. *The Shakespeare Tercentenary of 1864*. London: Society for Theatre Research, 1984.

Fox, Levi. "The Heritage of Shakespeare's Birthplace." *Shakespeare Survey* I. Ed. Allardyce Nicoll. Cambridge: Cambridge University Press, 1948. 79–88.

——. *The Shakespeare Birthplace Trust: A Personal Memoir*. Norwich: Shakespeare Birthplace Trust in association with Jarrold Publishing, 1997.

——. *A Splendid Occasion: the Stratford Jubilee of 1769*. Dugdale Society Occasional Papers no. 20. Oxford: Printed for the Dugdale Society by Vivian Ridler, 1973.

Fox, Levi, ed. *Correspondence of the Reverend Joseph Greene*. London: HMSO, 1965.

Freud, Sigmund. "Address Delivered in the Goethe House at Frankfurt," in *The Standard Edition of the Complete Psychological Works of Sigmund Freud*. Trans. James Strachey. Vol. 21. London: Hogarth Press and the Institute of Psycho-Analysis, 1964. 208–12.

——. *Civilization and Its Discontents. Complete Works*. Vol. 21. 64–145.

Garrick, David. "The Mulberry Tree," in *The Jubilee Concert: or, The Warwickshire Lad. Being a Collection of Songs Performed at the Jubilee, in Honour of Shakespear, at Stratford upon Avon, and at the Theatre Royal, Drury-Lane*. London, 1769.

Gillis, John R. *Youth and History: Tradition and Change in European Age Relations, 1770–Present*. New York: Academic Press, 1981.

Gray, George Jr. to his mother. May 1844. Collection of the Morgan Library and Museum, New York.

Green-Lewis, Jennifer. *Framing the Victorians: Photography and the Culture of Realism*. Ithaca, N.Y.: Cornell University Press, 1996.

Groth, Helen. *Victorian Photography and Literary Nostalgia*. Oxford: Oxford University Press, 2003.

Guide to Stratford-upon-Avon. Stratford-upon-Avon: John Smith, n.d.

Habgood, Francis E. C. and R. L. Eagle. *The Stratford Birthplace*. London: Bacon Society, 1940.

Hakewill, James. *An Attempt to Determine the Exact Character of Elizabethan Architecture*. London, 1835.

Hall, Stuart, ed. *Representation: Cultural Representations and Signifying Practices*. London: Sage in association with the Open University, 1997.

Halliday, F. E. *The Cult of Shakespeare*. London: Gerald Duckworth, 1957.

Halliwell, James Orchard. *The Abstract to the Title of the House in Henley Street, Stratford-upon-Avon, in which Shakespeare was born, drawn up by the Vendor's Solicitors, when the premises was about to be sold in the year 1847; the first document recited being the Poet's Will of 1616*. London: Thomas Richards, 1865.

——(-Phillipps). *A Brief Report on the Interchange of Books, Relics, &c., Between The New Place and The Birthplace Museum, and on the Re-Arrangement of The Library; Drawn up in Pursuance of Directions Given by the Trustees, May 5th, 1881. And Now Submitted to the Consideration of the Executive Committee*. Brighton, 1881.

——. *Collectanea Respecting the Birth-Place of Shakespeare at Stratford-on-Avon, Copied from the Manuscript Collections of the Late R. B. Wheler. With a few additions by J. O Halliwell. 1862*. London: Thomas Richards, 1865.

——. *A Descriptive Calendar of the Ancient Manuscripts and Records in the Possession of the Corporation of Stratford-upon-Avon; including notices of Shakespeare and his family and several persons connected with the poet*. London, 1863.

——. *Extracts of Entries Respecting Shakespeare, his family and connexions, carefully taken from the original parish registers preserved in the Church of the Holy Trinity, at Stratford-upon-Avon*. London, 1864.

——(-Phillipps). "A Letter Addressed to the Executive Committee of the Trustees of the Birth-Place of Shakespeare at Stratford-on-Avon, 31st May, 1880." Brighton, 1880.

——. *The Life of William Shakespeare*. London: John Russell Smith; Warwick: H. T. Cooke, 1848.

——. *A New Boke About Shakespeare and Stratford-on-Avon.* London, 1850.

——(Phillipps). *New Evidences in Confirmation of the Traditional Recognition of Shakespeare's Birth-Room, A.D 1769–A.D. 1777.* Brighton, 1888.

——. *Shakespearian Facsimiles; a collection of curious and interesting documents, plans, signatures, etc., illustrative of the biography of Shakespeare and the history of his family; from the originals chiefly preserved at Stratford-upon-Avon. Facsimiled by E. W. Ashbee. Selected by J. O. Halliwell.* London, 1863.

——. *Stratford-upon-Avon in the Times of the Shakespeares, illustrated by extracts from the Council Books of the Corporation, selected especially with reference to the History of the Poet's Father.* London, 1864.

Halliwell, James Orchard, ed. *A Brief Hand-list of the Collections Respecting the Life and Works of Shakespeare: and the history and antiquities of Stratford-upon-Avon formed by the late Robert Bell Wheler . . . and presented . . . to be preserved . . . in the Shakespeare Library and Museum.* London: Chiswick Press, 1863.

Hand Book for Visitors to Stratford-upon-Avon. Stratford: Edward Adams, 1860.

Hawthorne, Nathaniel. *The English Notebooks 1853–1856.* Ed. Thomas Woodson and Bill Ellis, in *The Centenary Edition of the Works of Nathaniel Hawthorne.* Vol. 21. Columbus: Ohio State University Press, 1997.

——. *Our Old Home: A Series of English Sketches,* in *The Centenary Edition of the Works of Nathaniel Hawthorne.* Vol. 5. Columbus: Ohio State University Press, 1970.

Haydon, Benjamin Robert. *The Autobiography and Memoirs of Benjamin Robert Haydon.* Ed. Tom Taylor. 2 vols. London: Peter Davies, 1926.

Heather, Rev. W. *Church Restoration: A Paper Read Before the Herefordshire Philosophical, Literary, and Antiquarian Society, November 15 1864.* Hereford: R. Redman, 1864.

Hendrix, Harald, ed. *Writers' Houses and the Making of Memory.* New York: Routledge, 2008.

Heywood, Abel. *Illustrated Guide to Stratford-on-Avon.* Manchester: Abel Heywood; London: F. Pitman, 1892.

Hodgdon, Barbara. *The Shakespeare Trade: Performances and Appropriations.* Philadelphia: University of Pennsylvania Press, 1998.

Holderness, Graham. "Bardolatry: or, The Cultural Materialist's Guide to Stratford-upon-Avon," in *The Shakespeare Myth.* Ed. Graham Holderness. Manchester: Manchester University Press, 1988. 2–15.

Howitt, William. *Homes and Haunts of the Most Eminent British Poets.* Vol. 1. London: Richard Bentley, 1847.

——. *Visits to Remarkable Places: Old Halls, Battle-Fields, and Scenes Illustrative of Striking Passages in English History and Poetry.* 1840. London: Longman, Brown, Green, Longmans and Roberts, 1856.

Hugo, Victor. *William Shakespeare.* Trans. A. Baillot. London: Hurst and Blackett, 1864.

Hunter, Joseph. *New Illustrations of the Life, Studies, and Writings of Shakespeare.* Vol. 1. London: J. B. Nichols and Son, 1845.

Hunter, Michael, ed. *Preserving the Past: The Rise of Heritage in Modern Britain.* Gloucestershire: Alan Sutton, 1996.

Hunter, Robert E. *Shakespeare and Stratford-upon-Avon, A "Chronicle of the Time": Comprising the Salient Facts and Traditions, Biographical, Topographical, and Historical, Connected with the Poet and his Birth-Place; Together with a Full record of the Tercentenary Celebration.* London: Whittaker and Co.; Stratford-upon-Avon: Edward Adams, 1864.

Ingleby, C. M. *Shakespeare's Bones: the proposal to disinter them, considered in relation to their possible bearing on his portraiture: illustrated by instances of visits of the living to the dead.* London: Trübner and Co, 1883.

——. *The Still Lion: Being an Essay Towards the Restoration of Shakespeare's Text.* London: Trübner and Co., 1874.

Ireland, Samuel. *Picturesque Views on the Upper, or Warwickshire Avon, From its Source at Naseby to its Junction with the Severn at Tewkesbury: with Observations on the Public Buildings, and other Works of Art in its Vicinity.* London: R. Faulder, 1795.

Irving, Washington. *The Sketch Book of Geoffrey Crayon, Gent.* 1819–20. Ed. Haskell Springer, in *The Complete Works of Washington Irving.* Ed. Richard Dilworth Rust. Vol. 8. Boston: Twayne, 1978.

James, Henry. "The Birthplace," in *The Better Sort.* London: Methuen, 1903.

——. "In Warwickshire," in *Portraits of Places.* London: Macmillan, 1883.

Jaques. "Modern Corruptions of Shakespeare's Text. A Letter to a Friend on the Subject of 'Cassell's Illustrated Shakespeare.'" London: Printed for private circulation, 1869.

Jephson, J. M. *Shakespere: His Birthplace, Home, and Grave. A Pilgrimage to Stratford-on-Avon in the Autumn of 1863.* London: Lovell Reeve, 1864.

Jerrold, Douglas. "Shakespeare's Home Preserved to the People," in *The Wit and Opinions of Douglas Jerrold. Collected and Arranged by his Son, Blanchard Jerrold.* London: W. Kent and Co., 1859.

——. "Shakespeare's House. (1847.)," in *The Wit and Opinions of Douglas Jerrold. Collected and Arranged by his Son, Blanchard Jerrold.* London: W. Kent and Co., 1859.

Jordan, John. *Original Memoirs and Historical Accounts of the Families of Shakespeare and Hart, deduced from an early period and continued down to this present year 1790. With drawings of their dwelling-houses and coats of arms.* Ed. J. O. Halliwell. London, 1865.

Karim-Cooper, Farah, and Kate Rumbold. "Literary Heritage: Stratford and the Globe," in *Authors at Work: The Creative Environment.* Ed. Ceri Sullivan and Graeme Harper. *Essays and Studies 2009.* Cambridge: D. S. Brewer for the English Association, 2009. 147–54.

Knight, Charles. *Old Lamps, or New? A Plea for the Original Editions of the Text of Shakspere: Forming an Introductory Notice to the Stratford Shakspere, Edited by Charles Knight.* London, 1853.

——. *Passages of a Working Life During Half a Century: with a Prelude of Early Reminiscences.* Vol. 2. London: Bradbury and Evans, 1864.

——. *William Shakspere; A Biography.* London: C. Knight and Co., 1843.

——. *William Shakspere: A Biography.* Revised and augmented. London: J. S. Virtue and Co., 1865.

Lanier, Douglas. *Shakespeare and Modern Popular Culture.* Oxford: Oxford University Press, 2002.

LaPorte, Charles. "The Bard, the Bible, and the Victorian Shakespeare Question." *ELH* 74 (2007). 609–28.

Lee, Sidney. *The Alleged Vandalism at Stratford-on-Avon.* London: Archibald Constable, 1903.

——. *A Life of William Shakespeare.* 1898. London: Smith, Elder, and Co., 1908.

Leyland, John. *The Shakespeare Country Illustrated.* London: Offices of "Country Life Illustrated" and George Newnes, 1900.

Lockwood, Allison. *Passionate Pilgrims: The American Traveler in Great Britain, 1800–1914.* New York: Fairleigh Dickinson University Press, 1981.

London Committee for the Purchase of Shakespeare's House. London, 1847.

Lucy, Mary Elizabeth. *Mistress of Charlecote: The Memoirs of Mary Elizabeth Lucy, 1803–1889.* Intro. Alice Fairfax-Lucy. Ed. Elsie Burch Donald. London: Orion Books, 1983.

Marder, Louis. "The Birthplace Auction—1847." *The Shakespeare Newsletter* 15:4 (September 1965). 32.

——. *His Exits and His Entrances: The Story of Shakespeare's Reputation.* London: John Murray, 1963.

Marshall, Emma. *Shakespeare and his Birthplace.* London: E. Nister, 1890.

Marshall, Gail. *Shakespeare and Victorian Women.* Cambridge: Cambridge University Press, 2009.

Marshall, Gail and Adrian Poole, eds. *Victorian Shakespeare, Volume 1: Theatre, Drama and Performance. Volume 2: Literature and Culture.* Basingstoke: Palgrave Macmillan, 2003.

Martin, George. "To G. I. at Stratford-on-Avon," in *Marguerite; or, the Isle of Demons and Other Poems.* Montreal: Dawson Brothers, 1887. 279.

May, George. *A Guide to the Birth-Town of Shakspere and the Poet's Rural Haunts.* Evesham: George May, 1847.

Miele, Chris. "The First Conservation Militants: William Morris and the Society for the Protection of Ancient Buildings," in *Preserving the Past: The Rise of Heritage in Modern Britain.* Ed. Michael Hunter. Gloucestershire: Alan Sutton, 1996. 17–37.

Mill, John Stuart. *Principles of Political Economy with Some of their Applications to Social Philosophy,* Book III. 1848. London: Longmans, Green and Co., 1900.

Miller, Hugh. *First Impressions of England and Its People.* 1847. Edinburgh: William P. Nimmo, 1873.

Moncrieff, W. T. *Excursion to Stratford upon Avon: With Historical and Descriptive Notices of the Town, Church, Shakspeare's House, and other Remarkable Buildings; Together with a Compendious Life of Shakspeare, Being by far more complete than any hitherto published. Copious Extracts from The Shakspearian Album; Account of the Far-Famed Jubilee; Catalogue of the Shakspeare Relics; With the Controversy on their Authenticity, And an Analysis of the Proceedings of the Proposed National Monument to the Memory of the Immortal Bard.* Leamington: Elliston, 1824.

Murphy, Andrew. *Shakespeare for the People: Working-Class Readers, 1800–1900.* Cambridge: Cambridge University Press, 2008.

——. *Shakespeare in Print: A History and Chronology of Shakespeare Publishing.* Cambridge: Cambridge University Press, 2003.

Murphy, Arthur. *The Life of David Garrick, esq.* London: J. Wright, 1801.

Neil, Samuel. *The Home of Shakespeare Described by Samuel Neil and Illustrated in Thirty-three Engravings by the Late F. W. Fairholt.* Warwick: Henry T. Cooke and Son, 1871.

Nelson, Harland. "Dickens and the Shakespeare Birthplace Trust: 'What a Jolly Summer!'" in *A Humanist's Legacy: Essays in Honor of John Christian Bale.* Ed. Dennis M. Jones. Decorah, Iowa: Luther College, 1990. 72–80.

New Shakspere Society's Transactions. London: Trübner and Co., 1874.

Nora, Pierre. *Realms of Memory.* Trans. Arthur Goldhammer. Vol. 1. 1992. New York: Columbia University Press, 1996.

Novy, Marianne. *Engaging with Shakespeare: Responses of George Eliot and other Women Novelists*. Athens: University of Georgia Press, 1994.

Orgel, Stephen. *Imagining Shakespeare: A History of Texts and Visions*. Basingstoke: Palgrave Macmillan, 2003.

Ousby, Ian. *The Englishman's England: Taste, Travel and the Rise of Tourism*. Cambridge: Cambridge University Press, 1990.

Parris, Leslie, ed. *The Pre-Raphaelites*. London: Tate Gallery, 1984.

Particulars of Shakespeare's House at Stratford on Avon, For Sale by Auction by Mr. Robins. London, 1847.

Payn, James. *The Talk of the Town*. London: Chatto and Windus, 1885.

Peltz, Lucy. "Aestheticizing the Ancestral City: Antiquarianism, Topography and the Representation of London in the Long Eighteenth Century," in *The Metropolis and Its Image: Constructing Identities for London, c. 1750–1950*. Ed. Dana Arnold. Oxford: Blackwell, 1999. 6–28.

Phillips, David. *Exhibiting Authenticity*. Manchester: Manchester University Press, 1997.

Poole, Adrian. *Shakespeare and the Victorians*. London: Thomson Learning, 2004.

Pressly, William L. *A Catalogue of Paintings in the Folger Shakespeare Library*. New Haven: Yale University Press, 1993.

Pringle, Roger. "The Rise of Stratford as Shakespeare's Town," in *The History of an English Borough: Stratford-upon-Avon 1196–1996*. Ed. Robert Bearman. Gloucestershire: Sutton in association with the Shakespeare Birthplace Trust, 1997. 160–74.

"Prologue Written for the Occasion by Mr. Charles Knight, and Spoken by Mr. Phelps," in *The Shakespeare Night, in Aid of the Fund for the Purchase and Preservation of Shakespeare's House. Tuesday 7 December, 1847, at the Royal Italian Opera, Covent Garden.*

Rhys, Ernest. *Everyman Remembers*. New York: Cosmopolitan Book Corporation, 1931.

Rosenthal, Michael. "Shakespeare's Birthplace at Stratford: Bardolatry Reconsidered," in *Writers' Houses and the Making of Memory*. Ed. Harald Hendrix. New York: Routledge, 2008. 31–44.

Rozmovits, Linda. *Shakespeare and the Politics of Culture in Late-Victorian England*. Baltimore: Johns Hopkins University Press, 1998.

Ruskin, John. "A Letter to Count Zorzi," in *The Works of John Ruskin*. Ed. E. T. Cook and Alexander Wedderburn. Vol. 24. London: George Allen; Longmans, Green and Co., 1903–12. 405–11.

——. *The Opening of the Crystal Palace Considered in Some of its Relations to the Prospects of Art*, in *The Works of John Ruskin*. Ed. E. T. Cook and Alexander Wedderburn. Vol. 12. London: George Allen; Longmans, Green and Co., 1903–12. 415–32.

——. *The Seven Lamps of Architecture*, in *The Works of John Ruskin*. Ed. E. T. Cook and Alexander Wedderburn. Vol. 8. London: George Allen; Longmans, Green and Co., 1903–12.

Sabin, J. F. and W. W. Sabin, *Shakespeare's Home; Visited and Described by Washington Irving and F. W. Fairholt . . . With Etchings by J. F. and W. W. Sabin*. New York: J. Sabin and Sons, 1877.

Santesso, Aaron. "The Birth of the Birthplace: Bread Street and Literary Tourism Before Stratford." *ELH* 71:2 (Summer 2004). 377–403.

Savage, Richard and William Salt Brassington, eds. *Stratford-Upon-Avon from "The Sketch Book" of Washington Irving. With Notes and Original Illustrations*. Stratford-upon-Avon: Edward Fox, 1900.

Scarfe, Norman. "Shakespeare: Stratford-Upon-Avon and Warwickshire," in *Shakespeare: A Celebration 1564–1964*. Ed. T. J. B. Spencer. London: Penguin, 1964. 15–29.

Schoch, Richard W. *Not Shakespeare: Bardolatry and Burlesque in the Nineteenth Century*. Cambridge: Cambridge University Press, 2002.

Schoenbaum, S. *Shakespeare's Lives*. Oxford: Oxford University Press, 1970.

Shafer, Yvonne. *The Changing American Theatre: Mainstream and Marginal, Past and Present*. València: Universitat de València, 2002.

Shakespeare, William. *The Complete Works of Shakespeare*. Ed. Peter Alexander. London: Collins, 1951.

Shakespeare Birthplace Trust. www.shakespeare.org.uk

"Shakespeare's Houses and Gardens." Stratford: Shakespeare Birthplace Trust, 2009.

"Shakespere's House; and Thou Art Gone From My Gaze." E. M. Hodges, n.d. Collection of the Folger Shakespeare Library, Washington, D.C.

Shakspearean Club. *A Circular Relative to the Restoration and Preservation of the Bust and Monument of Shakspeare*. Stratford-upon-Avon, 1835.

A Shakspeare Memorial. London: S. O. Beeton, 1864.

Shaw, Christopher and Malcolm Chase, eds. *The Imagined Past: History and Nostalgia*. Manchester: Manchester University Press, 1989.

Shelley, Henry C. *Shakespeare and Stratford*. London: Simpkin, Marshall Hamilton, Kent and Co., 1913.

A Short and Plain Pocket Guide with Map, to Stratford-on-Avon. Stratford-on-Avon: W. Stanton, 1894.

A Short Descriptive Guide to the East and West Junction Railway, Being the Shortest and Most Direct Route from London to Stratford-on-Avon via London and North Western Railway. London: Macfarlane and Co., 1886.

Smith, C. Roach. *Remarks on Shakespeare, His Birth-Place, etc. Suggested by a Visit to Stratford-upon-Avon, in the Autumn of 1868*. London, 1868–69.

Smyth, Albert H. "The Alleged Vandalism at Shakespeare's Home." Philadelphia, 1903.

Staunton, Howard. *Memorials of Shakspeare*. London, 1864.

Stochholm, Johanne M. *Garrick's Folly: The Shakespeare Jubilee of 1769 at Stratford and Drury Lane*. London: Methuen, 1964.

Stowe, Harriet Beecher. *Sunny Memories of Foreign Lands*. London: Sampson Low, Son and Co., 1854.

Tanner, Tony. "The Birthplace," in *Henry James: The Shorter Fiction: Reassessments*. Ed. N. H. Reeve. Basingstoke: Macmillan, 1997. 77–94.

Taylor, Gary. *Reinventing Shakespeare: A Cultural History from the Restoration to the Present*. London: Hogarth, 1990.

Tennyson, Alfred to Emily Sellwood. C. 8 June 1840, in *The Letters of Alfred Lord Tennyson*. Ed. Cecil Y. Lang and Edgar F. Shannon, Jr. Vol. 1. Oxford: Clarendon, 1982. 182.

The Tourist's Picturesque Guide to Leamington and the Surrounding District. London: Simpkin, Marshall and Co., 1872.

Trollope, Anthony to Kate Field. 11 April 1878, in *The Letters of Anthony Trollope*. Ed. N. John Hall. Vol. 2. Stanford: Stanford University Press, 1983. 770–72.

Wakeman, Geoffrey. *Victorian Book Illustration: The Technical Revolution*. Detroit: Gale Research, 1973.

Ward, Artemus [Charles Farrar Browne]. *Artemus Ward in London, and Other Papers*. New York: G. W. Carleton and Co., 1867.

Ward, H. Snowden, and Catharine Weed Ward, *Shakespeare's Town and Times*. London: Dawbarn and Ward, 1896.

Ward and Lock's Illustrated Guide to and Popular History of Stratford-upon-Avon. London: Ward and Lock, 1881.

Watson, Nicola J. *The Literary Tourist: Readers and Places in Romantic and Victorian Britain*. Basingstoke: Palgrave Macmillan, 2006.

——. "Shakespeare on the Tourist Trail," in *The Cambridge Companion to Shakespeare and Popular Culture*. Ed. Robert Shaughnessy. Cambridge: Cambridge University Press, 2007. 199–226.

Watson, Nicola J., ed. *Literary Tourism and Nineteenth-Century Culture*. Basingstoke: Palgrave Macmillan, 2009.

Watson, Robert Spence. *Joseph Skipsey: His Life and Work*. London: T. Fisher Unwin, 1909.

Wheler, R. B. *A Brief Hand-list of the Collections Respecting the Life and Works of Shakespeare: and the History and Antiquities of Stratford-upon-Avon formed by the late Robert Bell Wheler . . . and presented . . . to be preserved . . . in the Shakespeare Library and Museum*. Ed. J. O. Halliwell. London: Chiswick Press, 1863.

——. *Collectanea Respecting the Birth-Place of Shakespeare at Stratford-on-Avon, Copied from the Manuscript Collections of the Late R. B. Wheler. With a few additions by J. O. Halliwell*. 1862. London: Thomas Richards, 1865.

——. *A Guide to Stratford-upon-Avon*. Stratford: J. Ward; London: Longman, 1814.

——. *History and Antiquities of Stratford-upon-Avon: comprising a description of the Collegiate Church, the life of Shakespeare, and copies of several documents relating to him and his family never before printed . . . To which is added, a particular account of the Jubilee . . . in honour of our immortal bard . . . Embellished with eight engravings*. Stratford-upon-Avon: J. Ward, 1806.

Williams, James Leon. *The Home and Haunts of Shakespeare*. London: Sampson Low, Marston and Co., 1892.

Willis, Nathaniel Parker. *Romance of Travel, Comprising Tales of Five Lands*. New York: S. Colman, 1840.

Winter, William. *Old Shrines and Ivy*. Edinburgh: David Douglas, 1892.

Wise, John R. *Shakspere: His Birthplace and Its Neighbourhood*. London: Smith, Elder and Co., 1861.

Wordsworth, Charles. *Man's Excellency A Cause of Praise and Thankfulness to God. A Sermon Preached at Stratford-upon-Avon on Sunday, April 24, 1864*. London: Smith, Elder & Co., 1864.

Yeats, W. B. "At Stratford-on-Avon." *Ideas of Good and Evil*. London: A. H. Bullen, 1903. 142–68.

Zemgulys, Andrea. "Henry James in a Victorian Crowd: 'The Birthplace' in Context." *Henry James Review* 29:3 (Fall 2008). 245–56.

Ziegler, Georgianna. "Accommodating the Virago: Nineteenth-Century Representations of Lady Macbeth," in *Shakespeare and Appropriation*. Ed. Christy Desmet and Robert Sawyer. London: Routledge, 1999. 119–41.

Material in the Collection of the Shakespeare Birthplace Trust

Edward Gibbs Holtom of Stratford-upon-Avon. 1862–64. Typescript notes compiled by Edward Gibbs Holtom concerning the career of Edward Gibbs, architect.

Fairholt, Frederick W. *Shakespeariana, Consisting of Portraits of the Poet, Views at Stratford on Avon, Autographs and Miscellanies Connected with the Sale of His Birthplace in 1847.* 3 vols. 1829–52.

From St. Paul's in London, to St. Peter's in Manchester, on Foot and Alone; with Rough Notes of What I saw, Heard, and Thought, What I Liked and Disliked on the Way: Being a Diary of Eleven-Days' Travel, Through Seven English Counties, in the Leafy Month of June, 1876.

General Regulations for the Management of Shakespeare's Birthplace, &c., Trust, Comprising Shakespeare's Birthplace, Anne Hathaway's Cottage, and New Place. May 1904. *Additions to and Alterations of Regulations.* 1906–7.

Gifford, Sanford R. Typescript copies of letters to his father. July–August 1855.

[Graham, F. T.]. "Graeme's Wanderings: Stratford-on-Avon." Article from the *Metropolitan* mounted in a booklet with a letter from F. T. Graham of Chicago to Richard Savage. 22 October 1896.

Hank, J. Newman. Letter to "Dear Sister Havenner." 6 September 1858.

Hunt, W. O. Correspondence: Hunt Papers. May 1856–January 1860.

Minute books. 1847–90.

Paul Morgan Ephemera. 1521–2001.

Purland, Theodosius. *Boke of Scraps Relating to Shakspere His House.* 1847–1864.

Reynolds, Lucy M. *Shakespeariana.* Scrapbook of a visit to Warwickshire. 1892.

Rowley, Fanny D. *Stratford-upon-Avon in the Seventies.* C. 1950.

Stratford-upon-Avon Ephemera: material relating to the Shakespeare Birthplace Trust and Shakespeare. 1897–98.

Wheler, Robert Bell. Letters to Robert Bell Wheler: Wheler Papers. 1841–47.

——. "Collectanea": Wheler Papers. c. 1790–1850.

Whitefriars Club, London. Printed program for a "Pilgrimage to Shakespeare's Country." 23 June 1900.

Newspapers, Magazines, and Periodicals

All the Year Round
Annual Register
Art-Union (succeeded by the *Art Journal*)
Athenaeum
Belgravia: a London Magazine
Bentley's Miscellany
Blackwood's Edinburgh Magazine
Chambers's Journal of Popular Literature, Science and Art
Daily News
Eclectic Magazine of Foreign Literature, Science, and Art
Edinburgh Review
Evening Sun
Examiner
Fraser's Magazine for Town and Country
Funny Folks
Gentleman's Magazine
Glasgow Herald

Illustrated London News
London Society
Man in the Moon
Manchester Times and Gazette
Mirror of Literature, Amusement, and Instruction
Monthly Magazine
Morning Chronicle
Musical World
New Review
New York Times
Nineteenth Century: A Monthly Review (succeeded by *Nineteenth Century and After*)
Pall Mall Gazette
Prospective Review
Punch, or the London Charivari
Quarterly Review
Reynolds's Miscellany of Romance, General Literature, Science, and Art
Rose, the Shamrock and the Thistle
Royal Leamington Spa Courier and Warwickshire Standard
Saturday Review
Shakspere Newspaper
Sharpe's London Magazine
Stratford-upon-Avon Herald
Temple Bar
The Times
Train: A First-Class Magazine

Index

Acknowledgments

This book has drawn on the resources of numerous libraries and archives. I am indebted to staff at the Folger Shakespeare Library, the Morgan Library and Museum, and Yale University Libraries. Closer to home, Peter Keelan and Alison Harvey helped with material and images in Special Collections and Archives, Cardiff University. This book could not have been written without the assistance and expertise of those working in the Shakespeare Centre Library and Archive, in particular Robert Bearman, Mairi Macdonald, and Helen Rees. For financial support for visits to these libraries, I am grateful to Martin Kayman and the English Literature research committee, Cardiff University. A Young Researcher Travel Scholarship from Cardiff University allowed me to make the trip to Yale. I gave papers on aspects of this research at Exeter University, Oxford University, the Shakespeare Institute, Stratford-upon-Avon, and at the Literary Tourism and Nineteenth-Century Culture conference organized by the Institute of English Studies and the Open University. The audiences at these events gave feedback and asked questions that often made me rethink my ideas. Other anonymous contributors are the readers for University of Pennsylvania Press, who commented in detail on drafts of the manuscript and have made the book far better than it would otherwise have been.

There are so many people with whom I have discussed this project that it is impossible to name them all, but I am especially grateful to Maurizio Ascari for sharing his thoughts on the Birthplace, even before they were published; Neil Badmington, who claims to know nothing about Shakespeare, but, fortunately, knows a lot about referencing, copyright, and Roland Barthes; Catherine Belsey for listening patiently to all my woes; Heather Birchall for information about Henry Wallis; Paul Crosthwaite for advice on Victorian economic models; Jim Cheshire; Paul Goldman; Tim Killick, who discussed this book on a long, hot walk back from Arlington Cemetery and helped me with *The Sketch Book* (so thank you, Tim, for Washington and Irving); Anthony Mandal, who I am hoping will publicize this on the CEIR blog; Kate McLuskie; Becky Munford; Leonée Ormond for J. M. Barrie; Jonathan Osmond; Tomos Owen for Ernest Rhys; Carl Phelpstead; John Plunkett for information about stereographs of the Birthplace and Michelle Allen for finding them; Andrew Prescott, who identified all the Stratford Freemasons; Kara Tennant; Ailbhe Thunder for commerce; Nicola J. Watson; Jessica Webb for starting to write a thesis on empire and finding lots of stories in the *ILN* in the process; Richard Wilson for C. Roach Smith's *Remarks on Shakespeare*; and Paul Young for *William the Conqueror*. I cannot thank David Skilton enough for countless references and anecdotes and for knowing so much, along with his willingness to act as my research assistant on several occasions to track down attributions. The University of Pennsylvania Press has been an absolute joy to work with. Thank you to all those who have helped to turn this into a book, and especially to Jerry Singerman.

An earlier version of Chapter 2 was published as "Bidding for the Bard: Shakespeare, the Victorians, and the Auction of the Birthplace," *Nineteenth-Century Contexts* 30:1 (September 2008). I am grateful to Taylor and Francis for permission to reproduce this material. An earlier version of Chapter 3 appeared in Nicola J. Watson, ed., *Literary Tourism and Nineteenth-Century Culture* (Hampshire: Palgrave Macmillan, 2009) and is reproduced here with permission of Palgrave Macmillan.

Sometimes distractions are as important as the actual research. It was good to have the company of the Mirage Mummers, even in the rain. Peter Smith and Anne Lazarus will have to buy this book now that they appear in it. In my birthplace, or at least in my childhood home, there is a framed photograph from the late 1970s showing me and my brother posing at the base of the Gower monument in Stratford. I am very grateful to my parents for those holidays, even if we stayed a tent. Most of all, thank you to Stuart, who has always done Stratford in style, and for so many other things (enthusing about this book, formatting the pictures, fixing computer crashes, to name just a few of his day-to-day responsibilities). A pint in the Dirty Duck does not come near to expressing my love and thanks. Jude wanted to see his name in this book, so here it is, with memories of him eating his first ice cream outside Shakespeare's Birthplace.